MANNING

MANNING

ARCHIE AND PEYTON MANNING

WITH JOHN UNDERWOOD

HarperEntertainment

An Imprint of HarperCollins*Publishers*

JH TH FH

All photographs courtesy of the Manning family.

HarperCollins books may be purchased for educational, business, or sales promotional use. For information please write: Special Markets Department, HarperCollins Publishers Inc., 10 East 53rd Street, New York, NY 10022.

FIRST EDITION

Designed by Charles Kreloff

Printed on acid-free paper

Library of Congress Cataloging-in-Publication Data

Manning, Peyton.
    Manning/ Archie and Peyton Manning with John Underwood. — 1st ed.
        p. cm.
    ISBN 0-06-105136-5 (alk. paper)
    1. Manning, Peyton. 2. Manning, Archie, 1949– . 3. Football players—United States—Biography. 4. Fathers and sons—United States. I Manning, Archie, 1949– . II. Underwood, John, 1934– . III. Title.

GV939.M289 A3 2000
796.332'092'273'dc21
[B]
                                                                        00-040847

00 01 02 03 04 ❖/RRD 10 9 8 7 6 5 4 3 2 1

To my mother, Sis, who is the most
courageous and caring person I know.
And, of course, to my dear Olivia, the
"Great Equalizer," a fantastic mother,
and an all-pro wife.

—Archie Manning

ACKNOWLEDGMENTS

First of all, I would like to thank John Underwood. Although I did not know him personally before we started working on this book, I feel truly bonded to him. We were constantly on the same wavelength, maintaining the same views. I deeply appreciate all he has done for this book and I know that in him I have found a lifelong friend.

I would also like to thank my family and friends. When I think of them, I am often reminded of the Kris Kristofferson song "Why Me?" I know that I am extremely blessed to have such a wonderful family and hundreds and hundreds of friends.

And finally, Peyton and I would especially like to thank our coaches. Coaching is a special brotherhood for which we have the utmost respect. Over the years we have had the pleasure of working with many amazing men. We want to thank all of those coaches who have touched us, as well as those men who have graced the fields with us.

—Archie Manning

Biographies and autobiographies are only as good as their subjects are honest. Which is to say, if you are looking for truth and insight, you should know going in that you are getting full access to the thoughts, mindsets, and reasons for actions of those being written about. No holds barred. The Mannings gave me that. Weaving through and harnessing into prose the experiences of a family of five very interesting, loving, highly motivated people required total candor, or no real book would have come out of it. They complied, and for that I am grateful—and the reader should be as well. It was a complex journey that I would not have joined had Archie and Peyton Manning not been so willing to link arms and forge ahead. And had not my beloved wife and critic, Donna Simmons Underwood, been there to ride shotgun. I am indebted to all three. And to Mauro DiPreta, a writer's editor.

—John Underwood

INTRODUCTION

For reasons forever his own, Archie Manning's father turned a shotgun on himself on a summer's day in 1969. Archie was the first to find the result, draped backward across the bed in their little house on Third Street in Drew, Mississippi, where Archie grew up. The shotgun and the stick Buddy Manning used to activate the trigger lay incongruously on the floor in front of the dresser drawer he had pulled out to serve as a brace. It was the gun and the stick that caught Archie's eye as he passed the bedroom door, and when he turned back to look closer he saw the red spreading out from beneath his father's body. The implications swept over him like an avalanche.

Archie had come home ahead of the family from a wedding that Buddy Manning had chosen not to attend. It was later assumed that his dad planned it that way, hoping it would be Archie who found him rather than Archie's mother or sister, knowing that Archie would "take care of it," but Buddy Manning was never big on weddings anyhow, so that was speculation. Archie could only guess what prompted so drastic a decision. There were no precursors. Buddy's health wasn't great; he had had a stroke. But that was five years before and the effects seemed minimal. Business wasn't good, but that wasn't new either. Buddy ran the Case Farm Machinery shop in Drew but, like the town itself, had never really known an economic winning streak. Apparently it was an accumulation of things. His last words to Archie had been immaterial, something like "See you back at the house."

They had last talked freely a couple days before, when Buddy drove up to Oxford to bring Archie home from the

University of Mississippi for his short summer's break before football started again in the fall. Archie had completed his sophomore year, and had emerged as the team's starting quarterback, with favorable reviews. Buddy seemed pleased. No signs of depression then either.

But Archie would remember that his dad kept so much inside. He would remember—sadly, then, because there would be no more chances—that Buddy had never once told him he loved him. "I knew he loved me, he had ways of showing it, but he just never said it." He remembered the times his father had begged off attending Archie's games growing up, blaming work, and then along about the third inning or third quarter of this contest or that, Archie would look up and there would be Buddy, kibitzing with friends in the stands, and watching.

Through tears, Archie called the doctor and the ambulance that day, and made sure a friend diverted his mother and sister so that he could clean up before they got home. It was mostly a blur after that. Archie would remember that a man from Case came around with a check, and that his daddy's salary figured out at $6,000 a year. It would occur to him much later how insignificant that would be—spill-off, really—to professional football players today; that a year of his dad's labors wouldn't cover the down payment on one of their automobiles. The inequities still nag him.

Then after the funeral, Archie took his mother, Jane Manning, aside and told her he would not be going back to Oxford. That his football career was over. That he would get a job, maybe be a coach of some kind (he had lettered in four sports in high school), and would stay home to help the family make ends meet. He was, after all, not the stereotypical dumb jock. He had been valedictorian of his senior class, and his reliability was already well established on and off the playing fields of Drew.

"But you really didn't *tell* my mother anything," Archie says. "'Sis' is what everybody called her; one of those very independent ladies you just naturally respect. I get my size from her side of the family. Not from her directly—she was short like my daddy, but as they say in basketball, she played tall. She had a job as a legal secretary, which she kept until she was eighty, and she had a broad practical streak. She would park her car unlocked in front of the house with the keys in the ignition, and if you questioned her about it she'd say she would rather somebody steal it there than come in the house looking for the keys.

"Her priority was people. She was always there for those she loved, and even for some she didn't. But this was a new kind of challenge. My older sister, Pam, was in her senior year at Delta State, and Sis had to count the pennies. But when I told her I wasn't going back to college, she wouldn't have it. She said her needs were small. That when it came to living costs, Drew wasn't exactly Beverly Hills, California. She said she had her job, and that I had my Ole Miss scholarship. That I should get my education, and continue to play football like I wanted, which is what she wanted, too. Unlike my dad, she had seen every game I ever played growing up—I mean *every* game, in *every* sport, at *every* level. She said for her to be deprived of seeing more would be compounding the tragedy.

"So I went back to Oxford, and back to football."

Decisions at pivotal moments made even willy-nilly have a way of becoming profound. Stand for a moment at this melancholy bend in a road already traveled and project ahead to what would *not* have happened had Sis Manning accepted her only son's offer that day to sacrifice college for family responsibility.

The Archie Manning years at Ole Miss would have been over before they really started. Archie would not have twice made All-America, and Bear Bryant would not have had reason to call him "the most athletic quarterback I've ever seen." He would not have become the sports paradigm that he is in Mississippi, "a legend larger than life," according to the novelist John Grisham, a fellow Mississippian. Grisham named characters in his books after Archie. And there would not have been all those years in the National Football League, where he shone so brightly in spite of the teams he played for, primarily the woebegone New Orleans Saints.

And because the circumstances would have been so badly skewed, it would not have followed that he would marry his college sweetheart, the lovely, long-legged Olivia Williams of Philadelphia, Mississippi, who two years later when Archie was established as Ole Miss's lead player was the university's homecoming queen.

And from such undeniable genes would not have come their three sons, so alike in physical endowments—all three of them six-feet-four or better, with faces practically inter-changeable—yet so wonderfully different in style and content. No effervescent, slightly madcap first son Cooper to help channel second son Peyton into football even after his own aspirations were dashed by a life-threatening spinal disorder. No driven, courtly Peyton to set the stage for third son Eli, laid-back and matter-of-fact but by early indicators just as gifted, having shadowed Peyton's records at Isidore Newman High in New Orleans to become, now, the quarterback-in-waiting at their dad's old school, Mississippi.

And the University of Tennessee would not have bene-fited so grandly from Peyton's matriculation (thirty-nine vic-tories in three-plus seasons; two national college passing records; eight Southeastern Conference records, thirty-three school records, et cetera, et cetera; and for good measure, Peyton a Phi Beta Kappa graduate in three years). And America would not be enjoying now the spectacular liftoff of the third stage of his apotheosis—where in two years as the central jewel of the Indianapolis Colts, he has become so respected at the most demanding position in all of team sport that one breathless National Football League analyst said in 1999 that Peyton Manning had paved the way for his team to be "the next dynasty in [pro] football." Peyton took Indianapolis on the giddiest U-turn in the history of the league, from three victories and thirteen defeats in 1998 to thirteen won and three lost in the '99 regular season, a ten-game swing into the black. No NFL team had ever done that.

But those who know the Mannings even superficially would argue that although all of this is very good, it's not the best part. That the part you would least want to be deprived of since Sis Manning made her stand three decades ago is the Archie Manning *family*. One you can cheer without qualification, and lift up and rally round without a second thought. Indeed, in the erratic environment of modern American sport—where it is almost fashionable to be dysfunctional, and quirks and jerks with more money than sense leap regularly from the headlines onto police blotters—you would have to conclude that sport *needs* the Mannings. And all reasonable facsimiles thereof.

In New Orleans, where the boys were born and the family nested for good when Archie played for the Saints, they have achieved an enviable status, with a lifestyle Buddy Manning would never have dared dream of. There, since he quit playing, Archie has prospered in business, been a radio and television regular during football seasons, and is a much-in-demand stand-up speaker. Olivia, too, when she wasn't occupied at control central for the boys' upbringing, became a willing conduit for all manner of charitable causes. They are New Orleans fixtures, even as they stick out in such a toddling, freewheeling town as, well, *saintly* by comparison.

To be sure, the Mississippi Delta is still warm on Archie's and Olivia's speech, and they retain a Southern charm most Southerners only think is genetic—the charm of being generous without being unctuous, and of being interested without fawning. Their handsome antebellum house in the Garden District is an amiable anchorage where friends of the family have been flocking for years in ever increasing numbers, knowing that the warmth is drawn from more than just electric current and the table talk will flow freely beyond the tables and rooms.

When the sons were tots, football in miniature was played on the living room rug, Archie on his knees serving as tutor and foil. When they were older, there were raucous games in the yard and around the basketball hoop near the pool, a favorite being something Cooper and Peyton called "Amazin' Catches," which required the quarterback (Archie) to lob passes "downfield" so that the receivers (Cooper, Peyton, et al) had to make acrobatic leaps to reach, sometimes stretching full-body-out over the pool to come down with a gratifying splash, and sometimes actually catching the ball. The gatherings evolved in time into teenage happenings, with invitations at a premium. Peyton tells of discovering a gate-crasher at one and taking his grievance to Olivia. "She said, 'Oh, I know that. Let him be. There's enough to go around.'"

Random testimony on how well the family's synergy works has gotten wide currency over the years. In Peyton's case, a woman in Florida who was his camp counselor when he was ten said that "from the first day, every time the mail came Peyton would walk away with a fistful of letters from home." Friends tell of Archie and Olivia being there for him—for all three—at every sports event or school function growing up, Archie missing them only when his own games interfered. Even then he seemed always to find ways (odd-hour commercial flights, friends with jet planes) to make it back for an opening kickoff or tip-off or first pitch. In such a nourishing atmosphere, the boys' own bonding emerged, sometimes in extraordinary ways. Peyton, who according to Cooper is now "like a second father" to Eli, keeps as an heirloom a moving, heartfelt letter from Cooper, written as encouragement when Cooper's own football life died aborning at Ole Miss. In the letter, Cooper said he would from then on "live" his football through Peyton, and would always be there for him. He closed with "I love you, Peyt," and "Thanks for everything." (Ironically, the letter helped Peyton decide *not* to go to the University of Mississippi, and instead to Tennessee, a dramatic turnabout in itself and one that would lay bare for an unsuspecting Archie Manning the dark side of fan adulation.)

What makes all this even better, friends say, is that the

caring has had a way of spreading beyond familial borders. In Tennessee, they still rhapsodize over Peyton's inspirational talks to schoolkids when he was an undergraduate, his visits to children's wards in hospitals, his tireless autograph sessions—the things Archie's friends remember *him* doing as he made his way in sport. When Peyton got all those millions of dollars to play for the Colts as the NFL's number one draft choice in 1998, scarcely any of it was spent before he had set up a foundation to help give much of it away.

But what most commonly impresses are the little things. The kindnesses, the courtesies. A sportswriter visiting the Indianapolis locker room for a story during the 1999 season was so surprised when Peyton got up from his stool to fetch him a chair that he made it the focus of his story. Who, after all, could imagine such a thing? Late in the season, a mother in another town wrote to thank Peyton for the generosities he had extended her stricken son in the days before his death—calls, visits, autographed memorabilia. She said they had buried him in a Peyton Manning jersey, and told Peyton, "You now have an angel watching over you."

But we must be careful here not to take this too far. As Peyton himself has complained when the portrayals got uncomfortably close to squeaky-clean, "trying to do the right thing" is not the same as *being* an angel. Peyton, for one, has a rather abrasive stubborn streak that more than once has put him at odds with his superiors—notably, his basketball coach in high school, his athletic director in college, and even his current pro football coach, Jim Mora. Moreover, he has rankled teammates at every level with his near-obsessive work ethic and his impatience with slackers—which is to say, those who don't pay enough attention to the coaching that's going on around them or share his willingness to spend hours and hours of extra practice time "doing what it takes to win." And when his ire is up, says Mora, Peyton doesn't make his arguments with the benign euphemisms that usually mark his speech ("shoot," "dadgummit"). The contrast can burn your ears, says Mora. Which is probably the point.

At Tennessee, Peyton was implicated in a harassment suit when he mooned (showed his backside to) a woman athletic trainer in the training room, but that proved mostly exaggeration. He was aiming at somebody else, and so was the trainer. She was suing the university over job grievances. Archie was philosophical about it. "I knew he wouldn't have done it deliberately, because that's not Peyton's style," he said. "Now, if they'd told me it was *Cooper* . . . " Well, of course, Cooper. On a bet he allegedly lost, the irrepressible Cooper Manning once streaked (ran *au naturel*) down sorority row at the Mississippi campus. On a school day. At high noon. His concession to decorum was a telephone call to Archie's answering machine just before he took off "to let me know where he could be reached in case he got arrested."

And young Eli, the quiet one, *did* get arrested, briefly, at Ole Miss in February of his freshman year. For "public drunkenness" . . . outside the Sigma Nu house . . . during initiation week. He and another freshman player were being inducted into Archie's old fraternity, and the celebration quite literally spilled onto the lawn. A campus cop drove by at just the wrong moment. Eli called Archie early the next morning and gave him a play-by-play of the extenuating circumstances, including his being doused with alcohol by his new fraternity buddies ("honest, Dad, I wasn't drunk"), but Archie told him to cool it and take his medicine, which included a fine and, from the Ole Miss football coach, a curfew for the rest of the semester. "He got off cheap," said Archie. "It was a good lesson." At the time, Peyton was in Honolulu for the Pro Bowl, and when a television camera caught him on the sidelines during the game he lifted a cup of Gatorade toward the lens, winked, and said prescriptively, "Eli?" When Cooper heard about the incident, he was said to have only smiled.

Archie Manning has eased into middle age now. His eyes are latticed with laugh lines, well earned, and when he is hard into a subject his eyebrows lift to give him a look of luminous contentment, as though he has figured out some important things about life that you haven't. He is actually better-looking now than when he was a player. Then he favored long, decorative sideburns in the style of the day, and with his freckles and red hair he resembled nothing if not a contemporary Huckleberry Finn. Sports publicists got him to dangle straw from his mouth for pictures.

Now as the family's graying eminence, Archie is no longer lean and lithe, but he stays fit with regular workouts. Whenever possible, father and sons (and Olivia, too, when the agenda suits her) golf together, hunt together, travel together; and if the activity warrants including a friend or two or three—some of Archie's date back to high school— why, by all means, they bring 'em along. Though he is tall enough to top out most groups, it pleases Archie to note that all his boys are now taller. He stands next to them for pictures, and looks up, and smiles. They smile back.

Buddy Manning never told his son he loved him. Archie never stops telling his. It is a shared sensitivity, openly expressed, as genuine as breathing. The "I love yous" punctuate every parting, round off every phone call. It doesn't matter if anyone else can hear, they say it anyway. The communication lines stay open, even at those inevitable times when displeasing words are said and sometimes have to be reexamined. Even then the awkwardness never lasts for long. Peyton called home almost every night the four years he was at Tennessee, and still calls regularly and after every Colts game that Archie and Olivia miss, sometimes sotto voce from a team bus heading for an airport in some far-off city. Cooper, married in 1999 and working for an investment firm in New Orleans, calls daily or drops by. He and Archie now have their own weekly radio talk show, and all three brothers join with Archie every spring to operate a popular instruction camp for quarterbacks (what else?).

In the high-ceilinged family room in the big house on First Street, they still gather whenever their schedules mesh to chow down and watch televised sporting events, Archie writhing on the floor in his designated spot in front of the huge screen, the others with their wives or girlfriends scrambling for softer spots as convenient to Olivia's food outlays as possible. In the display cases arching around and over the TV, the trophies of father and sons crowd every shelf, a glistening metallic army affirming their status as athletes.

But when he is alone with a visitor, Archie's exploits grow stale on his tongue, and he ignores his own hardware to point out Cooper's award for this, Peyton's for that, Eli's for another. By the pool outside the back door, he sips a beer—he is not *that* saintly—and says he knows how lucky they've been. How gratifying it is to have had such a family and such a life. As a Christian with an active, viable faith, he thanks God for it every day. Sometimes, though, other memories squeeze in and he thinks how nice it would have been if *his* father had been able to see some of it: Archie's fulfillment at Ole Miss, his fitful journey through the pros, and the unfolding of his sons' achievements. "I could have taken him along on so many things. I think he would have enjoyed it, especially now with the kids doing so well. I think he would have been proud."

Archie Manning is content, now, with his last in college and the nest emptied, mainly to watch—and to provide with Olivia a resource for whatever might come along. Letting go, therefore, turns out to be a relative thing. Archie serves as schedule monitor for Peyton, helping him through the multitude of opportunities and requests. But at those times—as when Peyton is offered $100,000 just to make an appearance—he realizes again that the draw for each life is never quite the same, and worries what Cooper must think when he hustles to make his own family's budget and Peyton, "who never worked a day in his life," soars above it all on the wings of a game they tied to in childhood. It soothes Archie to know that Peyton thinks the same things, and reacts accordingly. His wedding gift to Cooper and wife Ellen was a honeymoon in Paris.

At such reflective times, Archie Manning's more deep-rooted convictions surface. He is an instinctively polite, even-keeled sort of man, not given to pro-nounce-ments; but while he may temper the way he expresses it, he tells you exactly what he thinks, holding nothing back. For example, there are things within his beloved game he says need fixing. College recruiting, for one, and the various rituals of bribery that sully the process. And the money madness that infects all of big-time pro sports, alienating fans, confusing loyalties, and making gypsies of players and coaches (and franchises, too, as they bounce from city to city). From the front office to the field, "it's not just how much you make anymore, but where you can run off to next to make more."

In matters relating to on-field conduct (i.e., sportsman-ship), he is an unabashed purist. He hates the posturing and the end zone discotheque that mark NFL games, "especially when you look up at the scoreboard and the guy who's doing all the dancing is 21 points behind." He laments the fact that white boys aren't playing football in the numbers they used to. He blames this on the overstructuring of the game at the lower levels that "has taken a lot of the fun out" and sent kids scurrying into other sports, "sports we didn't even have when I was a kid—roller hockey, lacrosse, those things. You never see white kids playing football in the street anymore. It's sad."

On this line, he is proud that he never pushed his boys into *any* sport, even as the evidence—their proficiency— might have indicated otherwise. He believes when you are a kid that you do sports for fun, period, just as he had, and that that consideration should be the only prerequisite for par-ents. He had strict rules against his three playing in organized leagues at too early an age, rules he put in when he found youth league sport to be mostly an adult conspiracy to nose in on child's play. He said that any game that requires grow-ing children to sit on benches in expensive costumes while others played was obscene.

All three—Peyton, Cooper, and Eli—sing the same song: that for all Archie's willingness to "be there" for them, even to participate when he could lend a hand or teach a technique

(how to throw a better spiral, how to make a three-step drop),
he never made football a must. The fact that they all wanted to
play it in the end is no doubt attributable in part to his example, and the aura of his long-running stardom; but for them it
was always just a fun thing to do—on the field, in the yard, on
the rug. He made sure of it. Evidence that the methodology
also bound them closer can be mined directly from their conversation. It is not unusual for Peyton in the middle of a dis-
cussion to say, "My dad taught us . . . ," or "As my dad used to
say . . . ," or, "I asked Dad about it and he suggested. . . ."

In so favorable a cocoon, the drive to excel flourished
without the familiar negative side effects. During Peyton's
dreadful 3–13 first season with the Colts there were no
accompanying alibis, no shifts of blame, no busted water
coolers. Neither the young quarterback himself nor his old
quarterback dad would deny that the losing was torture.
"Peyton doesn't laugh off defeats," said Archie, "he examines
them, over and over, like laboratory specimens." But he got
through it with poise and with renewed convictions about
the value of hard work, and was not ashamed to say that his
phone talks with Archie helped ease the way. It was in
notable contrast to the actions of Ryan Leaf, who coming out
of Washington State had been thought of as Peyton's equal for
the honor of being first choice in the 1998 NFL draft. Leaf
was picked second, by San Diego, and had a similarly painful
start in the pros, but whereas Peyton kept his cool, Leaf lost
his—throwing tantrums, accosting media, even dressing
down the club's general manager, Bobby Beathard. The latter,
in a subsequent friend-to-friend chat with Archie Manning,
asked if he could "send Ryan to live with you for about six
months."

Peyton Manning might not even be capable of such out-
landish behavior, given what we know of the prototype.
Archie Manning's own passion for winning was legendary in
Mississippi, where from childhood he "wanted to be first in
everything I did." But in his fourteen years as a pro quarterback, his teams never had a record better than .500, never

won more than eight games; and even while the losing got more oppressive with the passing years, Olivia Manning will tell you that Archie never brought it home with him, never took it out on those he loved, never stopped being a class act. When the 1999 Colts won their *ninth* game, Peyton was asked if it pleased him that he had surpassed Archie's "best" in just his second year. "I don't compete with my father," he said. "I learn from him."

Later in the season, a popular sports magazine accompanied an account of Peyton's quantum leap into NFL preeminence with a cover title that read: "So Good, So Soon." About the same time, a national radio commentator said that Peyton's singular talent should not be considered a genetic spin-off, that his success was his alone to claim because in so many ways he had brought to the quarterback position a markedly singular talent and devotion. In both accounts, the phraseology was good, the perceptions skewed. Peyton Manning is as much an extension of his father and his family as a man's hand is of his arm. They are as connected as pipeline. Moreover, when you see the way Peyton handles himself now, you pretty much see the way he has been handling himself since childhood. The present development has a well-developed past. See Peyton play this game, with such breathtaking competence, and you see why he was succeeding long before success became such a profitable factor in his life.

To extract a fuller appreciation and understanding of this, however, you really must go back—back to where the Mannings and football first intersected. You must go back to the fickle soil of the Mississippi Delta, to a time and place where the game was played not as a means to an end but an end in itself. You must go back to Drew.

1

If you were to ask Archie Manning what there was about football that made it so defining, so important to him early on, he would tell you that it wasn't. Not then. For a boy growing up in Drew, Mississippi, football was one of the games you played, that's all; one of the fun things you did, no goals intended. . . .

From as early as I can remember, I played every sport available to me in school and on the playgrounds, which in Drew meant four: football, basketball, baseball, and track. Sports dominated your thinking if you were the least bit athletic, and more than a few of us went from one to another, season to season, like migrants. We were the embodiment of what used to be called (with great pride) the "Four-Letterman," the high school or college athlete who won letters in all four. You never hear that term anymore, except as it relates to a dubious vocabulary, because even at the lowest levels the seasons intrude or overlap and force you to make choices. If a kid plays two "organized" team sports now it's a lot.

But in Drew, and I daresay in most small towns in America in the '50s and '60s, there wasn't anything else. Only the big four. No soccer, no lacrosse, no field hockey. No swimming. Swimming was something you did in a lake or a pond in the summertime. Wrestling was something you watched on television. Forget about golf. Drew had no golf courses. No tennis either, to speak of. In the whole town there was only one tennis court, snugged in behind the Little

League baseball field, mostly just taking up space. The net was always torn or down.

Drew is a farming town, founded in 1898 by officials of the Illinois Central Railroad. It squats in the middle of what maps call the "Delta" in northwest Mississippi. The Sunflower River meanders by to the west and the Tallahatchie to the east, and the in-between is as flat as an ironing board. Cotton country, and soybeans and rice when the growing was good. Memphis qualifies as the nearest city—120 miles north into Tennessee. The Drew population stagnated a long time ago at just over 2,000, a figure that still includes my eighty-one-year-old mother, who wouldn't live anywhere else. Asking Sis Manning to live in New Orleans would be like asking her to live on Mars. In Drew, you can count the stoplights on the fingers of one hand and still have a finger left over to point out that one of the lights didn't have a yellow caution in the middle until recently.

Our house was right across the street from the high school, and within walking distance of Main Street. *Every* house was within walking distance of Main Street. It was a walk-everywhere kind of town, surviving pretty well when I was a kid, but now on the ropes with the farming so bad. They had a fire downtown a couple years ago that took out five stores, and the stores never got rebuilt. But Drew has always been a safe, easy place to grow up, terrific for kids like me who loved the freedom of being outdoors at any and all hours. Its only notoriety, if you can call it that, is that the state penitentiary is eight miles up the road at Parchman. Most of the kids whose parents worked there as guards and administrators went to school in Drew. My sister Pam's husband, Vernon Shelton, an Ole Miss history major, teaches the prisoners there now. (Pam won't live anywhere else but Drew, either. Must be in the genes.)

Occasionally as a boy I'd go up to Parchman myself to spend the night with a friend, and it always gave me an eerie feeling. They put hardened criminals in the penitentiary there, and every two or three weeks somebody would escape (the security was less than maximum), and when that happened, they'd make scary announcements on the radio: "A convict's out! Lock your doors!" But my daddy always said it wasn't something to lose sleep over because "if they break out of Parchman, they sure as heck aren't gonna stop in Drew." Most Drew people practiced what Daddy preached by never locking their doors. I'm not sure many of them even had locks.

Baseball, not football, was my first love, as it was with most kids I ran with in those days. It's the all-American game, where you don't have to weigh 250 pounds or be seven feet tall or run a ten-flat hundred to compete. An advantage baseball has over football when it comes to full-fledged team involvement (as opposed to backyard pickup games) is that no matter what position you play, you still get to do all the fun things: you get to hit, you get to field, you get to throw, you get to run the bases. And if you're a pitcher—the closest thing to quarterback—you get to pitch, too. But in football, if you're a guard or a tackle on either side of the line of scrimmage, you could go through life without ever touching the ball. In all but a handful of positions in football, you *never* do what most people (me included) would think of as the fun things: run the ball, pass it, catch it. Blocking and tackling are every bit as crucial, but you shouldn't have to do those things exclusively until you've at least had a taste of the others.

I mean, we played and played and *played* baseball, not just in its time slot on the school calendar, but all summer, too. At one point growing up, we actually made our own field, laid it out, and grassed it in, just like Kevin Costner in *Field of Dreams*. An old cotton patch had lain fallow between my house and my idol's, an older boy named James Hobson, and we put it there. The Hobson house was about two hundred yards from ours, giving us plenty of room, and we built a real field, with a pitcher's mound and everything. We filled burlap sacks with dirt to serve as bases and mowed a line at the outer limits of the outfield grass to serve as a fence. It had some lumps and bumps, but all the measurements were correct, and as far as I was concerned, it was beautiful.

When the baseball season started, we played pickup games there every chance we got, even if we could only muster five or six to a side. Pickup games are the best teachers when you're young and learning. You don't need parents hanging around scrutinizing when you're getting your feet wet in a sport, you need to be free to "fail" without it being a big deal. Who wins isn't important either, when you know there'll be another game tomorrow—or right after the one you're playing. Organization, and all the position channeling that comes with it, can happen later, when the appropriate skills are more clear-cut. That's especially true in football when speed and size factor in.

I remember the times we had on that field like it was yesterday. In the summer of 1961, when Roger Maris and Mickey Mantle of the New York Yankees were in that famous home run race that wound up with Maris hitting sixty-one, a kid named Jerry Knox hit sixty-eight homers in our little park—seven more than Maris! All that was important to me because the Yankees were my team and I was a typical obnoxious Yankee fan. I used to daydream about playing for the Yankees: "Archie Manning, shortstop, Drew, Mississippi. Bats left, throws right. Good speed, good arm, great bunter." Actually, the bunting part came later, when I got some specific tutoring (from a Drew High coach named "Tooter," if you can imagine), and, in my mind's eye, became a world-class bunter.

Saturdays in the summer were big in my house because that was the day the baseball Game of the Week was on television. I especially looked forward to it because my dad watched with me. He managed the Case Farm Machinery store in Drew, and on Saturdays he'd shut down at noon to come home for the games, and I'd be there waiting. I'd get butterflies waiting. It didn't have to be the Yankees. It could be any team, just so it was baseball. Just so it was sports. Just so it was the two of us.

Daddy was "Buddy" to all of us, but his real name was Elisha Archie Manning, Junior, my namesake. (I used to write it as "Archibald" instead of "Archie" until I saw the birth certificate.) He was a stubborn, feisty little guy, about five-seven, but he was good-natured and well-liked, too, and was the central figure at the Case store, which was a gathering place for fathers and farmers—the place to go to bullshit, if you want to know the truth. They called it the "Case Place." The farmers would come in and drink their nickel Cokes and just hang out. Even when Cokes were selling in machines for a dime or a quarter, my dad would still sell 'em for a nickel.

Buddy never pushed me in sports. They didn't mean as much to him. He'd played some football as a high schooler, without distinction, and when they wrote him up in the year-book it was mainly for his spunk: "When the fights broke out, Buddy was there." He was the youngest of five Manning children from the family homestead in Crystal Springs, Mississippi, down near Jackson, but he was nine years older than my mom when they married, and the difference seemed to grow with the years, because he was never all that healthy. He smoked and didn't exercise, and was always struggling—with his health, with his job at Case, with life generally.

The job was a hassle because the farming was iffy and a lot of the farmers had a peculiar mentality about paying their bills. They'd grow their crops and sell them, take the money and go right out and spend it—buy a Cadillac, take a vacation in New Orleans, go to the Ole Miss games and party, do everything Right Now, and never mind making the payments for the tractor they bought or the machinery they got fixed at Case. The kind of mentality that lived for the day. And I know that affected my father, because he was in a business that had to show results, and too many of his customers just flat-out didn't pay. I remember my mother going with him to collect from some of them, and how frustrating and embar-rassing it was.

So Buddy was usually "too busy" to be involved, but I didn't mind all that much because I was a consummate sports nut and really didn't need any props. But reinforcement in one form or another is necessary for every kid, as are role models, because so much of the learning process in athletics is imitation. You watch a good athlete do the things he does best and you copy. Which is where James Hobson came in.

I think it's universally true that every great athlete, even the best of the professionals, can tell you chapter and verse on a better one they knew and idolized growing up. James Hobson was that to me. I never told him, and I wish I had, because we've lost contact now, but he was the best. A few years ago when I was voted Mississippi's all-time "Greatest Athlete," I thought, "Boy, if they had only seen James Hobson."

James was three years older than me, and his father worked as a mechanic for my father at Case. He was the best player on the baseball team, the quarterback on the football team, a pretty fair basketball player, and a track star. I thought he hung the moon. I also thought he would wind up lighting up the scoreboards at some place like Ohio State, but it didn't happen. Drew was not exactly a hotbed for college scouts, and James wound up in junior college, then moved on to Delta State fifteen miles away in Cleveland. My dad and I sometimes drove over to watch him play. I lost track of him after that.

But when I try to pinpoint when football grabbed me, James Hobson's name keeps coming up, even if indirectly. We all played some version of the game when we were very young, mainly in the yard, and I thought it was okay. Something else to do. Then in the fifth grade I went out for a team in what was called the "Peewee League," open to fifth- through eighth-graders who weighed 120 pounds or less. It really wasn't a good mix, pairing fifth-graders who were maybe ten or eleven years old with eighth-graders who were fourteen, and I don't recommend it at all. Maturity is much more than a matter of weight, and the fifth grade is way too early to start organized play in football. Besides, I still thought baseball was a better game, and that I was better suited for it.

But I went out because I was eligible, even though at the time I weighed about 70 pounds dripping wet and was so scrawny and limby and white-skinned that I was ashamed to take my shirt off, even to go swimming.

And I went out because even at that age I knew that running back or quarterback were the only positions I would have any interest in, and they let me play running back (which in that first year meant I got to carry the ball maybe twice a game).

And I went out because James Hobson was on the team. Naturally, he was the starting quarterback.

I always worshipped "older" athletes, a factor partly attributable to our living across the street from the high school. When I was more into football, I'd come home for lunch—we called it "dinner" because it was our big meal— and hang around outside keeping a lookout for Ronnie Steed, Drew High's star quarterback. Without knowing it, Ronnie was my fashion guru. Whatever he had on I'd try to wear the next day—blue jeans, a white shirt, whatever. Sometimes when the older guys got up touch football games at the high school on Saturday and Sunday, I'd hang around until they needed a body to even up the numbers and they'd invite me to play.

In sixth grade, you might say by popular demand, I became the quarterback of the 120-pounders. James Hobson had moved up to the junior varsity, so the position was open. I wasn't necessarily thinking along those lines, however, because we had a coach then who at the first practice would line you up and pick your position for you ("Okay, you're the fullback ... You play halfback ... You're a guard..." et cetera, et cetera). Not exactly democracy in action. On selection day I was down near the end of the line, scared to death he'd make me a left tackle, and when he got in front of me, the kid on my right blurted out, "Archie's got to be the quarterback!" The coach gave him a look, then looked back at me, then smiled and said, "Okay, Archie, you're our quarterback." Elected by acclamation.

I was a quarterback from that day on.

Which is as good a place as any to stop and ask, why?

Why quarterback? What is it about the position that makes it so appealing? I'm biased, of course, but I think anybody who ever played the game could cite the reasons. Counting the mental requirements with the physical, quarterback is by far the most demanding position in all of team sport, and undoubtedly the most glorified. It is the biggest attention-getter at all levels of football, and the best-paid in the professional leagues. Fans know their team's quarterbacks better than they know their elected officials. Successful coaches know their quarterbacks better than they know their own children. They make it a point to.

For me, the challenge of playing quarterback—and it is certainly that—was as thrilling as it was daunting. Nothing I know of in any other sport, baseball and basketball included, could match the breadth of the skills involved. Peyton will tell you the same thing. The physical requirements are enough, but there is so much to it beyond the physical. The position is made-to-order for athletes who are natural leaders, "coach-on-the-field" types who *want* to be at the center of the action, and *want* the ball when a game is up for grabs. At the more sophisticated levels, every time a quarterback comes to the line to initiate a play, he not only has to know what his ten teammates are supposed to do (and how well they figure to do it), but what the eleven *opposing* players are likely to do as well. The homework alone—watching film, poring over playbooks—is mind-boggling.

And I won't even dwell here on the skills you need to pass the football—to put it precisely where it has to go, when it has to be there, at varying speeds and varying distances, sometimes when you're on the run from opposing players bearing down, or at the last split second before several hundred pounds of hostile flesh cascade over you.

Then you have to factor in that the targets you have to throw to are all moving, all with their own sets of skills and idiosyncrasies. Peyton can tell you about the thoughts that swirl through your mind and have to be accounted for when you're dropping back to pass: how the flanker now in the game might be a second-stringer and two steps slower than the starter on this particular pattern, or how the running back missed bed check and looked like a man carrying a safe on his back in warm-ups, or how the defensive end on the side the play is supposed to move toward hasn't been blocked all game long, et cetera, et cetera.

Moreover, football is a sport that is always evolving. It never stands still. As Bear Bryant used to say, it's "a coach's game," and the best coaches are marvelous innovators and incorrigible tinkerers. As a result, what's hot today is old hat tomorrow. The single wing gives way to the T, the T to the split-T, then the winged-T, then the I, the wishbone, the veer, the pro set, and on and on, each one offering a whole new set of mysteries to ponder. For quarterbacks it is a game of ever shifting constants and an unlimited number of variables. Thus, when Peyton huddles up with the Colts for season 2000, he is in a world much more complex than I knew as a New Orleans Saint almost thirty years ago. And that, of course, means even more pressure.

The result is a flip side that you wouldn't wish on your deadbeat uncle's most disgusting child, much less your own son. Check it out the next time the old home team loses a game, and see who gets most of the blame (besides the coach). See who gets the most flak from unhappy fans (and unhappy media). And never mind that in the end, a quarterback is still just one of eleven guys on the field at one time— more important than the others in terms of responsibility, but still just one of eleven. No quarterback ever won a game single-handed. Or completed a pass, for that matter.

You naturally tend to exaggerate those feelings of failure when you screw up as a quarterback, but that's predictable, too. Chances are you really did fail, in one way or another. It goes with the territory. I felt more than a few times that I was the reason my team lost a football game—when I didn't make the plays that had to be made, or threw a key interception, or made a wrong decision near the end. Peyton has experienced those things, too, just not as frequently as I did. Thank God.

So if you survive as a quarterback, you will be accustomed to being the center of attention, favorable and unfavorable. If you're not willing to accept the catcalls with the accolades, both of which are usually exaggerated, you really should find another position. Or sport. It's been my experience that the positives outweigh the negatives, and this is why the best all-around athletes who take to football almost invariably gravitate to quarterback. And do so early, as kids. They emerge as smaller versions of same in the sandlots and little leagues. The star quarterback that you see now was the boy who was singled out when you were choosing up sides in a vacant lot—the one you knew would call the plays and throw the passes. Sometimes he might be the *only* one who could do all that, and he'd have to quarterback both teams. I used to have that happen to me occasionally, quarterbacking both sides in sandlot games, and I loved it.

It was at that stage during puberty that I latched on, and from then it was the only position in football I wanted to play. I didn't care about anything else. When I collected football bubblegum cards, I'd weed through and discard everything but the quarterbacks (and the bubblegum). My "keepers" were Johnny Unitas and Bobby Layne and Lamar McHan, and Bill Wade from Vanderbilt, and Jim Ninowski, Milt Plum, and Y. A. Tittle. And of course, Charlie Conerly, who had made All-America at Ole Miss before he got *really* big with the New York Giants. Charlie was from Clarksdale, Mississippi, only thirty miles up the road from Drew.

So quarterbacking that Peewee team was a milestone, and I couldn't get enough of it once I started. Mercifully, the size gap had narrowed, though I was still intimidated by some of the older players. The coaches didn't pay much attention to the weight restrictions, and I'd shudder when I'd see those big, hairy-legged, 130-pound eighth-graders, who'd been over the limit at the weigh-in, sneaking into the games in the second quarter. But at that point I could run and throw the ball pretty well, and I hung in. And by the seventh grade, I was able to make some plays, most especially a rollout-right that

I'd call every time we got close to an opponent's goal line. The coaches let us call our own plays—which is another fun thing that's been taken out of the mix at all levels—and whenever possible I exercised my prerogative: rollout-right. I scored a lot of touchdowns on that play.

That year Drew sprung for a new football field for the high school and was going to name it after Beef Maxwell, who owned the Western Auto store downtown. Beef had been a fullback at Mississippi State, and if the world didn't know it, Drew did, and was justly proud. The dedication was scheduled for a Friday night, but on Thursday afternoon we played a 120-pound game on the new field, and I ran (rollout-right) for the only touchdown in a 7–0 victory over Ruleville. It was the first touchdown scored on Beef Maxwell Field. Nobody in the entire state of Mississippi would remember that but me, but it's as fresh in my mind as when it happened—one of those golden moments that make participating in sports so wonderful and live forever in your mind. Of course, I also remember striking out as a Little Leaguer to end a crucial baseball game and crying like a baby in front of my daddy, just so ashamed. When you screw up, *un*-precious moments also live on.

In the eighth grade I thought I had it worked out where I could quarterback *two* teams at once: as the regular starter for the junior high, and as a ringer for the Peewees on game days. James Hobson had done that, so why not? I'd practice only with the junior high team, but play for both. Pretty good deal if it hadn't been so unfair, and so obvious in a little town like Drew. The first time I did it with the Peewees, we killed the other team—and moms and dads on *both* sides raised holy hell. I couldn't blame them, especially the parents of the quarterback who practiced all week just so he could sit on the bench when I came over. I was relieved of duty from the Peewees.

I said earlier that kids in the learning stages don't need parents monitoring their every game or practice. That wasn't meant to minimize the value of adult involvement. I feel blessed for the help I got from adults and family along the way, even when they realized what a fanatic I was. An added advantage I had living so close to the high school was that the school system had housing available in the area and there were always two or three married coaches nearby for me to pester. I got to know them immediately because one of my daddy's finer points was his neighborliness. Whenever anybody moved in he'd invite them to dinner. He might not ever invite them again, but he'd do it then. A one-man Welcome Wagon.

And since my parents were older than most of the parents of the kids I ran with, I'd tie to those young coaches and their families. They'd spend time with me, teaching me techniques, giving me an old ball, giving me an old helmet. They'd see me out in the yard throwing a baseball or a football to myself—up in the air, catch it; up in the air, run under it, catch it—and they'd take pity and play with me. The reason I came to think of myself as a world-class bunter was because a coach named Cecil (Tooter) Holmes came to Drew High from Dallas when I was in the seventh grade, and as a neighbor was always including me in things. Sometimes he'd even take me on scouting trips to see other teams play. But that first year, Tooter taught me how to bunt, and later when I was on his high school team, he helped me hone the skill so that it became a big reason I hit for high averages at Drew and later at Ole Miss. I mean, Tooter could *bunt*.

I got real good at insinuating myself on people that way. The Mannings on my father's side were natural targets, so with them I was an even bigger nuisance. All five of the siblings who came from Crystal Springs were there in Drew, the four besides my daddy living on the four-hundred-acre farm their father left them: Uncle Andy (also named Frank, so I called him "Uncle Andy-Frank"), Uncle Peyton, Aunt Lucy, and Aunt Mamie. One small fact that speaks volumes about their personalities is that not one of them ever married. Mamie and Lucy had taught school and were old maids when they died. My uncles had girlfriends but never got them to the altar, or vice versa. Uncle Andy-Frank ran the farm with tenant laborers, raised cotton and oats, had some cows. Uncle Peyton was his right arm. (Yes, my son's namesake—*my* Peyton was born on Uncle Peyton's seventy-fifth birthday. Actually, though, Olivia and I had already decided to name him that, even if he'd turned out to be a she.) All four treated me like I was their mascot.

From the fifth grade on, I was a regular at Drew High football games, and if the team was playing out of town, Uncle Peyton was my wheels. My dad would go to the home games, but he wasn't keen on driving fifty or sixty miles to see one, so when I asked, "Can we go to the game tonight?" he'd say, "Where?"

"Over in Winona."

"Call your Uncle Peyton."

Uncle Peyton usually brought four or five of his friends and we all crammed into his old Studebaker truck. My tagging along might have limited their drinking and cussing some, but I had no qualms about that. I'd sit right in the middle of them. And on those rare occasions when Uncle Peyton didn't go, my mother would say, "Call Mr. Hughes," referring to a neighbor. And I'd do that, too, and it always worked. What're they going to say to a kid with his hat in his hand— "No, you can't go with us!"?

With Uncle Peyton, who liked to stay to the bitter end, we might get back from a road game after eleven o'clock, so he'd drive us on over to Cleveland to eat breakfast. Sometimes he'd drive us there for a movie. Saturday nights in Drew were pretty much confined to everybody hanging out on Main Street. Uncle Andy-Frank worked at Joe Mims's clothing store on Saturdays, and after he got off work we'd join him there and get an ice cream or buy something at the five-and-dime. The truth, though, is that if it wasn't sports, I really wasn't all that interested. Even into high school, if a weekend came and I had a choice between a date or playing Ping-Pong, I played Ping-Pong.

I credit Uncle Andy-Frank for turning me into a left-handed batter. I'd go out to the farm when I could, to where they had a peach basket strung up for backyard basketball games and kept a couple gloves and a baseball handy, and one day Uncle Andy-Frank told me it would be to my advantage if I hit left-handed. He said most pitchers were right-handed (true), which gave left-handed batters an edge (also true), and when you bunted from the left side you were that much closer to first base (true again). So I learned to hit lefty. He also recommended I learn how to *pitch* left-handed. That part didn't take. Now, when about all I do athletically anymore is play golf, I betray the results of a lifelong confusion by hitting my woods and irons right-handed and my putts left-handed.

As I grew into adolescence, I'd sometimes hire on at the Manning farm to chop cotton or run the tractor for three dollars a day. What *that* taught me was respect for those who chopped cotton and ran tractors, and that I didn't want to do either for a living. It was the same with the image I carry in my mind of the bricks on the high school building across the street from our house. They are indelible because one summer the town tore down the elementary school to make way for a new one, and I got a job cleaning the old bricks—chipping and scraping off the concrete so they could be recycled. A hard, hot, boring job they'd let you do whenever you wanted and for as long as you could stand it because the payoff was always the same: half a cent a brick. I didn't think about playing professional sports for a living until much later, but I knew from that one experience that I'd do almost anything *not* to be a bricklayer.

Both my aunts, Lucy and Mamie, were headstrong like my daddy, but especially Lucy. She never forgave Olivia and me for not naming our firstborn "Elisha Archie Manning the Fourth." I said no, because if he wanted to play the piano instead of football I didn't want him saddled with "Archie." We cut it off there, and when our first came along we named him after Olivia's father, Cooper Williams. Even then Aunt Lucy wouldn't call him that. She called him "Jackrabbit." The preacher at her funeral referred to her as "a tough old bird," and my mother nodded in agreement. But Lucy took care of

Mamie without complaint for years when Mamie developed a form of Alzheimer's, and in the end Lucy outlived all her brothers and sisters and ran the farm all by herself. When she finally felt compelled to sell, I told her I'd buy it, and worked it out for her to live there as long as she liked. She died at age ninety-two. We still own the place, but it hasn't been a moneymaker in a long time.

Interestingly enough, my mother's mother was named Olivia, too. Jane (Sis) Manning was born in Humboldt, Tennessee, to Olivia and Brady Nelson, and was raised with an older brother, Brady Jr. I don't know what the odds are that I'd marry a girl with the same name as my grandmother, but they have to go pretty high when you consider the name is as rare as "Olivia." Grandma Olivia was tall with long, slim legs, and she outlived three husbands and was still doing her own gardening into her eighties. Tough old birds evidently ran in both sides of the family. I used to spend two weeks with her every summer in Humboldt, listening to her complain to her second husband, who was a carpenter and, mercifully, couldn't hear well. When he died she married her high school sweetheart and moved to Mississippi, too—to Hickory Flat, up near the Tennessee border and even smaller than Drew.

Altogether, I suppose if you judged everything by net worth, you'd have to say the Mannings of Drew were a long way from wealthy. But we weren't the poorest by any means, and certainly never thought of ourselves as poor. My dad had the job with Case, and some sporadic income from his share (eighty acres) of the farm, and my mother had her job as a legal secretary. She still drives a new Buick she gets every year, and never puts more than three thousand miles on it, sticking so close to home. About the only thing we've been able to tempt her to New Orleans with lately was Cooper's wedding in March of 1999.

So I never had any real problems growing up, and part of that was because I never created any. I did what was expected, when it was expected. Not that there was much to get into in Drew—maybe steal a few green plums was all. But I did have one small taste of notoriety that convinced me early that crime was overrated. Actually, it was more a swig than a taste. At the Little League baseball field before practice one afternoon, a bunch of us were hanging around the closed-down concession booth when, for some reason, I tried the door. It opened. (How typical of Drew. Another unlocked door.) The temptation was too much. Eight or nine of us went in and helped ourselves to Cokes.

The theft must have been pretty obvious because the next day before our game the concessionaire complained, and somebody who bragged about it helped somebody else figure out who the culprits were. The next thing I know, my daddy's marching me down to the office of the mayor, W. O. "Snake" Williford, an insurance man and a great guy when he wasn't intimidating child bandits. We all confessed and paid for the Cokes, and the next night went back to the ladies who ran the concession stand and apologized. I couldn't have felt more ashamed if I'd robbed the Illinois Central.

Peyton squirms now when anecdotes are told that make him sound like a goody-goody, but it could very well be in his blood, at least as far as appearances are concerned. For thirteen years I went to the First Baptist Church of Drew without missing a day of Sunday school, an all-time record. It was a wonderful church, right in the middle of town (and right next door to the Methodists'), and I liked Sunday school. We had great teachers. Between Sunday school and church, we'd go to the cafe nearby for doughnuts and sneak 'em up into the balcony for the service. Sundays were fun.

But I have to say I wasn't participating for all the right reasons. I loved to compete, mainly. Getting those attendance pins was competition. I mean, I was valedictorian of my high school class and there were at least five or six kids who deserved it more than I did. I just competed harder. I didn't even take chemistry or physics or solid geometry my last couple years. I didn't want to, being so involved in all the sports (you *could* make a case that I was the most athletic), so I worked around the tougher subjects and got the grades that made me number one.

I joined the church when I was twelve, when it was "time." I knew the difference between right and wrong, but I think at that point I was joining just to be joining. I know when I went to college I didn't go nearly as much. The commitment, and the understanding of that little mystery that separates belief from nonbelief, came later, when I gave it more thought and realized why it meant so much to my life. Besides the singular faith in Christ, which is the most important thing, I think the things I learned as a kid in Sunday school took on more significance, and opened me to a greater awareness when I was into adulthood. My boys are finding the same thing now, when the teachings of the Church are central to coping in life. You don't get that kind of guidance and feedback sitting on a rock staring at the ocean.

But for a kid growing up in a small Bible Belt town like Drew, church activities come one after another (Sunday school, "Training Union," "Vacation Bible School"—I did 'em all), and I chafed when they interfered with my athletics, which was often. So did other things my folks pushed on me. The piano, for example. My daddy was a frustrated singer, and he loved to have my mother play the piano so he could sing Cole Porter songs with her. I think he expected me to follow my mother's lead, but at best my interest was marginal. The biggest whipping I ever got, and I didn't get many, was for missing a piano recital. It was scheduled for a Sunday at four o'clock, but after lunch ("dinner") I'd gone over to a friend's house for a touch football game, and the next thing I knew it was after five. Subconsciously, it might have been that I just lost my guts because I didn't know the piece I was supposed to play, but I didn't show up at the recital. And my daddy did. And he probably didn't want to be there either. Reasons enough to get out the belt. It was a major league whipping.

Not long afterward, I was "allowed" to quit piano. My folks realized it was no use. Now, of course, I'd love to be able to play, but I don't see it happening at this late date. Peyton is probably our last chance for musical redemption. He loves to sing, even though he can't sing a lick, and he says he's going to learn to play the guitar. He has one thing going for him: his persistence. He already cut one CD with a country music star, Kenny Chesney, for the NFL. Peyton sings in spite of himself, and if people laugh, he doesn't care. He loves it. I tell him Buddy and Aunt Lucy would be proud.

Baseball was still first with me into high school. But football had been closing the gap, and when I was in the ninth grade we didn't have enough players to field a junior high team, and I got invited to play on the high school varsity as the backup quarterback—right behind James Hobson, then a senior. Nothing glamorous about it, though. In practice all I did was imitate the other team's quarterback, running plays against the defense. But into the season, the coach told me he was going to use me in a play that involved moving James to halfback. I couldn't have been more excited. And the next day in practice I broke my right arm. I was out of the game, and out for the season. I was always nursing some kind of injury, but this was the worst.

At the beginning of my sophomore year I was six feet tall and still weighed less than 135 pounds, and began thinking maybe I'd had it with football. Too tough on the body. But a new coach for the varsity came to town, Gerald Morgan, and during one of my summer baseball games he took me aside and told me I was his "quarterback of the future." Morgan had quarterbacked at Ole Miss. We had another, shorter guy named Matt Land at the position, and Matt was a junior and tough as nails, but Coach Morgan had a mind to play me at quarterback and Matt at flanker, which was also to Matt's liking.

But the coach took it slow, didn't just throw me to the wolves. As the season went by I played more and more at quarterback, and by the time we finished I was doing pretty well. I started the last game.

So my junior year was going to be it. I'd start, Matt would

play flanker. Then in the third game of the new season, another disaster. A guy plowed into me full force as I was going down and shattered my left arm. Just crushed it. End of season for Manning. Same sad finish. When it came to football I seemed always to be wearing casts and splints. Too brittle, that's all. Not enough flesh and muscle around the bones. I broke my ankle (in the eighth grade). I broke my arms. I had a real bad break of the same left arm when I was at Ole Miss.

At Drew, though, when you lost a player for any reason it was an emergency because we only had a handful on the team. If a couple dozen guys came out in the fall, it was a crowd. Playing "both ways" (offense *and* defense) wasn't an honor, it was a necessity. My senior year we started with a twenty-five-man roster, and I think there were only two of us who didn't go both ways. We had another new coach, Paul Pounds, and he was afraid I'd get hurt. So was I. I was now a comparatively robust six-two, 160 pounds, but not at all confident that it would last. I had been up to 170 before we started workouts.

As it turned out, next to most Drew football seasons, that last one was a lark. We played our butts off to win five out of ten games, the first time Drew hadn't finished in the red in years, and won the fifth on the last day, beating Cleveland. I made it through the year without a single visit to the emergency room. But all that effort took its toll on the rest of the team. When our seven seniors went out for the coin toss, there were only eleven more Drew players on the sidelines. We were down to eighteen, all inclusive. Cleveland had twenty-seven *seniors*!

Coach Pounds lived next door to us that year, and when the season was about to start, he cracked a door I hadn't even thought of opening. He said, "This might surprise you, but I think you're college material. I think you're good enough to get a scholarship." There'd been some feelers. And the more I thought about it, the more excited I got. I had actually gotten faster, and felt I was stronger now, too, with a little added muscle from—I hate to admit it—helping a bricklayer.

Nonetheless, I wasn't counting on anything. Basketball season was starting, and I loved basketball. I averaged almost 30 points a game that year, and we made the state tournament. And then would come baseball, my first love. People in Drew who had seen me play, and some who hadn't, kept pumping me up with talk about my being a big league prospect (thanks in no small measure to Tooter Holmes), and I wasn't about to contradict them. Then there was track, in which I ran the sprints and the relays. And I was advancing toward graduating as valedictorian and class president, and being named "most versatile" and, to top it off, "Mr. Drew High." Altogether pretty heady stuff for an seventeen-year-old.

But as far as future play was concerned, I knew deep down my options were limited. No major league baseball team was beating down my door with a contract, and most of the college baseball programs didn't offer scholarships. The only real hope I had to further my education was through football, preferably at a school where I could play baseball, too. The catch was, I was only lightly recruited for football—nothing like the interest shown Peyton and Eli coming out of Newman High in New Orleans their senior years. Comparing my recruitment with theirs, where the "feelers" alone numbered in three figures, is like comparing a tidal wave to a leaky faucet. I wound up getting asked by only three universities—Mississippi, Mississippi State, and Tulane—for obvious reasons: My resume was loaded with risks. I was from a small school, on a very small team, at the bottom of a twelve-team conference. I was tall, skinny, and injury-prone.

With my three sons' recruitment a generation later, I got a good look at what recruiting for big-time college football programs has come to, and it's every bit as crazy-wild as it's made out to be, and unbelievably intense, and not always pretty. But for me coming out of Drew High it was mostly serendipitous. Like, "What have we here?" And it seemed as if everybody in town got in the act. One Friday afternoon when we were into the basketball season, Snake Williford called and said, "This is a little unusual, Archie, but I need you. Somebody over in Greenwood has stolen a car, and he's kidnapped two policeman, and they're heading our way." I reminded him we had a game that night, but he said, "Don't worry, this shouldn't take long."

You have to understand that the Drew police department is more *Andy of Mayberry* than *NYPD Blue,* so you couldn't exactly take anything for granted. They had a "day" man and a "night" man, and Mayor Snake moonlighted in emergencies. Evidently this was one. He picked me up in the police car and drove me out to Highway 49 at the edge of town, where he said we'd just "sit here and show our force" when and if the kidnappers came through. He had what looked like a machine gun in his lap, and was talking on the radio to somebody who kept saying things like, "They've passed Ruleville . . . looks like they're still coming . . . "

Then as we're waiting, Ol' Snake starts talking to me about going to Mississippi State. About all the advantages I'd have playing there. And he kept on, and after we'd been sitting there for half an hour, it hit me: he was recruiting me for State. My own mayor was trying to bait me!

Snake Williford aside, Mississippi State did try harder than the other two. The first time I'd ever been on an airplane was for a recruiting trip to Starkville. After that visit, they were driving eight of us recruits back to the airport in a van, and seven had committed to State. I was the only holdout. My dad tried to stay neutral, but not very hard. He said he was pulling for both, but a little more so for Mississippi State because it was "a farmers' team."

But of course, I didn't go to Mississippi State. I went to Ole Miss. It was my first choice from the get-go. I liked the school, the campus, the people. I liked the tradition. I liked the fact that Ole Miss was winning eight games or so and going to bowls every year while State was winning three or four and going nowhere. And probably as much as anything, I liked the idea of playing for Johnny Vaught, a coaching legend who ranked in the South with Bear Bryant of Alabama,

Bobby Dodd of Georgia Tech, and General Bob Neyland of Tennessee. Vaught had a reputation for developing great quarterbacks (Jake Gibbs, Charlie Conerly, Glynn Griffing) and I was told at the time that he was very much in the market for fresh blood. Mississippi's quarterback play had slacked off.

Johnny Vaught never came to see me in Drew. I wasn't enough of a catch to bring him. But he sent a longtime assistant named Tom Swayze, who'd played for the Rebels in the '30s, and had the final say on quarterbacks. I didn't get the impression I was high on Swayze's list, however. He came to the house to talk to me after a basketball game on a Monday night, and it was almost as if he wasn't exactly sure why he was there. He was a cocky kind of guy anyway, and he kept saying, "Well, what do you think about Ole Miss?"

And I'd say, "I like Ole Miss."

And he'd say it another way, as if he couldn't bring himself to say "We want you." Like he wanted me to say it first: "I wanta come to Ole Miss."

In those days, you could sign a Southeastern Conference letter of intent for a football scholarship on December 10, even though by National Collegiate Athletic Association rules you still had until February to sign anywhere else. And right at the end, when I'd signified my intentions, one of the Mississippi State coaches told me there were seven other quarterbacks committed to Ole Miss. He pointed out how tough the competition would be, and how in the past Johnny Vaught would recruit quarterbacks and then switch them to other positions. *That* got my attention.

But then came another Drew assist. Frank Crosthwait is our lawyer, and was a close friend of the family there for years. He was also well connected at Ole Miss. One night during the recruiting period, Frank called and asked if I wanted to join him for a trip to Oxford to see an Ole Miss basketball game. I said, "Sure." Oxford was only an hour-and-fifteen-minute drive.

So we went up, and after the game Frank said, "Let's stop

by the athletic office on our way out, I wanta check on something." It was nearly ten o'clock, and I couldn't imagine anybody being there that late. But there was. The whole coaching staff was there, Coach Vaught included. And they talked, and I listened, and that clinched it.

But it didn't end the dramatics. The freshman coach at Ole Miss was a wonderful character named Wobble Davidson—tough, funny, and so much a campus fixture that a book was written about him. Wobble had a colorful way of communicating, with a real vulgar tongue, and boy, he could get to you. He had nicknames for everybody. I was "Ichabod Crane" to Wobble Davidson the whole time I was at Ole Miss. He died not long ago, and I don't know anybody in the state who didn't mourn.

But Wobble didn't like to involve himself with incoming freshmen because he knew he'd be busting their asses on the freshman team. So he had a graduate assistant, Roy Stinnett, do the sweet-talking. Roy had coached high school at Clarksdale and was getting his graduate degree, and his recruiting area was the Mississippi Delta. He came to see me before Swayze, and then looked after me when I visited the campus at Oxford.

On the weekend of the signing date, I was playing basketball for Drew in a tournament in Clarksdale, against some bigger, better schools. I had worked it out with Roy Stinnett that I would sign with Ole Miss on Saturday, the last day of the tournament. And when we got to Clarksdale and started play, one of the tournament game officials turned out to be . . . Roy Stinnett!

Sure enough, we won on Thursday night, won on Friday night, and won on Saturday morning to make the finals that night. I signed between games, and then we won the final. Little Drew had beaten all those big teams. A major upset.

Now, I'm not about to say that our good fortune had anything to do with my recruitment, or that Roy Stinnett was anything but a totally fair and honest official in that tournament. I believe he was certainly that. But every time I had the ball the last two games, which was often, if an opposing player got within my zip code he was called for a foul. I shot forty free throws those two games, and scored a lot of points. And when it was all over and we'd won, I was named the tournament's Most Valuable Player.

If you want to jump to any conclusions about that, feel free. Either way, I'm not returning the trophy.

2

Peyton Manning fell in love with college football listening to tapes of his dad's Mississippi games almost twenty years after the fact. He was seven or eight years old when a friend of Archie's sent a collection of Ole Miss audio broadcasts from the seasons of 1968, '69, and '70, and Peyton soon had them squirreled away for his own. In the privacy of his bedroom in New Orleans, he committed the scenes to memory (and to the whims of his imagination, "since I could only hear the action, not see it"). Years later, when he passed up a chance for a lot of money to turn professional early so that he could play a fourth year at the University of Tennessee, it was generally assumed Peyton took the risk in order to give himself another shot at the Heisman Trophy. Not quite so. He wanted one more year of college football, primarily. He wanted a "senior season," hoping to extract a measure of the joy his father had known. . . .

I listened to those tapes over and over, like I was hearing them for the first time every time. It was a kick whenever they mentioned his name. "Manning of Drew rolls right . . . He throws downfield to Franks of Biloxi . . . Complete! Touchdown, Ole Miss!" "Manning eludes a tackler, he shakes off another . . . He's gonna run! . . . He's free! . . . He's at the ten, the five . . . Archie Manning scores again!"

I know that sounds corny, but it was fun. And it was happening at a time and place where college football was *it*. What made the play-by-play so intimate was that all the players were from Mississippi. All they had to say was "Manning of Drew" and you knew. I memorized them all: "Mitchell of Columbus," "Winther from Biloxi," "McClure out of Hattiesburg." You can't do that now because every major college team has players from all over. There's not as much allegiance to place. At Tennessee we had them from throughout the South, from New Jersey, from Texas, Ohio, Illinois, Oklahoma, even California.

From the radio tapes I could re-create the games myself, adding things about Dad: "Ole Miss comes to the line . . . Manning of Drew, the elusive six-three redhead with the rifle arm, is under center . . ." Later we got some videos of the games that had been televised, but I liked radio better because I could embellish. I did it even when we played in the yard, dubbing over the action like it was Dad instead of me with the ball. When I moved up to eleven-man teams, Mom said I'd come out of the huddle and up to the center with that same bowlegged stride Dad had.

Funny, but I never thought of it as imitation. It was, of course, and it shows the awe I must have felt. Dad's days at Ole Miss were life-shaping. For me, they were magical. If I could be a fly on the wall in time, I'd want to go back to when he played. Follow him around, do the things he did. I used to pester him for details. "What did you do on dates at Ole Miss?" "What did you do after a game?"

I'd have loved to make an entrance into a fraternity party on one of my lineman's shoulders, the way he did one night after a big game. It never happened to me, and it's not something you could ask for. (You can't say, "Hey, Joe, put me on your shoulders and carry me inside.") But I imagined what a trip it would be.

I'd love to have played a game where I got hurt in the second quarter and then came back and won it in the fourth, like he did against Georgia. But I never got hurt until the very end of my college career, and there were no heroics afterward, just the season winding down.

I wanted all the things my dad had. I wanted to have the girls look at me twice like he did, and walk through campus and have people I didn't know smile and say hello. He used to go to Memphis, to a restaurant called the Rendezvous, to eat with his buddies on a weekend. I wanted to go there and hear people say, "Yeah, your dad used to come in here." Not an ego thing, a fun thing.

Staying that fourth year in Knoxville helped, and it was good because I could relax and go with the flow more. I had worked hard to get my degree in three years. But when you combine a heavy class load with a full-fledged football commitment, you leave yourself very little breathing room, and those first three years went by in a blur. I had missed a lot. I wanted that senior year to sum up, but I also wanted to slow down the excitement so that I could savor every minute. I wanted to *walk* to class, and *walk* to practice, instead of sprinting everywhere. I did, too. And I went out to eat more, or hung out at fraternity parties to listen to the bands, and I did karaoke at somebody's house.

Sure, by playing another year I was gambling that I might get injured and blow the chance to make it in the NFL. I didn't, though, and when it was over I think I came as close as I could have to duplicating Dad's college days. I'm just not sure you could ever again completely experience what he had then. It was a different time. He made his deepest friendships, friendships for life, those four years in Oxford, and later they retired his jersey and he was voted a "Living Legend." All of it was magical. I wish I could have been a fly on the wall.

The University of Mississippi in Oxford is an hour's drive south of Memphis into the lap of William Faulkner country. It is a Deep South rendering of antebellum sophistication that held together with the school itself after the turmoil of mid-'60s desegregation to become a respected, integrated seat of higher learning, which would seem to coincide with what the earliest residents had in mind when they bought the land in 1836 from a Chickasaw Indian woman named Ho-Kab. The grand plan then was to replicate the learning center at Oxford,

England. The university was founded twelve years later. "Ole Miss," the favored name for those whose affection for it goes beyond buildings and books, now boasts more Rhodes Scholars than all but six U.S. universities—and a football program that has successfully made it from Then to Now with its achievement quotient intact. The Ole Miss teams were all-white when Archie Manning went there, but were already playing teams with black players; and they, too, were integrated the year after he left. They are now well-marbled, as the football program stabilized into a kind of working amalgam of past and present. The Confederate flag isn't flown at Ole Miss games anymore, but its teams are still called Rebels and its bands still play "Dixie." For Archie Manning, however, all that was incidental to more personal matters when he matriculated in the fall of 1967. Being there was just half the battle. Staying there was the thing. . . .

I was excited about going to Ole Miss, even if I didn't see myself as some cool guy about to make a splash at the biggest university in the state. It's a very social place, which you have to deal with when you don't have a lot of money to spend. But I was excited about making new friends, about playing sports in that environment. I also knew that everything depended on how well I did in football, because even if you're on a four-year scholarship, also-rans at big-time college programs have a way of slipping through the cracks and then not getting their degrees. You're there, then suddenly you're not, and all the hype you might have gotten coming in goes into the recycling bin. I didn't think that would happen, but I was ready for anything.

Seven other freshman quarterbacks came in with me in 1967, and that wasn't as unusual as it sounds. In those days, Division I schools could sign forty new players a year, and, with walk-ons, might very well field freshman teams of sixty or more players—more than an entire NFL roster today. Some coaches with the biggest budgets were notorious for stockpiling, for signing players just to keep them from going to a rival school. But they couldn't *keep* forty players a year because that would mean 160-man rosters. Clearly, some weren't expected to last. Those from smaller schools were long shots. Drew ordinarily wouldn't send a scholarship player to a Division I university like Ole Miss more than once in ten years.

I had that in the back of my mind when I got ready to go to Oxford, along with the very real possibility that Coach Vaught would do what he had a reputation for doing: move some of us to other positions. He was always looking for the right peg for the right hole, and he didn't mind messing with your preferences in the process. But that summer I got a break that boosted my chances. I was selected for the Mississippi High School All-Star game, to play for the North team coached by Bob Tyler of undefeated Meridian High, and Tyler liked to throw the ball. His quarterback, Bob White, another Ole Miss signee, was a high school All-American and, of course, was all set to be Tyler's starter in the game.

But Bob White had a bad knee, and early in the game he got hit hard and had to come out. I took his place—and immediately fumbled away the first snap. Fortunately, the North team's third quarterback wasn't a passer, so Coach Tyler left me in, and before the night was over, I had thrown for four touchdowns and ran for a fifth, and we won 56–33. When I was awarded the Most Valuable Player trophy afterward, I couldn't help thinking that I might not have played at all if Bob White had been healthy.

It happens all the time. In sports like football (baseball, basketball, et cetera) that are played nationwide by thousands of kids on thousands of teams, it's axiomatic: the line between those who make it and those who don't is paper thin. I'm not talking about superstars here, the ones who are head and shoulders above the rest (a Michael Jordan, a Wayne Gretzky, a John Elway), I'm talking about that huge second tier of really good athletes who arrive at crucial points in their lives with virtually the same credentials and potential, and very often make it or not depending on the luck of the draw. That line *is* paper thin. If it weren't, pro sports teams wouldn't be holding tryouts every year looking for talent that was overlooked or passed over somewhere along the way. They wouldn't spend so much time giving rejects a second, third, or fourth chance. Kurt Warner, the St. Louis Rams' quarterback and Super Bowl 2000 Most Valuable Player at age twenty-eight, was bagging groceries for $5.50 an hour in Waterloo, Iowa, five years ago.

Wobble Davidson saw that high school All-Star game, and there's another example of how thin the line is. Wobble had his own arbitrary ways of deciding who would play ahead of whom on the freshman team. Before his first practice, based solely on what he and his coaches had seen at these games or on film, Wobble would select his teams and designate position rankings by jersey color: red for the first team, blue for the second, white for the third, and so on. (The jerseys also had "UMAA" stenciled on the front, so they were hot items for the players to peddle to other students for spending money. The NCAA would *not* have approved. Welcome to the real world.)

On the first day, we eight quarterbacks arrived to be counted, each of us sporting a shaved head from the freshman hazing process, and all of us scared to death. We waited for the jerseys to be passed out.

And when they were, mine was red. I was first-string.

Was I the best? I like to think so, but I'll never know and neither will they, because not only was I proud of that jersey, I was possessive of it, too. I stayed number one throughout the freshman season. Would I have climbed up to first-team status if they'd given me the color jersey the eighth quarterback got, knowing that you don't get nearly as many repetitions in practice when you're not number one? I like to think so, but we'll never know that, either.

Staying "in the red" wasn't easy, though. Freshman players, by NCAA rule, were separated from the varsity then, as they should be still—freshmen have enough trouble adjusting to college life without heaping on the demands of varsity play. The freshman team had only a four-game schedule, so we practiced more than we played. But Ole Miss practices were long and tough, and making it tougher was that the freshmen played one-platoon then, meaning every player had to go both ways—offense *and* defense for half the season.

As a hedge against possible injury, quarterbacks played safety on defense, the farthest point from the ball we could get and still be in the game, but there was a lot of hitting, a lot of tackling, a lot of hard work. I weighed 170 pounds at the start, but Coach Wobble ran us like mad, and whenever I gave them my weight numbers ("170 pounds," "169") it was wishful thinking. I was below 160 most of the time. Besides that, freshmen didn't get the best-fitting equipment, and I dug a deep purple crease across the bridge of my nose from my helmet banging down every time I made a tackle. The crease lasted the season. I thought of it as a combat ribbon.

Peyton's heroic recollections aside, I had my share of downers those first weeks. The kind freshmen can expect when they're suffering through learning pains and homesickness at the same time. In our opening game we got beat 28 to nothing by LSU's freshmen, and at free safety I guessed wrong on a pass play that resulted in an LSU touchdown and got my ass chewed by Wobble Davidson. We had a break after that game and the freshman players were allowed to go home for the weekend. Some never came back. I had thoughts along those lines myself. In fact, on Sunday when it was time to drive back to Oxford, Buddy said, "You ready to go?" and I gave him one of those long pauses.

But I had never quit anything I'd started, so what came out instead of "no" was "I guess so."

I had no more doubts, and a lot more fun, after that. The next week I intercepted three passes against Alabama and we won, and then threw for four touchdowns when we beat Vanderbilt. Our last game was against Mississippi State. The night before, we met with the varsity and got our marching orders. Our hair was finally growing out, and one of the varsity players said, "I guess you know this game means more than all the others combined. If you don't win, we're gonna cut off your hair again." We won.

Peyton likes to think I was an easy rider from the moment I stepped foot on the Ole Miss campus, but the truth is my eyes were big as dinner plates over everything that happened that first year. Playing freshman ball. Going to class on a beautiful campus swarming with sharp-looking students. Seeing girls I'd like to meet, but thinking they were much too sharp for me. I mean, I wasn't from Memphis or Jackson, or even Yazoo City. I was from Drew. Plus I had that shaved head from the hazing, which was a bummer for a confirmed longhair who never considered himself handsome in the first place. I thought long hair helped me hide the fact.

It was the kind of indoctrination that automatically makes you cling to your peers, in this case the freshmen football players. Our rooms at the athletic dorm were our refuge from varsity players hounding us to get them food or wash their cars or shine their shoes for ROTC. To avoid them (and just about everybody else), we'd lock ourselves in a room and talk, as quietly as possible. And we really did bond, so much so that several of us have been the closest of friends ever since. Two were from the same school in Jackson: Skipper Jernigan, a guard, and Billy VanDevender, a safety; and Jim Poole, a tight end, was from Oxford. Billy was my roommate from my second year on and was best man at my wedding. Jim came from a family of football greats, including a much-celebrated end named Barney Poole who made All-America at West Point on the great Blanchard-Davis teams, then came back to Ole Miss in 1948 and made All-America there, too.

That summer I got the news I wanted most, but hadn't dared expect so quickly. Coach Vaught declared me his starting varsity quarterback for the upcoming season. It was unusual for him to go with a sophomore, so he really must have been hurting for quarterbacks, but I had no objections. He seemed to enjoy it as much as I did, because for years afterward he got a kick out of recounting an incident he remembered as a reason for his choice.

Of the eight quarterbacks he had brought in as freshman, only three were on the spring roster for our sophomore year.

(What did I tell you?) Bob White never recovered from the knee injury. A couple of guys quit. A couple more changed positions, doubtless on Vaught's orders. Besides being the head coach, Vaught also coached the offense, and in the spring of my freshman year when the other players divided up into groups at the dorm for after-lunch meetings, Coach Vaught took the quarterbacks over to his office where we could also watch film.

On that first day, he walked the three of us out to his car, which was like a pickup truck in that it was basically a front-seater with an open-air place in the back. Vaught led the way, and I was lagging behind when the other two quarterbacks hurried in with him, filling the front seat.

But I wasn't about to be relegated to that little bench in the back.

I didn't say anything, just squeezed into the front with them. Like it was the only appropriate thing to do.

Vaught said later he was watching to see what would happen, and that I did exactly what he hoped. He made it sound as if I wouldn't have been his starter if I'd let myself get pushed to the rear. The symbolism must have been a factor.

Johnny Vaught was a special coach and a special human being and one of the great men I've known. Old school, to be sure, but a relentless competitor, right up there with Bryant, Dodd, and Neyland. His very first Mississippi team (1947) won the Southeastern Conference championship, and he won five more after that, plus the school's only national championships in 1960 and 1962. His assistants worshipped him. He kept every member of the same staff together for about twenty years, sometimes in the face of great temptation. One year Bruiser Kinard turned down the head coaching job of the Buffalo Bills to stay on as his offensive line coach. You'd think it couldn't happen, but it did. Vaught kept his coaches close. When my daddy died, every single one of them came to the funeral in Drew.

The private Johnny Vaught was a gentleman in every sense of the word, courtly, very bright, very sharp. He wouldn't say anything bad about anybody, so you had to gauge his true feelings sometimes by how much "good" he said. For three years he advised me on everything from the length of my hair (he didn't like it long, probably because of his own shortcomings) to the possibilities of my becoming a pro. He screened my "contacts" to protect me from opportunists. Vaught had an air about him, like a tough but friendly bank president. He was a snappy dresser who looked good in sports coats, and he had an impressive selection of shoes made from the skins of reptiles. He wore brimmed hats to cover up his baldness, but after he quit coaching he switched to a hairpiece. I'd have stuck to the hats, but either way, he looked elegant.

The one worm in him was that he couldn't remember names. Over the years, he had coached so many players who came from the same schools or the same areas of the state that he'd get them mixed up. Reggie Dill was a linebacker on our 1970 team. His brother Kenny had been an All-America at Ole Miss eight years before, so Reggie was "Kenny" to Coach Vaught from the first day to the last. Other players heard him call me "Jake" a few times, which didn't hurt my feelings any. "Jake" was Jake Gibbs, his All-American on the 1960 championship team.

Like Peyton (and yes, like me), Coach Vaught loved to reminisce—about past games, about past players, about other coaches he admired. My favorite Ole Miss quarterback was Gibbs, and Vaught would tell me stories about their big games with LSU when LSU had Billy Cannon, and him coaching against Dodd and Bryant and Paul Deitzel. I doubt many players get to talk to their head coaches about the past anymore, or would even take the time to. The love for reminiscing is not likely to be there when you haven't been weaned on the tradition. Peyton found that out at Tennessee. Few of his teammates knew anything about General Neyland.

Coach Vaught was an offensive genius, but an unlikely one. He'd been an All-America guard at TCU, and you just don't expect guards or tackles to know that much about the

game overall, especially when offenses got to be so complicated that everybody but the quarterback (who *has* to know
the total picture) was hard-pressed to keep up with his own
assignments. But when Vaught got into coaching, he
devoured everything he could learn about offense and was
way ahead of most of those he competed against. It helped
that he was an unabashed, unrepentant pirate of other
coaches' ideas.

One of his jobs as Ole Miss's offensive coordinator ordinarily would be to break down the film of an opponent's
defense the week of a game to determine how and where to
exploit it. But not Coach Vaught. He watched the other
team's *offense*, to find formations and plays he could use
himself. Houston was a good source for him in those days—
an outlaw school when it came to the rules, but with good
players under a master of innovative offense, Coach Bill
Yeoman. Coach Vaught would pore over the Houston films,
and when he saw something he liked, he'd take it for his
own. Nothing illegal about it, of course. Coaches in all sports
borrow from one another all the time. Vaught just laughed it
off. "Coaches are great plagiarists," he'd say.

Johnny Vaught is rightfully credited for putting his particular spin on the sprint-out pass, which happened to be my
long suit. But he also liked the veer option that Yeoman
worked so well at Houston. Vaught would say, "If we could
ever combine the veer and the sprint-out, we'd be unstoppable."

He was probably right, but I didn't think of myself as the
quarterback to do it. I was not a convert to the veer at all. It's
an option offense, essentially, a derivative of the old split-T,
and I didn't like the option because quarterbacks get clobbered almost every time they run it, whether they keep the
ball or not. The veer isn't for injury-prone, six-foot-three-and-
a-half-inch stringbeans (although I was then pushing 200
pounds); it's for tough, wiry five-foot-eight-inchers who can
run better than they can throw. I had no desire to be an
option quarterback. I felt if we were going to concentrate on

anything other than the sprint-out it should be the drop-back pass, which is what the pros do ninety percent of the time. But Coach Vaught kept slipping it in on me, mixing the veer with some play-option passes.

In those days, college quarterbacks called most of their own plays. You were drilled in meetings to be the coach's voice on the field—to think like him, to call the plays he'd call. I could do that with Coach Vaught. I understood what he had in mind. He said his confidence in me was such that "anything Archie wants to do, anywhere on the field, is all right with me." On those occasions when he'd send in a play he *really* wanted called, I got so I could anticipate what it would be, depending on the game circumstances (the down and distance, the score, the time to play, et cetera).

But he made one mistake. He gave me latitude to over-rule him. So whenever he sent in an option play, I'd almost always check out of it at the line of scrimmage—not to go against him so much as to do what he had me in there to do, with the skills and body God gave me. I mean, Houston could run the veer because that was Houston's offense, and Yeoman recruited for that purpose. If Coach Vaught had wanted to run the veer, I was the wrong man to be his quarterback.

We actually started a slew of sophomores on offense that 1968 season, all of us green as grass, and when we played Memphis State in the first game, we were so scared we were bumping and stumbling into one another like baby chicks. Memphis State was real physical, and we let it get to us. We made one first down in the first half. But then in the second we straightened out. I made a long run and threw a couple of touchdown passes, and we won, 21–7.

We had our moments that year, and beat some good teams—most notably Alabama, by 2 points. But we lost to a better Georgia team, and lost to Houston. Then in Baton Rouge, in Tiger Stadium, we came from behind to beat LSU, and a big part of it was a pass-or-run option play (of all things) that Coach Vaught installed. It was one I had to call at the line of scrimmage, depending on how the defense lined up.

LSU never got it right. We won, 27–24, with a touchdown pass off a sprint-out option at the very end, and I was named National Back of the Week. A first, and a big thrill. But Coach Vaught deserved the credit.

Two weeks later, we went to Knoxville to play Tennessee, and got slaughtered, 31–0. I threw six interceptions.

High school, college, or pro, it was the worst game I ever played.

We did a lot of drop-back passing that day, and I never was the drop-back passer I'd like to have been. It's funny, but I actually know the mechanics now better than I did then. And on that day the wind was whirling, which played havoc with my passes, and Tennessee whipped us up front, and everything combined to make it a total blowout. Twenty-some years later when he was a freshman at Tennessee, Peyton dragged out that game film, and after watching it to the bitter end had it transferred to videotape. He sent the tape to me, with a note: "Dad, you were awful." He was being kind.

Nevertheless, that first year we finished 7–3–1, including a Liberty Bowl victory over Virginia Tech in Memphis. What made it encouraging was that Ole Miss hadn't threatened for the SEC championship in five years, and Coach Vaught was getting tired of making excuses. He felt maybe we had turned the tide.

There was something else turning in my life then, too. Making an impact in ways football never could. A budding relationship with an Ole Miss coed, who before we left school as graduating seniors would be my wife, and who would later become the mother of my three sons. A girl who when she first laid eyes on me thought I was absolutely obnoxious.

Olivia Williams of Philadelphia, Mississippi, saw me long before I saw her. Which if you knew Olivia then (as now) you'd have to say was definitely my loss. But on the night in question, I was on the basketball court in Philadelphia, leading an underdog Drew High team to what sportswriters like to describe as a "stunning" victory over Philadelphia High, her school. It was a big embarrassment for Philadelphia, a town almost three times the size of Drew, and compounding the embarrassment was me.

But let Olivia tell it:

"I was a big basketball fan, and basketball is huge in Philadelphia. We were hosting the regional tournament, which we almost always won to go on to the state finals in Jackson. But that night we got upset by this little Drew team, and there was Archie, as cocky-looking a player as I'd ever seen. Long red hair. Tall and skinny. Dribbling the ball behind his back like a Globetrotter. Making shots from every angle.

"Anybody who knows Archie would tell you there's nothing cocky about him, but that's the way he came across. I know losing to Drew probably colored my thinking, and if he'd been doing the same things for us instead of to us, I'da been cheering, but he had a style that just made me cringe.

"I came back with my dad two nights later to watch the finals, and in that game the Drew team put on what was known as a 'freeze,' where you try to beat a better team by stalling. Holding the ball, passing it, and dribbling it endlessly, and almost never shooting. Stalls were legal then. There was no mandatory shot clock. Drew lost, 4 to 2, but the thing I remembered was Archie dribbling, dribbling, dribbling to keep the ball away from the other team. I told my friends I not only didn't like him, I despised him. He dribbled all night long.

"That summer, a bunch of us went over to Jackson for the North-South All-Star football game, and there he was again. It was known then that he was one of the high school recruits signed to play at Ole Miss. He didn't start the game, but he wound up being the star and getting the MVP trophy. I couldn't stand it."

The princess and the loathsome pauper met at Ole Miss the next year. It was the only school Olivia applied to, the only place she wanted to go. Her older brother, Tommy, was there, her dad had been there before Barney Poole played, and her dad's sisters had been in the same sorority she wanted to pledge, Delta Gamma. And it turned out that one of the guys she knew when she came to Oxford that fall was Jim Poole, who by then had become a good friend of mine.

One afternoon Jim and I were walking across campus and Olivia pulled up in the new white Ford LTD she'd talked her daddy into buying her. (There wasn't much she couldn't talk her daddy into, and he could afford to indulge her.) She said, "Where you heading, Jim?"

"The drugstore."

"Get in, I'll drive you."

"Both of us?"

"Sure."

She introduced a girl who was with her in the front seat, and when Jim introduced me, she said, "Oh, I know who *you* are. You're the one who beat Philadelphia our senior year." Like it was something I should be ashamed of.

Naturally, I was impressed.

But who wouldn't be, really? She was pretty. She was tall and willowy, like a model. She was vivacious. She was smart. And she knew football. Not the X's and O's, but the essence of the game. It came naturally. Her daddy, Cooper Williams, had played some at Ole Miss as a walk-on, and her cousin, Frank Trapp, was then a junior linebacker lettering for the second straight year. In fact, her whole family was athletic. Her mother, Frances, had made all-state in high school basketball, and brother Tommy was a junior on the Ole Miss basketball team. There wasn't much about sports that she couldn't talk about.

Our one significant difference was economic. My dad was struggling, hers owned a Standard Oil distributorship, a cotton gin, and most importantly, a one-of-a-kind country store named "Williams Brothers" that he had taken over for his father as a teenager. Williams Brothers sold everything from groceries to bib overalls. It had one clerk who did nothing all day long but slice slab bacon and hoop cheese for the customers. The store was written up in the '30s by *National Geographic* for selling more snuff than any place in America, and had a reputation for adjusting to its clientele. Once, for example, it had a room where only Nike shoes were sold.

Williams Brothers had always been a family operation, which meant the whole family profited. Which also meant I never saw Olivia in the same dress twice. Nor the same car for more than a year or so. First she drove the LTD, then a new Mercury, then a new Caprice. She admitted once that her daddy enjoyed spoiling her so much that she was allowed to drive at age thirteen. But you couldn't resent any of it with the Williamses because they were all so warm and gracious, with so much trust in people and each other. Olivia's younger brother, Sid, runs the store now, and Tommy and her younger sister, Cynthia, still live in Philadelphia along with her parents. Her dad drove carpool for his grandkids for years—picking them up at their homes, taking them to school, to the park, to wherever, then bringing them home. He said it was the best job he ever had.

Cooper Williams was my biggest ally from the start. He liked the idea of Olivia and me. She told me later that after we were going together for a while, she wanted to take a summer trip to Europe with some of her girlfriends and he wouldn't let her because he was afraid we might break up. I didn't know it at the time, but Olivia called him before our first date and said, "Hey, Daddy, guess who I'm going out with tonight?"

"Who?"

"Remember that show-off from Drew who beat us in basketball?"

"Archie Manning?"

"Yes. It looks like he might be Ole Miss's next varsity quarterback."

And her daddy chirped, "When are you gonna bring him home for dinner so we can approve of him?"

He's a delight, Cooper Williams. His grandkids call him "Paw-Paw," and when Peyton was at Tennessee, Paw-Paw would call the Nashville talk shows long-distance to get his two cents in. But he couldn't hear too well, and as he waited to be connected you'd hear him on the radio saying, *"Hello! Hello! Am I on! Hello! Am I live!"* When his namesake, our Cooper, got a radio show of his own in New Orleans in 1998, the station had enough range for Paw-Paw to pick it up in Philadelphia. One night when he was feeling his oats, he called the show. In a loud voice he said he wanted people to know there was a third Manning coming along *"WHO'S GONNA BE BIGGER AND BETTER THAN ANY OF THEM!"* He meant Eli. Cooper laughed and said, "Congratulations, Paw-Paw, you just got me fired." Olivia's mother laid the law down after that. No more calling talk shows.

Cooper Williams is in his eighties now but still gets around. He saw most of our games at Ole Miss, and several of Peyton's in Knoxville. When I was with the Saints he bought season tickets and made every home game, plus a lot of the road trips. If he couldn't get anybody to go with him, he'd go alone to wherever we were playing. He'd fly to San Francisco, watch the game, then grab a cab for the airport. He said he wasn't there to sightsee or spend his money at fancy restaurants, he was there to watch football. He loves it.

Olivia and I actually began our courtship very cautiously, no doubt because she still thought of me as public enemy number one. Our first "date" was hardly a date at all.

At the end of the freshman football season, I joined Sigma Nu, with Jim Poole and some other players, and one night we had a "swap" at the fraternity house, where pledges from Delta Gamma came over to dance. Olivia was one of them. I hadn't seen her since she gave us the lift in her car. We danced, and it was easy going because she could talk football. She said she was surprised (having already formed an opinion) that I was so quiet. A little like Eli is today. She said she probably should have just kept her own mouth shut, but she grew up loving football, and there was no keeping it inside.

I'd been dating, but not seriously, so I asked her out.

To the library.

On a weeknight.

Olivia said she figured it was because I was "so much more studious" than she was (she was studying elementary education, but halfheartedly). My budget was the real reason. She said the fact was she was glad it was the library because there was a ten-thirty curfew at the dorms (midnight on the weekends), and that was her "out" if a date didn't go well: "Sorry, gotta go home now. Curfew, you know." But despite the misgivings, we hit it off pretty well.

One date led to another, and that summer when I went home to Drew, she went to Texas to modeling school, to give herself an option if she didn't take to teaching, which there didn't seem to be much danger of. And I realized how much I liked her, how much I already missed her. Nothing was etched in stone, but at the start of our sophomore year, we began what Olivia would tell you was a very eventful courtship.

So let her:

"All of it was fun, and everything fit. At Ole Miss, you knew everybody, anyway—a walk across the campus was a series of thirty-second conversations—and my best friends were girlfriends of Archie's teammates. It was like having a club all our own. We hung around together, played and partied and studied together, did everything together.

"College football games in the South then were even bigger than they are now. Serious social events. I'd known that from going to the Ole Miss games with my folks, the men in coats and ties, the women in hats and gloves and wearing corsages. You dressed up for the college games and down for the pro games. I knew on Monday what I was going to wear on Saturday, and I knew that first Saturday what I'd be wearing all season. As Archie says, I wouldn't be caught dead wearing the same outfit twice.

"If we went to an away game, say to Nashville, we girls would go up together on Friday and go out to dinner (without the players, of course; they were back at the hotel getting their beauty rest). Then we'd shop all day Saturday right up to game time. One year I had a friend who spent every bit of her tuition money on clothes. After games, we'd meet the guys and do whatever you normally do with boyfriends, except that if an overnight was involved we had to be chaperoned. My home was only eighty miles from Jackson, and when Ole Miss played there, Archie would sometimes come home with me in my parents' car.

"Dating the star quarterback was a big deal, I won't deny that. Automatic status. But I'd always vowed I wouldn't marry anybody who wasn't 'tall, dark, and handsome,' and although Archie was certainly tall, and cute (he didn't qualify as good-looking until later), he was anything but dark. And he had that shaved head. And compared to me he was about as talkative as a stone. I fell in love with him anyway. Our whole family did. He was so nice, so straight. He had a great sense of right and wrong, and a spiritual side you had to admire. I couldn't help but love him.

"We bonded quickly, and in the three years we courted, hardly ever had a cross word. Archie isn't the squabbling type. He knows instinctively when not to say the wrong thing, and he'll avoid a fuss more often than not, usually with good reason. But we did break up once, after Mississippi State tied Ole Miss that sophomore year. The game was played on Thanksgiving, and Archie was supposed to come to our house afterward for dinner. But he was disgusted by the tie, more than I'd ever seen him. He admitted he was in an ornery mood, which was unusual because he doesn't take his setbacks out on others.

"One word led to another, and he finally said, 'You go ahead home, I'm going back to Drew.' And I did, and he did. But neither one of us wanted it, so it was a brief separation. A week at the most.

"I don't think our differing backgrounds ever worked against us during that time, but I really didn't get to know his side of the family until after his father's death. I hadn't spent any time in their house in Drew, and I couldn't say I knew his father at all. Later, I got to know and love and appreciate his mother, and we'd go to the games together, but there was a lot to fathom when his father committed suicide. My own conclusion was that he had weighed his bad health against the problems he had making ends meet, and decided he just couldn't go through life as an invalid.

"I know I'll never forget the day it happened. A hurricane had hit the Gulf Coast, Hurricane Camille, and it was a rainy, depressing day. A close friend of the Mannings, Louie Campbell, called to tell us the bad news.

"My family went to the funeral, but we had to stay at a motel in a nearby town because there were no accommodations in Drew. Afterward, we had lunch with the family at the house, and I remember thinking how strong Sis Manning was, and Archie's sister, Pam, home from Delta State. And Archie—really, really strong in the face of all that sadness. He didn't unburden on me except later to say how it hurt that his dad had never taken the time to tell him he loved him. He touched on the irony of it all—that he was just about to make his dad super proud at Ole Miss, and then if he went pro could maybe make his family's life a little easier. It bothered him that his dad had worked so hard with so little to show for it. He had to be thinking, 'Why now?'

"Archie more or less lost his sorrow in his football after that. But I know his dad's death drew us closer from then on. There were just so many unanswered questions. . . ."

The way it happened, I'd completed a semester of summer school after my sophmore year at Ole Miss, and Buddy had driven over to Oxford to get me for my two-week break. That night, he and my mother and I went down to Indianola, Mississippi, for an Ole Miss alumni meeting. Billy Mustin, who was on the staff at Ole Miss and had played there, was the speaker. Billy and his wife, Sue, ran the football dorm and lived there. At the banquet, he was very complimentary of me, saying something like, "I hope my son grows up to be like you."

When I pointed that out to a writer later, he took it wrong

and his story made it sound as if Billy's remarks might have triggered something in my dad. I didn't mean it that way at all, and certainly didn't believe it. The fact was, my dad was stoic about his poor health. He resisted treatment of any kind. When he'd had his stroke five years previously, he stayed home a week before he went to the doctor. He was stubborn that way. He didn't like doctors, didn't like medicine, didn't like to coddle himself.

He came out of the stroke with no grave aftereffects. No slurred speech. No noticeable impairment. But you could tell the way he moved that he wasn't well. He was only fifty-nine, but an old fifty-nine (he was past forty when I was born), and he wasn't in the best of spirits because business was so bad. But he'd seen several of my games that sophomore year (my mother saw them all), and he seemed in pretty good spirits on our ride home from Oxford and that night at Indianola.

The next day we went to a wedding, and then the wedding reception. Buddy stayed home. He said something about me coming back to "cook steaks" with him later. At the reception, a couple buddies of mine wanted me to ride over to Cleveland with them to drink beer, but I remembered about the steaks and I said, "No, I want to go on home. I'll hang around there this afternoon and catch up with you guys tonight."

And I went home, and was walking by his little bedroom to go to the bathroom when I saw my dad lying back on the bed, his legs stretched out with his feet touching the floor. It didn't register at first, and I kept going. Then it hit me, and I turned back. I see it now as a series of still shots, each one clear but incomplete. I see the gun on the floor, and the stick he used to fire it. And him lying there, faceup, very still. And a big blood spot on his chest. "Oh, God," I thought. "Oh, God, no." I was twenty years old, and my first thought was, "Thank God my mother's not here. Oh, God, thank you that my sister's not here."

I ran to the phone and called the doctor. I wasn't sure of

the gravity of it, but I said, "I think Buddy's dead." I called Louie Campbell, who was not only a family friend but one of my dad's hunting buddies. I said, "Louie, you need to find Sis and Pam right away and get them down to your house. Whatever you do, don't bring them here."

I cleaned up the house before they got home. And later I went through all the things you have to go through, the clothes, the papers, and did all the things I didn't want my mother to have to do. That's when I told her I was going to quit Ole Miss and stay home, find a job in Drew, and work to keep the family together. And that's when she told me she wouldn't have it. That I was going to get my college education, period. And play football, period. And "after that, we'll see."

I haven't talked about it much over the years. I never talked to my mother about it in any depth. I don't talk to my kids about it. Olivia and I have gone over it from every angle without any real conclusions. But I still *think* about it. A lot. When it's my mom and dad's anniversary, or the anniversary of his death, it comes back strong. Then I might mention it to my mom, and she'll say again that she thought he just didn't feel good anymore. That he couldn't see himself being a burden. She knew him better than any of us, of course. Maybe the only one who knew him well.

I know without a doubt that I'm a lot closer to my kids than I was to him, and maybe that's a generational thing. I look back and remember most of the kids I palled around with had daddies that were much the same as Buddy. Maybe that's why I'm so much closer to mine. Because I missed that with him. By the same token, I don't absolve myself completely of the blame. Buddy loved to hunt. During bird season, he hunted every chance he got, with that same twelve-gauge shotgun. And I seldom went with him, just once or twice a year. I didn't like it. But I regret, now, not going with him more. It would have helped me get to know him better.

Buddy Manning was actually a sharp, witty guy when he was in the mood. He'd gone to college at Bowling Green, Kentucky, and had taught English part-time somewhere. He knew poetry. He *really* knew the Bible, and could teach it. Our church's blue-hairs, the most devout people on earth, used to rope him into teaching a Sunday school class, and they thought he was great. But every Thursday they'd have to call him to make sure he wasn't going to play hooky and go hunting. My mother saw that other side quite well. Sometimes Buddy would sneak off to a little club in Drew to play poker with his friends, and Sis would steam. I remember driving over to the club with her at ten o'clock one night, and her sending in a message for him to come on home.

I guess because he and I didn't mesh as well as we might have makes me remember the harder images. He was definitely a taskmaster, and I think that was to my advantage in the long run. I'm one myself, albeit with a softer edge. But as a kid I didn't like it much. He had a rule about cleaning your plate (he said it was because he wanted me to get stronger, which I could appreciate), but I remember at age eight or nine walking to school and emptying my pockets along the way of the eggs I was supposed to have eaten for breakfast. One time I left a big helping of tuna fish on my plate and he practically forced it down my throat. I got so mad I called my Aunt Lucy and told on him, thinking she'd hustle right over and tell him off. She didn't, of course.

To this day I can only speculate why my dad did what he did *when* he did it. He'd never threatened anything like that. He was proud, and he was tough, and he just didn't seem the type. I do know that nothing in my life before or since has hit me like that. I've really had a wonderful, easy life by comparison, with no other life-or-death traumas until years later when we discovered Cooper's illness.

I don't think my dad's death really hit me until I was back in school at Ole Miss and we were practicing two-a-days for the fall. Then it got me: the impact, the loss. The things I thought about then were the things he and I *didn't* do, and might still have done. He had never shared in my life as much as I'd have liked growing up. We really had no mutual triumphs, on or off the playing fields. He never really praised me a lot either, but I think that had more to do with him not wanting to show favoritism over Pam.

He had ways, though, of letting me know he cared, and these I remember now.

Between my freshman and sophomore years, when it was announced I was going to be Johnny Vaught's first sophomore starter at quarterback, I was working at home for a bricklayer and turned over a load of bricks on my ankle. The ankle swelled up like it might be badly hurt, so I went to the doctor in Drew and he put an Ace bandage around it and gave me a pair of crutches to use. He didn't take X-rays; I'm not even sure he had an X-ray machine. So I hobbled on home, and when my daddy came in, he saw the bandage and just exploded. "What happened? What'd you do? Are you all right?"

He immediately called Bob Tyler, the receivers coach at Ole Miss. Tyler came to Drew the very next day, picked me up, and drove me to the Campbell clinic in Memphis for X-rays. Turned out to be nothing serious, but it gave me a better sense of my daddy's true feelings. It reminded me of the time Tom Swayze came to recruit me. I didn't think Buddy had any interest in my recruiting until then. Swayze arrived early and stopped by the Case place to see him. They went to the coffee shop and visited. Coach Swayze told me afterward how interested my daddy was about my going to college, and how much he seemed to care about me.

He attended some of my freshman games, and then the home games my sophomore year. When we went to the Liberty Bowl in Memphis, he and Sis drove the ninety miles to the game on the day it was played, then back that night. I remember it well because it was the last one he ever saw me play.

It was one of those bitter cold days that Memphis is famous for in midwinter—so cold, in fact, that the girlfriends of our group decided at the last minute to cut and go shopping, where they could warm up in the stores. They reappeared outside the locker room afterward, pretending they'd been at the game all along, but Olivia confessed later that they'd opted for comfort. It was considered such a sacrilege to miss a game that one of the girls didn't tell her future husband she'd skipped out until five or six years later.

Anyway, it was so cold that when the game started, a bunch of the mothers moved from their choice seats down to the end zone where they could face the sun. The dads stayed right where they were, having had the foresight to bring Jack Daniels and Old Granddad along for company. After the game, I saw Sis and Buddy before they took off for Drew, and there were no signs of frostbite so we said our good-byes. But when I called later to make sure they got home safely, my mother told me that when the car was warmed up good, "all that whiskey went to your dad's head and he was drunker'n a skunk."

By the time they got to Tunica, about thirty miles from Memphis, she had to take the wheel. She said, "We were lucky your dad didn't fall asleep before we realized what was happening to him. I drove the rest of the way."

I still think about him. I think mostly about the times we've missed since then. The pleasures we would have shared during my playing days, and those he would have had with his grandkids and *their* successes. The many things he and I could be enjoying now as father and son—going places, meeting people, going to NFL events where he could have been included. And to golf tournaments, banquets, and luncheons. And hunting.

At those times I get flashes of him, and I say to myself, "Boy, I wish Buddy were here."

Growing up, Peyton Manning had always been reluctant to ask his dad about Buddy Manning's suicide. It wasn't a subject readily pursued by anyone in the family, and Archie had not been inclined to volunteer. Then on a hunting trip after his first year with the Colts, Peyton and his father had driven back to Drew to visit Archie's mom . . .

I loved to visit the homestead because it has a lot of Dad's college memorabilia—the pictures, the letter jackets, the clippings. We were looking at team pictures, and he was telling us the funny nicknames everybody had. I'd say, "Here's Johnny Aldridge," and he'd say, "Oh, sure. Defensive end. 'Porpoise Face.'"

Drew, of course, had been hard hit by the farming failures at that point, and it looked it. As we drove through, Dad would pass an old place and say, "I used to get my hair cut right there . . . And right there was the best hamburger joint in Mississippi."

Then we drove by the cemetery. In terms of upkeep, the nicest place in Drew. We were kinda in a rush, but he wanted to stop, and he showed me the graves of my uncle Peyton, my aunt Mamie, Lucy, and so forth. Then he came to his father's grave. And we stood there, staring at it, not saying anything.

Before, I'd always hesitated to bring it up. We'd been on a lot of road trips together over the years, but it never seemed appropriate. He'd *tell* me things, all right, but only when he was good and ready, so I never asked. Mom had tried to fill me in, but at the time it happened she'd just started dating Dad regularly and wasn't close to the Manning family yet.

So we're standing there, and I just came out with it: "What was it like, Dad, what happened with your dad?"

He got a little emotional telling me about it. He said what a shock it had been, and how it seemed as if his father probably knew it would be Dad who'd find him. And how important it was that when he did, he protect his mother and sister from the scene.

He talked about his dad missing out on so many of his games, but coming, too, when least expected, and then sitting with his buddies in the stands. I asked him why, and he said it was the nature of his dad's job, having to work so hard, not being able to take anything for granted. He said his dad made the Ole Miss games, but not if he had to fly to one.

Then he said he knew his dad loved him but had never told him so, and I was reminded how often he tells us— Cooper and Eli and me. How he never ends a telephone call without letting us know. How they *both* do. Openly and often, as if they enjoy saying it as much as you enjoy hearing it. You never know when you're talking to one of them on the phone who might be there with them, or even if they're in somebody's office or at a meeting or something, because the conversation always ends with: "I love you, Peyt." "I love you, Coop." "I love you, Eli."

And when Dad told me how the loss had set in after the funeral, all that he would never be able to do with his father, it explained in part why he makes such a great effort to be there for us. How he's *always* been there for us. I think I really began to feel it when I was seventeen or eighteen and Cooper was nineteen, twenty, which was the corresponding time in his life that he lost his dad. I'd feel it when he put his arm around me. I'd feel it in the empathy and the caring that he always showed for what was going on in our lives.

So I understand now, and it's not complicated at all. What he missed he never wanted us to miss. But what explains *him* best is still the part we had already grown so accustomed to. The love part.

3

College football tradition, like election results and wartime dispatches from the front, is never taken lightly at those places where partisanship is entrenched. It is what gives the college game so broad a rooting edge over the more peripatetic professional version, both in terms of loyalty (college players don't bounce from team to team; college teams don't skip town when they're not given a new domed stadium) and in terms of endearment. Peyton Manning never tires of recollecting the joys of game days at the University of Tennessee: the team's traditional "Vol walk" from Gibbs Hall to ponderous old Neyland Stadium; the throbbing emanations from the school band playing "Rocky Top" inside; the crowds so huge and full-throated—numbering more than 100,000 each when he was there; and on a day in 1996, against Florida, 107,600—the largest ever to see a college game in America. Having experienced such frenzy, Peyton could never be intimidated by the smaller crowds of the NFL. And of course, he was already indoctrinated on the passions of the college game from hearing Archie Manning compare his experiences at Mississippi, where the stadium is barely half the size of Tennessee's but game days were just as compelling. . . .

'm prejudiced, of course, but I always thought Ole Miss was better because we had "The Grove"—an airy, ten-acre park with giant oak trees that the football team passes through wearing blazers and ties to get to the stadium on game day. There's an archway on brick pillars at the entrance that reads "Walk of Champions," and the fans line both sides of the path. The head coach leads the way, and the cheering at such close quarters raises the hair on your neck. It's right out of Cecil B. DeMille, except the triumphant processional is two hours *before* the conquest instead of after.

Thousands of fans tailgate in The Grove, but their vehicles aren't allowed. They carry everything in, and they spread their white tablecloths and flowered centerpieces and eat their gourmet meals with their best silver. I do that now with Olivia when we're there with friends to watch Eli. Up to game time, The Grove is always alive with revelers, even when Lafayette County was "dry" and you couldn't bring as much as a cold beer inside. Legally, on a nice day, it's not unusual for four or five thousand people to stay right there for the duration, never making the game. My sister Pam does that. She prefers the socializing to the football. That seems to be part of the tradition, too.

The Ole Miss campus as a whole is eye-catching without being imposing, and stately without being large. The enrollment is barely 10,000, a quarter of the size of schools like Florida. But by keeping the school that way, the natural beauty and intimacy of the campus haven't been compromised, and I hope it never gets any bigger. Most of the male students still wear ties to the games (for pledges it's required), and it wasn't that long ago that the women wore hats and high heels. The stadium was enlarged recently to 50,000, which is still not big by Southeastern Conference standards, but it wrings from Ole Miss fans as much cheering per capita as anybody's. It certainly could claim the largest *name* anywhere after Coach Vaught's was added to make it "Vaught-Hemingway Stadium/Hollingsworth Field."

Playing there, and in Jackson, our teams won thirteen of sixteen home games in the three seasons I started at quarterback, 1968, '69, and '70. Plus the tie with Mississippi State my sophomore year, which was memorable only for the spat Olivia and I had when I was "uncharacteristically gruff" after the game. I'm glad to say there were no complaints after that.

Our best year was the next one, my junior season, when we were picked to win the SEC championship. We came close despite a horrible start.

After an easy victory over Memphis State to open the season, we made a major tactical mistake. Or maybe it was psychological. If you know about mood swings in football, how they can hinge on almost any stimulus, you'd probably say both. We were scheduled to play Alabama at Birmingham in the third game, and under Bear Bryant, Alabama was always tough. It had already won three national championships in the '60s, including back-to-back in '65 and '66. The preseason buildup was huge. Mississippi versus Alabama would have the honor of being the first college game ever televised nationally at night.

Prime time.

The catch was, we had to go to Lexington to play Kentucky in our *second* game. And nobody—coaches *or* players—took Kentucky seriously. We were at least two-touchdown favorites. So Coach Vaught and the staff decided we should save ourselves for Alabama. We would show Bryant's scouts nothing in Lexington. Vaught even put in a series of power-I plays to keep our offense as inconspicuous as possible.

But Kentucky had a new coach, John Ray, who had been the defensive coordinator on Ara Parseghian's staff at Notre Dame, and Ray was a defensive genius. Not that he had to be that day. "Nothing" was exactly what the Alabama scouts saw. Kentucky played us to a standstill. We fumbled the ball away at the goal line on our last chance to win and got upset, 10–9.

The next week we went to Alabama and relieved our frustrations by throwing caution (and the ball) to the winds. I mean we really aired it out. I threw fifty-two passes, thirty-three caught by the intended receivers. Alabama didn't have one of its better defensive teams—Bryant said later it was during a period when he had gone to "too many golf tournaments in California"—but it was still Alabama, which meant that it also played good offense. It turned into one of those games where if you were in the stands you never sat down, and if you were watching on TV, you never left your set. For years afterward, when I'd go to Mobile or Birmingham or Tuscaloosa for an event or to make a speech, seven of the first ten people I'd meet wanted to talk about that game. Scott Hunter, the Alabama quarterback, even wrote about it. A good guy, Scott, and he had a great game. But my numbers were even better and still stand as an SEC record for a single game: 540 yards in total offense, 436 passing and 104 running.

The trouble was we lost that one, too, by 33–32.

It was mind-numbing. The team picked to win the SEC championship had started the season 0 and 2 in conference play. Two defeats by a total of two points.

But we rallied. During the following weeks I think we played as well as anybody in the country. We knocked off undefeated Georgia, then upset undefeated LSU. And when we got to Tennessee in mid-November, we were in the chase for a bowl bid and a top ten spot in the national rankings. Coming into the game, Tennessee was undefeated, too, and ranked third in the country. The Vols were said to be a shoo-in for the Orange Bowl. They had also embarrassed us—me especially—the year before by 31–0 in Knoxville. After that game Steve Kiner, their All-America linebacker, told the media he knew where I was throwing every pass. That I was "eyeballing" my receivers. I accepted the criticism as constructive. Thanks for telling me, Steve.

But Tennessee had no intention of letting us forget that debacle. When the SEC writers got to Knoxville on their annual preseason tour, they asked Kiner about Ole Miss being picked to win the SEC title. He replied, "Well, everybody says they've got the horses. But I think they're a bunch of mules." A comment guaranteed to make the locker room wall in Oxford.

The week of the game the fans got into the act. Ole Miss faithful wore buttons that said "Archie" on them, and when Tennessee fans got to Jackson they had buttons of their own: "Archie Who?" (A postal clerk in Magnolia later wrote a song

he called "The Ballad of Archie Who." The recording immediately sold 35,000 copies.) Kiner's put-downs resurfaced.
Every day that week an unidentified masked man rode a
mule around the Mississippi campus, drawing catcalls. Not
that Steve cared. He was utterly fearless. I know because I
also had to go up against him in the pros.

But you could feel an upset brewing. One afternoon late
in the week, a light plane flew over the practice field and
dropped a load of leaflets on us, each one with a nasty message purporting to be from Kiner or Jack Reynolds,
Tennessee's middle linebacker and another All-American.
There was no doubt in our minds where the leaflets came
from. Coach Vaught. It was corny, but it was his way of prim-
ing us. On the day of the game, he gave us one more incentive: "If you beat Tennessee today," he said, "I guarantee you
I'll get you into the Sugar Bowl."

We did. We killed 'em, 38–0. Everything we did was right,
making everything they did wrong. In Tennessee *and*
Mississippi, they still call it the "Jackson Massacre." I call it
sweet revenge. A new button emerged: "You Know Damn
Well Who."

Now flash-forward twenty-plus years to when Peyton
was finishing his senior year at Newman High and being
recruited (successfully, as it turned out) by Tennessee. Phillip
Fulmer had been a sophomore on the Tennessee team we
beat so badly that day in 1969, and now he was the Vols' head
coach and sitting in our living room in New Orleans trying to
convince Peyton to come to Knoxville. And Olivia couldn't
resist. With just enough sarcasm to nail the point, she said,
"Tell me, Phillip, do you ever see Steve Kiner? Does *he* come
to the Tennessee games?" Then she recited the "mules"
episode.

When Fulmer got back to Tennessee, he told a friend of
mine, Bobby Scott, who had played for the Vols and been my
backup quarterback with the Saints, "We're not going to get
Peyton Manning. He ain't coming to Tennessee."

Scott said, "Why not?"

"Because the mother makes the call, and this mother doesn't like us. He ain't coming."

So much for Phillip Fulmer's male intuition.

True to Coach Vaught's word, we got the invitation to the Sugar Bowl to play third-ranked Arkansas, which had concluded its season at 9–1. The Arkansas defense had given up only 7.6 points a game. But we were on a roll. We scored 24 in the first half and had another touchdown called back before finishing it off at 27–22. I passed for 273 yards and a touchdown and ran for another, and won the trophy as the game's outstanding player. We finished 8–3 for the year and wound up ranked eighth in the nation, the first time Ole Miss had cracked the top ten in six years.

There's no doubt in my mind that Coach Vaught's influence got us into the Sugar Bowl, just as he said. With a 7–3 record at the time, and our being ranked only thirteenth, there almost had to be some pull involved, and Vaught had pull. The bowl committees are generally made up of community leaders in the towns the games are played, and coaches like Bryant and Vaught and Bud Wilkinson of Oklahoma and Bob Devaney of Nebraska had contacts on the committees that they could massage. It worked both ways, of course. Sometimes the bowls lobbied the coaches. Regardless, you can't underestimate the influence big-time college football coaches had in those days. *Still* have, actually, although it's not as obvious now.

I think one of the reasons so much is made of the "inducements" college players get illegally during the recruiting process, or the "enhancements" when they've been at a school for a while and contributed on the field, has a lot to do with that: the stature of head coaches. The clout they have in dealing with a program's needs, and their own determinations on how those needs should be met. I don't claim to know everything about it, but I believe this: whatever is done, and *wherever* it's done, the head coach will know about it. The "chairman of the board," as Bryant called the job, always knows, because if he doesn't, his program is apt to spin out of control and take him down.

The mistake some people make in judging these things, however, is to believe that college football is totally corrupted by the process. Just one big happy cesspool that everybody wallows in for mutual gratification: the coaches, alumni, and "friends" who break the rules, and the players who profit by their being broken. I don't believe that for a minute. Sure, there have been excesses. Lots of them over the years. And there'll be more. College football at the top level is as vulnerable as any big business. With the pressure coaches are under to win, some are bound to take desperate measures. And some administrators will let them. Or even help them.

But I think the executive branch of this giant fishbowl we call intercollegiate athletics—the presidents, the athletic directors, the head coaches—is as honorable as you'll find in any field, if not more so, and if you really knew the particulars in most cases where infractions were penalized, you'd find at the center of the violation a poor (or certainly not well-off), unsophisticated kid who has had to scrounge to make ends meet. The system virtually forces him to. NCAA rules are just too restrictive. Administrators know it, coaches know it.

I'm talking here about rules that turn a free lunch into a capital offense. That make the tiniest transgression a cardinal sin. Some of the nit-picking the NCAA allows under the guise of policing conduct is ridiculous. For example, say you've had a kid at your campus for his last official recruiting visit. The next day you see him walking in the rain on the outskirts of a nearby town, thumbing a ride. You're going in that direction, so you stop and . . . Unh-unh, no you don't! Your travel limits have been exhausted. You can't take him anywhere, even to the bus station.

The rules also say you can only make contact with a recruit once a week during the recruiting period. That's fine, but if you call the house and the father tells you the kid isn't home and the conversation goes beyond that, too bad. It still counts as your one allowable call. Meanwhile, "visits" are a nightmare of restrictions. When Peyton was being recruited, David Cutcliffe was the first to come in from Tennessee. Cutcliffe is now the head coach at Ole Miss, but at the time he was Phillip Fulmer's offensive coordinator. When he had concluded his visit in New Orleans and was ready to go back to the airport, we offered to take him to lunch on the way. I suggested Olivia ride with him as navigator in his rental car and meet me at the restaurant. David said, "No, I can't do that. I can't give her a ride. It's against the rules."

Now, is that splitting hairs to the extreme? Is that totally absurd? Is the world round?

Again, I don't say the darker side of college football doesn't exist, and that players haven't been "bought" with whatever version of the shiny new red convertible they might have been offered. And there's no doubt such things poison the system and must never be allowed or excused. Universities compensate their scholarship athletes in the currency of an education, the most valuable thing they can offer. Anything beyond that must always be measured with the utmost care to keep the process as wholesome and practical as possible.

But let's not be naive here. Being paid with a scholarship is still being paid. The real reason colleges can't add "salaries" on top of that is twofold. One, they can't afford it. It would break the bank at most schools if they had to give their star athletes what star athletes get these days. (Not to boast, but I doubt even a successful program like Tennessee's would have been able to afford to pay Peyton what his contribution was worth those four years.) More important, if they did, it would kill the mystique of college sport, all the principles of "team first," and it would be anathema to purists like myself who prefer to believe that a football player chooses a university because the name on the shirt matters as much to him as it does to them. It's what glues the whole thing together.

The fact that the vast majority of NCAA violations have involved the athletes' struggles to get by is nothing new, of course. John Vaught was (is) one of the most honorable men I've ever known. But were guys being "helped" when I was at Ole Miss? You bet. It just wasn't flagrant and it wasn't beyond the reasonable. I knew of no one getting a lot of money or a new car. I do know by the time some players were juniors they were driving used cars they couldn't afford, and you had to wonder if maybe a car dealer somewhere had given their daddies or mamas a "deal." I certainly never got anything like that.

But I had a guy tell me to come by his clothing store in Indianola one time to pose in one of his suits for a picture, and afterward he gave me the suit. "Just keep it," he said. I did, too, but when I told Frank Crosthwait, our family's longtime lawyer friend, he went back and paid for it. Frank was what you might call my "older brother confessor" in those days, just as he now serves Peyton as a legal overseer. His father had been my Sunday school teacher in Drew growing up. Good influences all around. But the owner of a store in Canton, Mississippi, gave me clothes after that, and I parceled them around to other players who could use them. It didn't seem like that big a deal.

I heard of guys at other schools getting folding money from alumni in the end zone after games, but I never saw it happen. At Ole Miss we did have an alumnus who owned a drugstore and after a big win he'd come into the dressing room where the players were showering and hand out towels with $10 bills tucked inside. He wasn't a wealthy guy, but he was an avid fan. When he was around, we had players taking two and three showers, one right after another. Did the coaches know what was happening? I don't see how they couldn't have.

We also made some extra money selling our game tickets, which is a time-honored practice everywhere. For each game we got four free tickets, face value of six or eight bucks each, and usually had regular buyers at $25 apiece. Sometimes a gung-ho fan would take all four for the whole season. We also sold our "UM-AA" sweatshirts for $10 apiece, new, in the boys' *and* girls' dormitories. After a big victory, we got to keep our game jerseys, too, and they were eminently marketable. I had it down to a science. I'd change to a fresh jersey at halftime, then maybe another later in the game, and wind up using three that I could take out afterward and "give" to people, knowing I'd get thank-you notes with a little something inside. The note might say "This is for you to take your girlfriend to dinner." Which is about what the enclosure would cover.

All these things are NCAA no-nos, of course, but when you don't have much, you don't think of a hustled buck or two as contraband. We were scrounging for walking-around money, that's all, and the NCAA still hasn't found a way to make that palatable. To cut some slack beyond "tuition, board, and books" for scholarship athletes. There used to be a laundry allowance, something like fifteen dollars a month, but even that got taken away. The least the NCAA could do now would be to reestablish an equivalent, a regular stipend adjusted to the economics of the times. With all the money involved since television became such a huge contributor, they'd better, because one of these days the system is going to blow up in their faces.

Recruiting, as always, is the beating heart of the larger problem. Where the real sinning starts. I think it's undoubtedly true that a lot of it involves heat-of-the-moment decisions at the point of attack, when a recruiter is hundreds of miles from home and competing to "win" a coveted recruit. Joe Paterno used to say that every mile a recruiter puts between himself and the campus, the more pressure he feels to get the player, and thus the more tempted he will be to "bend the rules." Which I suppose makes a good argument for limiting the scope of recruiting—maybe require more extensive use of the phones and the mails. Or, now, the E-mails. It would be a lot cheaper, too.

Coaches say the player most likely to have his hand out fits a familiar profile: usually a kid from a low-income family, with questionable academic credentials, and with people around him who make it clear he "needs help." More often than not, he's been getting help for years (grades, favors), ever since his athleticism drew public acclaim. He learns to expect it. The recruiter on the road, meanwhile, doesn't want to come home empty-handed—or has been *told* not to come home empty-handed—after spending all that expense money, so he says things, or does things, he shouldn't.

I had that happen one time when I was being recruited. A coach from another school asked me right out, "What do you want?" I thought I'd made it clear I was going to Mississippi, and he must have figured he had to come up with a bigger ante. I didn't know how to respond so I just shook my head. I suppose you instinctively know when an inducement has gone too far, and he'd crossed that line. My dad practically kicked him out of the house.

I didn't have to worry about any of that with our three boys, not even Peyton and Eli with all the recruiting attention they got, because everybody knew they weren't for sale. They didn't fit the profile. We had no "needs" beyond making the right choice of schools, and weren't looking for anything except that. If it had been offered, I would have been offended.

Ironically, Ole Miss got nabbed for some serious (and inexcusable) recruiting violations the year after Peyton chose to go to Tennessee, which made that decision seem even stronger in retrospect. Again, I think it had to do with the pressure coaches feel when expectations have been greater than achievements. Billy Brewer was the Ole Miss coach then, a friend I'd known since he coached in high school. He'd given our Cooper a scholarship to Ole Miss when other schools were saying he was too slow-footed to make it as a college receiver. I admit that I was more than a little disappointed when Billy wasn't successful in recruiting Peyton for Ole Miss, which became such a bitter issue after the fact. I'll get to that.

Billy had played on three of Coach Vaught's better teams in the late '50s, including the 1959 Sugar Bowl winner that wound up ranked second in the national polls. But when he came back to Ole Miss to coach, he told me more than once that the playing field was "no longer level." That the Tennessees and the Alabamas had more advantages—which, of course, they do: bigger stadiums, bigger support groups, bigger budgets. Some coaches consider that kind of thing a challenge, others despair over it. I suppose it depends on how much success you've had beating the odds.

Billy had been the Rebels' head coach ten years when the NCAA lowered the boom in 1993. He'd had some good seasons, winning nine games three times and going to the Liberty and Gator Bowls. But he never quite reached the summit. No top ten finishes, no SEC championships, no major bowls. The pressure undoubtedly grew, and with it the missteps. "Little things" became big things. Boosters engaged in a number of activities that weren't kosher, including squiring junior college recruits around Memphis, taking them to strip joints and the like. The NCAA started sniffing around, and the charges multiplied. Ole Miss drew a two-year penalty— no television games, no bowls, a reduction in scholarships— and Billy Brewer was fired. It was a downer all around, but I was sorry for Billy because he was as much a victim of the system as he was a facilitator. The walls closed in.

As I said, I think as a college player you can almost sense what you can (and should be allowed to) get away with. I made it through Ole Miss without raising any eyebrows because I walked that line. All the "big" money I earned working in the summer (*every* summer) for the bricklayer in Drew, and hating every minute of it. My dad had made a deal with me early on that he'd pay for everything else when I was home if I'd save my earnings for incidentals at school—to buy clothes, or go out to eat, or take Olivia to the movies.

That was especially important because Olivia was now a fixture in my life. The all-seasons variety. That summer between our junior and senior years, when I was visiting for a weekend with her family in Philadelphia, I asked the appropriate question and she gave the anticipated answer and we got engaged.

Almost from the beginning—which is to say, once she got over the shock that I wasn't the loathsome basketball player she thought I was from high school—we knew where the relationship was heading, and if there were any doubts on either side, or from either family, I never heard them. Despite some rather obvious economic differences, we had the kind of compatibility you pray your children will have when they make their marriage commitment. Some of our best friends at Ole Miss were on the same track (six of the eight couples who partied together regularly were married that first year), and our nights and weekends were like celebrations.

As an added bonus in the euphoria, Olivia was crowned Ole Miss Homecoming Queen at the Houston game the fall of that senior year. She said she was "shocked" to be selected for the honor. I said she was a shoo-in.

Making it even sweeter was that we won the game—the only time we beat Houston in three tries. The downside was I broke my left arm in the third quarter, so severely that it required surgery (a steel plate and four screws had to be implanted to hold it together) and a week in the hospital. It turned that final season into an anticlimax. We had won six out of seven to that point, losing only to Southern Mississippi in a game where I threw more passes (57) than I ever had, completing 33 for 341 yards and two touchdowns. But I also had three interceptions, which tells you something about how deceiving gaudy passing numbers can be.

I was out for the next two games, including a loss to Mississippi State, and then tried to come back too soon against LSU at Baton Rouge on national television. The doctors who had first predicted I'd be sidelined for the year fitted me with a bulky plastic sleeve, and it was so cumbersome I could hardly go to my left at all. We got blown out, 62–17, and then lost to Auburn, 35–28, in the Gator Bowl. For that one I had recuperated enough to wear a lighter protective sleeve, and wound up having a pretty good day. But I also had to do a lot of scrambling, and I got badly winded and wheezed through the second half. It felt like I had the hospital bed on my back.

The silver lining was that by playing my last college game I had seen the last of my college injuries, a technical rundown of which would probably require a medical glossary. Among the more prominent over the four years were, in layman's terms, a concussion, two cracked ribs, two jammed thumbs, a severe groin pull, the shattered arm, and a badly bruised elbow.

The X-rays alone would make a novel.

So we finished that final season at 7–4, not great but not bad either, when you consider the alternatives. Over the next decade or so when I was playing in the NFL, you can't imagine how good 7 and 4 sounded.

Having Olivia (and our future) waiting on the other side helped me through those last painful weeks. But I gave up another love in the interim: baseball, my *first* love in sports. It was a final parting. I started at shortstop for two seasons on the Ole Miss varsity, and we had some success. We got to the College World Series my sophomore year, when I batted about .270. My junior year I was just under .400, and a lot of the hits were bunts. Tutor Holmes should have seen me then.

But baseball was a different game at that level. At Drew, we barely had enough players to suit up a team, and we played only fifteen or sixteen games a year, not nearly enough to make the improvements in skills needed from level to level. I hadn't even competed in American Legion ball in the summertime because it was only available thirty miles away and I was working with the bricklayer. Once I got to Ole Miss, I realized how much I had to learn. I had athletic ability, but I was a long way from being an accomplished player.

I didn't even *see* a slider until I got to college. I was consoled later when I read that it was the pitch that pretty much sent Joe DiMaggio into retirement, but knowing about it is not the same as hitting it.

So I skipped my senior year of eligibility, ostensibly to concentrate on the new "Big Two": the upcoming marriage to Olivia, and the NFL draft. The former was much more important, of course, and if you are looking for proof in the outcome, check the box score: my NFL career lasted fourteen years; my marriage, twenty-nine and counting. More is better.

Olivia and I were married in Philadelphia, Mississippi, on January 21, 1971, a Thursday night, and if you were to ask disbelievingly, "Who in the world ever got married on a Thursday night? In *January*?" I'd say, "Well, it fit. Barely."

Consider the whirlwind we rode during that time period.

The Gator Bowl was played January 2. The next day Olivia and I, my mother, her mother and dad, Frank Crosthwait and his family, and several other friends all flew to Honolulu for the Hula Bowl game, where I was the starting quarterback and participated without further damage to my person, thank you very much.

We were there a week. We returned and hurried through all the prenuptial preparations and events, then the wedding, and then the next day (January 22) Olivia and I flew to Acapulco for our honeymoon, during which I acquired what had to be one of the ugliest, most painful sunburns ever inflicted on human flesh. Not the kind of handicap you'd want to deal with on a honeymoon. *Especially* on a honeymoon. My feet were so badly swollen I had to go in my stockinged feet to the flight home.

We got back on the twenty-seventh and moved into our off-campus apartment, and on the morning of January 28 I was awakened by the Ole Miss sports information director and told that the NFL wanted me at the athletic office by nine o'clock to be available for the 1971 NFL draft. In those days, the draft wasn't a televised event, and was much more low-key. When Peyton was chosen, they flew him to New York in advance to be on hand—and in front of a national television audience—when the selections were announced. For me, it was a short wait by a telephone on the SID's desk in Oxford.

At nine-fifteen, I was called there by the head coach, the general manager, and the owner of the New Orleans Saints, in that order, with the news that I was their first pick and the second player chosen in the draft—right behind Jim Plunkett of Stanford, picked by New England, and just ahead of Dan Pastorini of Santa Clara, picked by Houston. It would be the only time three quarterbacks were ever drafted one-two-three by the NFL until Tim Couch of Kentucky, Donovan McNabb of Syracuse, and Akili Smith of Oregon were one-two-three in 1999.

After the phone call from the Saints, an AP photographer took a picture and I gathered up my books and went to class.

Oh, did I mention that somewhere through there Olivia and I crammed in a week of final exams? As I remember, it was before the honeymoon, but feel free to insert it wherever you can find room.

As for the wedding, only Olivia could give a description justice:

"My mother and her friends, and practically the whole town of Philadelphia did the planning and put it together. All we had to do was show up.

"The wedding was at the First Baptist Church downtown, and the reception was so big they had to hold it at the National Guard Armory. Our only country club wasn't much more than a large room because Neshoba County was dry and there wasn't any real demand for that kind of environment. So my mother, Frances Williams, had them convert the armory into a kind of Mississippi version of Windsor Court. It was beautiful. The best-looking armory you ever saw.

"No invitations were sent out locally because it wasn't necessary. The local paper, the Neshoba County Democrat, ran a full-page picture of me with an announcement at the bottom: 'Friends and Family are Invited through the Medium of the Press.' If you thought you were a friend, you came. To add a little class, they took the 'National Guard' off the reception card and made it just 'The Armory.'

"We got rooms in Meridian for a lot of our out-of-town guests because Philadelphia didn't have nearly enough hotel space to accommodate everybody. The Ole Miss coaching staff came, and the governor had two plainclothes detectives there to watch out for us. Newspapers from as far away as

Memphis covered the wedding, and the Memphis Press-Scimitar ran pages of pictures.

"Archie and the best man and eight or ten groomsmen (ushers) had rooms in Meridian. The wedding was at 6:30 P.M., so it was left to Archie and a highway patrolman to get them on the road in plenty of time. But Archie let them stop on the way at this little honky-tonk, Ed's Beer Joint the time got a little tight. So did several of the groomsmen. They didn't want to leave. We had that happen at one of our friend's weddings, Freddy Brister's, about the same time. Some of his groomsmen stopped for a beer, and one beer led to another, and they never made it to the wedding.

"But after our guys had been at Ed's for a while, the highway patrolman came in and insisted they go back to the cars. Archie had told him not to let them be late to Philadelphia under any circumstance. So they arrived an hour and a half before the wedding. The doors weren't even open yet. But the front lawn of the church was packed with people, and about the time they pulled in, a friend of Archie's, Hubert Blanton, came driving up honking and waving, and everybody was waving back, and Hubert rammed right into the back of the police car Archie and Billy VanDevender were riding in. Fortunately, there were no injuries. The groom was saved for the sacrifice.

"Both the church *and* the armory were packed. People were lined up outside at both places. The joke was they were scalping the reception invitations. The governor, John Bell Williams, said he got a couple hundred bucks for his (he couldn't make it). When the doors opened, a storm.of people rushed in. The wedding party had to scramble for their seats at the reception. Souvenir hunters among the 'guests' walked away with the decorations, the tablecloths, anything that wasn't nailed down. When Archie complained to my dad that some of them were taking bottles and even cases of champagne, Daddy said, 'That's okay, let 'em.'

"Otherwise, surprisingly, everything went off without a hitch. At least I think it did. I went through it in a cloud.

"In Acapulco, we stayed at a resort, Las Brisas, where every room had a swimming pool and every couple was given a pink and white Jeep to drive around. The pool was about as big as a dining room table, and the water as cold as ice, but the Jeep was fun to drive. Archie's sunburn took some of the edge off at the end, but we were still in a contented fog when we got back to Oxford. We'd missed a couple days of classes, and when I finally went to one, the professor called the roll and had to repeat 'Manning' about three times before I realized he was referring to me.

"As for the NFL draft that followed, and Archie's selection by the Saints, the only thing that stuck with me was a newspaper columnist's opinion the next day. He wrote, 'Archie Manning is going to the cesspool of the NFL.' Hmmm."

For newlyweds still in college, we actually had it pretty easy. Academically, we were both on cruise control. Olivia was driving twenty-eight miles to Batesville for her practice teaching, so she had to hustle more than I did, but I took some speaking engagements and did some endorsement-type things—I could make money at last!—and altogether it was a nice way to start a marriage.

A month later, in February, Drew had a "day" for me. When I first heard about it, it was going to be one of those simple little get-togethers where a hometown sets aside a few minutes for a ceremony and a lunch and the presentation of a plaque. But Ole Miss got into the act, and then Frank Crosthwait, and then the mayor, and then somebody suggested adding a parade, and before long it was a statewide tribute. "A" day became "the" day for me. I think it's safe to say Drew hasn't seen anything like it before or since. Not because it was me, but because it was so wonderful. Snake Williford, the ex-mayor who had tried to con me into going to Mississippi State was one of the prime movers of the event. He took me aside afterward and said, "I've never been so proud." Neither have I.

They gave me a new Lincoln, a big old white Mark III with leather interior, the first car I'd ever owned. In fact, our family had always driven secondhand Chevrolets, purchased on the cheap through one of the owners of the Chevrolet dealership, Johnny Stacy. Johnny probably should have felt insulted. He was a close family friend, and after my dad died he and his wife drove Sis to every Ole Miss home game. In Chevrolets. But somebody asked me what I wanted, and without thinking I blurted out, "A Lincoln." Sort of going for the moon, since I really wasn't sure they were gonna do it.

But they did.

Drew was doing okay then as a farmers' town, and all twenty stores on Main Steet were still operating. Each one was decorated, and each had a collection of pictures, showing my life in chronological segments, starting with baby pictures at the drugstore. For the parade, Olivia and I sat in the backseat of an open car, and at the ceremonies they gave us a little ski boat to go with the Lincoln.

Ole Miss players were there, and school dignitaries, and members of the coaching staff. The Saints' head coach, J. D. Roberts, also came, and there was a lineup of celebrities including Dizzy Dean, the Hall of Fame pitcher who used to do the national TV Baseball Game of the Week, and Senator Jim Eastland from Doddsville, at the time one of the most powerful men in the U.S. Senate.

The climax was a ceremony at the high school football field, and it must have meant something to people who were there because for years after, I'd run into adults who would say, "I was there, I was at 'Archie Day.' I was twelve. My folks brought me." That's what they'd called it, "Archie's Day," and they put up signs at the entrances to town, "Home of Archie Manning." That kind of recognition fades, of course. When the signs wore out, they didn't replace them.

Olivia and I were now into the first-time task of making a life independent of parental supervision or a head coach's "suggestions." For me it wasn't hard because I'm a planner and I'd already been laying the groundwork. I set up my academic year (as a business major) so that all the harder subjects were covered during football season, when I'd be disciplined to handle them. After that I knew the income opportunities would take us just so far and I'd need to concentrate on getting my pro football contract settled and signed. The last semester, I carried only nine hours of courses. I got my degree easily, but I really hadn't been as dedicated a student as I'd been in high school, making B's instead of A's. My true major was football. And don't ever think that's not typical. What the NCAA calls "student-athletes" in Division I are really "athlete-students." If you doubt it, you don't understand the priorities.

And the demands aren't just internal. A college football player with "star status" (if you'll pardon the expression) has a lot of requests for his time, even beyond alumni meetings and banquets and the like. The media has needs, and you're expected to meet them with a good attitude. As you should. It helps the program. Other times you might get called on in matters affecting the school in general. The chancellor at Ole Miss pulled me out of class four or five times to take me to the state legislature with him. He was lobbying, getting money for one department or program or another, and he'd have me go along to meet people, shake hands, maybe say something. I didn't mind. I was proud to be asked.

But now it was time to get on with being a New Orleans Saint. To sign a contract, do whatever I needed to get in good shape (I still had that plate in my arm), go to camp, start the new season.

But the pros don't do these things with dispatch. They drag their feet, and hesitate, and postpone, and turn the whole thing into a drill. I'm convinced it's a game they play, trying to wear you down. Instead of a mutually gratifying meeting of minds that resolves things quickly and amicably, you get a drawn-out battle of wits and wills. Very tiresome, very (I thought afterward) unnecessary. I suppose management would say it's what they've had to do to protect themselves since players started getting so much money, and since high-profile, big-ego agents started crawling all over sport, but what both sides seem to miss is the resentment it causes. And sometimes the resistance.

Worst of all, it makes the whole relationship adversarial. You against them. Not good karma for a "team" sport.

About the only thing positive I can say about it is that it's guaranteed to make you realize you are now most definitely in the football *business*, with all that implies.

I got Frank Crosthwait on board at the outset of negotiations. On the morning of my wedding, I brought out a big box of letters from agents and attorneys that I'd kept under my bed and gave it to him. I said, "Frank, this represents two years of offers. I've talked to some of these guys on the phone, and they all sound good to me. I need your help. Pick one, or tell me what to do."

Frank went through everything, and couldn't believe some of the illegal solicitations from lawyers. He made some calls, interviewed some of the agents, and we visited with some. Mostly, we eliminated. We finally decided on Ed Keating of Mark McCormack's agency, International Management Group (IMG), a class act. Mark was the brains behind the early marketing of Arnold Palmer, Jack Nicklaus, and Gary Player that lifted professional athletes into a new realm of income opportunities. IMG was broadening into team sports, but doing it carefully. Keating said they'd made it a policy to handle only three players from any one team. They were getting the best, too: in Miami, Larry Csonka, Jim Kiick, and Paul Warfield of the Dolphins, for example.

IMG wanted Frank Crosthwait to stay involved, so we put our heads together and came up with what we thought I should get as my first contract. Although hardly earthshaking by today's standards, and probably too restricting, it had a nice round sound to it: ten years at $100,000 a year. But we really wanted the Saints to make an offer first. So with Coach Vaught's blessing, we set up a meeting at the Vaught ranch right outside Oxford. Vaught had had a heart scare and was taking it easy, and seemed glad to have us come by for a little diversion. The Saints sent Vic Schwenk, their general manager, and a lawyer.

Their first offer was so low it was ridiculous. Coach Vaught is from Texas, but he always talked like a Northerner, and I'll never forget it. In his best Yankee voice, he said, "Damn it, gentlemen, Archie made more than that playing here!" I had to laugh.

So we didn't get anywhere, and parted company without agreeing on anything. And time passed. Olivia was teaching, and I was driving around in my Mark III, which was guzzling gas at a rate I couldn't afford without a job. I didn't know what to think, and was too naive to even guess what might be happening. Olivia and I took side trips to New Orleans occasionally, just for fun, and one weekend Frank came along and we met with the Saints again. IMG had agreed that we ought to take a "country lawyer" approach for a while, with Frank the lead voice. But again, nothing.

After that, we met (unsuccessfully) in New Orleans and now it was summer. We were over on the Gulf Coast, where Frank had asked me to speak before a bar convention when we met again, and it was bizarre. We were in his suite at the Broadwater Beach Hotel in Biloxi, with the curtains pulled, and I could see some of his friends in silhouette outside, trying to eavesdrop. And newspeople were there, too, awaiting word. To no avail. Another standoff. Meanwhile, to my surprise, I had been drafted by the Kansas City Royals of Major League Baseball, and early on Frank contacted them. They told him they couldn't pay pro football salaries, but if we wanted to use them as leverage in our negotiations with the Saints, they'd make an offer. So in June Frank threw the Royals at the Saints, suggesting we might decide to talk to them about switching to a baseball career.

The trouble was, this was six months after the original big league draft, and unbeknown to me there'd been *another* draft, a follow-up, with all unsigned players back into the "eligible" pool.

A reporter called me. He said, "You aren't really gonna talk to the Royals, are you, Archie?"

I said, "Maybe. Why?"

"Because you now belong to the Chicago White Sox. If anybody's going to sign you for baseball, it has to be them."

Oh, boy. (Altogether, I got "drafted" four times by big league baseball teams, which tells me that I was either over-rated by the scouts or underrated by myself. The jury will forever be out.) The foot-dragging went on and on. I had pretty much decided the Saints were just cheap, but from what we heard, they were doing the same thing with all their draftees, and evidently so were most of the other teams. When it came time to report for training camp, I still hadn't signed. I wasn't too worried about coming in late though, because in those days they were still playing the College All-Star game in Chicago, matching a team of the best college players against the NFL champion, and I had been picked to play, along with Plunkett and Pastorini. Which would mean I would be three weeks late to training camp anyhow.

But when it was time to fly to Chicago and I still hadn't signed with the Saints, I decided not to go. Frank had checked and found the league only insured you for a career-ending injury. Not worth it. When Plunkett heard, he made a comment that if it were him he'd be there regardless, "because it's an honor to play in this game." Jim's a good friend, so good that when Peyton went to Stanford's football camp before his senior year in high school, he and a buddy stayed at the Plunketts' home in Palo Alto. But I bristled at the remark and pointed out that it was easy for him to say because he'd already signed his contract with New England. His money was in safe harbor.

In the meantime, the Saints had moved their training camp to Hattiesburg, in south Mississippi (I have no idea why), and J. D. Roberts invited me to come down and at least watch some of the practices. J. D. was an old Oklahoma All-American who had coached under Wilkinson and had been brought in the year before when the Saints fired Tom Fears.

In J. D.'s first game, Tom Dempsey of the Saints kicked the all-time record 63-yard field goal, but it was one of only two games the Saints won all year. Roberts sounded as anxious as I was to get this thing resolved. So I went. Secretly.

Under the rules, I couldn't work out with the team as long as I was unsigned, so J. D. arranged for me to train with some Southern Miss players during the day, and at night he'd come to my room at the Holiday Inn and we'd meet with his offensive coordinator, Ken Shipp. It was like a James Bond movie, everybody tiptoeing around and looking over their shoulders and around corners. Shipp provided me with a projector and every night brought me team films so I could watch on my own. I wasn't entirely unfamiliar with his offense. I'd been to a minicamp in the spring in New Orleans and studied some of the basics, and in June I'd worked out with a couple of Saints players when we were over there, so I had a pretty good idea what was going on. But it was uncomfortable. I felt like a sneak. The only car I had was the Lincoln, which was more than just obvious. I was careful not to park around the practice field where people might see it. I could have used a car from an auto dealership I'd signed to endorse, but that would have been worse: a red Corvette. And there were so many people around. The National Guard had a summer installation in Hattiesburg, and every day there'd be a big contingent out watching the Saints' practice, along with the usual numbers of fans and media. I had to be careful not to be seen, and it got to be really awkward. Every day for two weeks I prayed for deliverance.

As it happened, probably not by accident, John Mecom, the team owner, was staying at the Holiday Inn in Hattiesburg. Mecom was barely in his thirties, not much older than most of the players, and was easy to talk to and easy to like. We ate together a couple times, and finally one night he said, "We need to get this thing done, Archie. Get Frank Crosthwait down here and the three of us'll do it."

And just like that, we did.

Frank came, and we sat in Mecom's room and ironed out

the details. Frank ran the terms by Ed Keating by phone (IMG preferred to stay a step removed). And I signed what was, for me, an end-of-the-rainbow deal: five years for $410,000, broken up into salaries of $30,000 the first year, $40,000 the second, and so on to $70,000, with a signing bonus of $160,000. It was a whole lot of money at the time, and made headlines: the biggest contract ever for a rookie. Bigger even than Plunkett got from New England. I was more than satisfied.

Now I was anxious. I wanted to start practicing, start playing. I'd never been a drop-back passer and I'd have to be, to be a Saint, so I wanted to get going.

But we still had to wait another week. This was just before the All-Star game, and because I had been booked for that, the commissioner, Pete Rozelle, ruled that I couldn't start practicing until after the game was played. I finally went into camp "officially" on a Saturday morning in early August, and immediately was greeted by a heavy dose of rookie hazing. The veterans were tired of all the other rookies' singing, so they made me stand up and sing at every meal.

I didn't mind. I sang my lungs out. I was a professional football player at last.

4

The time he spent quarterbacking the New Orleans Saints would be, for Archie Manning, forever bittersweet. The Saints had gone nowhere in their first four years in the NFL, and over the next twelve, Archie's contributions did little to disturb this consistency. While he became a mostly beloved New Orleans fixture—and materially well off—the Saints continued to be losers, and not particularly lovable ones at that. One of his coaches called him "a franchise player without a franchise." The vindication of playing well enough to make All-Pro teams and the Pro Bowl and to win MVP awards was squeezed dry by the relentless scoreboard. Meanwhile, and as a result, he experienced a new sensation in life: boos. Or rather, being *booed.*

We laugh about it now, this hard-to-define thing we call my "pro football career." Not that it was ever funny in progress—fun, sure, much of the time, but never funny—and not that it was ever taken any way but seriously. The fact that I *can* laugh is probably because I made up my mind I'd never let it make me bitter, which I have seen happen with professional athletes who got mired on losing teams and woke up one day realizing they were fresh out of time to do anything about it. Except get the hell out.

But the truth is that, even after so many disappointments, year after year after year of hopes raised and then dashed, I can still say with all candor that pro football was a good thing for me to have done, and definitely beneficial to the Mannings—if for no other reason than the wonderful friendships we enjoy and the rewarding life we were able to provide our boys in a great, if somewhat erratic, city.

But in retrospect, it *was* funny. But *only* in retrospect.

Olivia was the first casualty, so to speak. She had never heard me booed, which was new to me, too, but it is something even the most successful pro quarterbacks have experienced and should be willing to go through (for the millions they're paid). When it really began to get to her, she said, "Archie can take it, but I can't." First she stopped sitting with other wives in the stands, where they were such easy targets, and moved with Cooper and Peyton—when they were old enough to be "fans," too—to more inconspicuous seats. Ones belonging to her father.

Being the consummate Southern belle, Olivia held her composure. When she heard the gripes at close quarters, she sat there in silence, or tried to be kindly with her responses. It didn't help, she said, that every time she opened her mouth, I'd take that exact moment to throw an interception. One day she finally confronted a guy in front of her who kept yelling, "Manning stinks, get him outta there! He stinks!"

In that soft, sweet voice, she said, "Please don't say that. He's my husband."

The guy turned and looked at her for a second and said, "You have my sympathies, lady, but I don't care. He still stinks."

Near the end, she quit going altogether.

Ah, but the boys. Storehouses of one-liners for my speeches later on. The complaining fans didn't bother them. They thought it went with the territory. Cooper came home from a game one Sunday and said, "Dad, is it all right if I boo, too?"

Once when the situation on the field was deteriorating rapidly and the squawks from the stands were intensifying, Olivia was sitting there hunched under the deluge when she suddenly heard piercing voices mixed with the booing from behind. She turned around and saw that it was Cooper and

Peyton. "Boo! Boo, Archie! Boo!" At ages seven and five, they had taken matters into their own hands.

Young boys are always brutally frank, of course. It's part of what makes them boys. When the media started calling the Saints "Ain'ts" and the fans started wearing brown paper bags over their heads to show their collective embarrassment, Cooper and Peyton wanted to wear the bags, too. They thought they were cool. I came home one Sunday night after an unusually successful road trip (i.e., we won) and sort of casually asked if they'd watched the game on TV. "Naw," they said. "We watched the Dolphins."

I finally got it. The Saints weren't even their favorite team. Cooper liked San Diego. When somebody asked him to name his favorite players, he said, "Lance Alworth, Lynn Swann, and J. J. Jefferson," three wide receivers. When asked who his favorite Saint was, he named another wide-out, Wes Chandler. "But my second favorite is Dad," he said. "Dad's my favorite *quarterback*." When asked who *his* favorite team was, the younger Peyton said, "Wes Chandler!"

All of it was guaranteed to keep me humble.

At the beginning, of course, the thought of making a career out of losing was furthest from my mind. I know it's true that you always think you're going to do better than the team did last year, or *you* did last year, but I really felt we had something going. J. D. Roberts was in his second year as head coach, a good man with a good pedigree, and although the Saints had won only twice in 1970, hopes were up.

In other words, we felt what every bad team feels: that the situation will get better, one day soon. That we will be a winner, one day soon. It's the nature of team sport. Usually you just don't realize how bad you are. When you're practicing against only yourselves, you feed on any improvement, even if it's illusory. Such optimism prevails before every new season. If you went around to the training camps in the NFL (or for that matter the NBA, the NHL, or Major League Baseball) and read every local paper and listened to every local sports show, especially the call-in variety where people who don't always know what they're talking about talk to people who don't know the difference, you'll invariably come away thinking, "Ah, this team is on the move."

It's all in the perspective. Talk to the defensive players on the Packers and they'll tell you how good the Green Bay offense is going to be. Talk to the quarterback of the Chargers about the defense and he'll say how good it is. And the quarterback of the Bears will say the same thing as the quarterback of the Chargers, who'll say the same thing as the quarterback of the Raiders. All the same. You've got six months building up to the new season—the coaches put their people in place, work hard, make *you* work hard, and even if it's just practice you think, "It's going to happen." And you *believe* it's going to happen.

But it doesn't.

Not for a lot of teams.

Under J. D. Roberts that first year, 1971, we doubled the victory total: from two to four. We also tied two and lost eight. The NFL was playing fourteen-game seasons then. I came into camp after the All-Star game in time to suit up for the first exhibition, at Buffalo. Two things happened, arguably more comical than historic.

J. D. took me aside before the game and said, "I'm not going to play you tonight. You've only been with us a week so I'd rather you just watch." He gave me a clipboard and had me stick with him on the sidelines while Bobby Scott, the rookie I'd played against when he was at Tennessee, and two other quarterbacks took the snaps.

J. D. was an ex-Marine, a hard-core, no-frills guy, and I liked him. But you couldn't tell sometimes if he was ill-informed or just *acting* like he was ill-informed. I'm following him with the clipboard, watching and listening and taking notes, and on the field O. J. Simpson is starting his third year in Buffalo with a vengeance. He hadn't torn up the league yet, but he was still O. J.: Heisman Trophy winner, two-time All-American, first pick in the NFL draft, et cetera, et cetera. He opens with a good run, then another. I'm moving down the sideline with J. D. trying to keep up. On his third carry, Simpson jukes a defender out of his shoes and runs about thirty yards before our guys push him out of bounds.

And J. D. turns to me and says, "I don't know who that number thirty-two is, but he's a damn good-looking running back!"

I said to myself, "Well, here I am in the NFL, and the head coach doesn't know who O. J. Simpson is."

I really think J. D. knew, all right, it was just his style. You came to expect it. But the next thing I know, I'm in the game, which I *didn't* expect. Five or six minutes to play, we're trailing by 7, and J. D. turns to me and says, "Get in there!"

I thought, "What do I do now?"

What I did was revert to type, to my high school and college days. On the first play, I sprinted out and tried to throw deep to Danny Abramowicz. Not even close. I threw again, incomplete. Call 911, we have an emergency here. Luckily, the clock was on my side. It was winding down. I finished 0 for 4: four passes, no completions. Welcome to the National Football League.

But in the next week's exhibition against Dallas in the Cotton Bowl, I played the entire second half and made some things happen, mostly off busted plays. I felt better. The third week I started against Kansas City in our first home exhibition. The Chiefs were defending Super Bowl champions. I never saw so many big guys on one team. The field shook when they ran on. And early in the game, I scrambled out of another busted play—they were commonplace with the Saints—and at the end of the run got slammed into a sideline dugout. A *concrete* sideline dugout. The Saints were playing in the old Sugar Bowl (Tulane Stadium) then, and they still had those dugouts. I rammed the arch of my foot into the concrete. For the next couple weeks I could barely walk.

I made it back for the last pre-season game, and afterward J. D. Roberts named me to start the season opener—against the Los Angeles Rams, who had been picked to win the NFL

championship. And why not? Roman Gabriel . . . Deacon Jones
. . . the "Fearsome Foursome." *Those* Rams. But game day was
oppressively hot in New Orleans, and the heat seemed to
bother them more than it did us. We got charged up, and they
didn't play well, and as luck would have it, we won on the last
play of the game, with the rookie quarterback from Mississippi
scoring the winning touchdown. But not by design.

We were trailing by 3 points with four seconds to play
when we reached the Rams' three-yard line. I called time out
and went to the sidelines to talk it over with the coaches.
Obviously, we had time for only one play. A field goal would
tie it (there was no overtime provision in the NFL then), and
a tie with the Rams would have been like a victory for the
Saints.

But when I came to the sidelines, the first thing J. D.
Roberts said was "We're going for it!"

Great. Let's do it.

Except, J. D. didn't have a play in mind. We stood there
strategizing, trying to determine what might work. Ken
Shipp was the offensive coordinator, a smart man and a good
coach. Ken is retired now and lives in Murfreesboro,
Tennessee, where he became one of Peyton's biggest fans, and
he still calls me every other week or so. But he's also a delib-
erate, slow-moving kind of guy, and he hadn't really told me
what they wanted when the referee came over and said,
"C'mon, men, let's play!"

I wandered back onto the field, glancing over my shoulder
in the forlorn hope of getting some kind of sign. Abramowicz
met me at the huddle. "What are we gonna do?"

I said, "I don't know. They never told me."

Well, what the heck. I called a run-pass option to the left,
another old standby, and I probably should have thrown, but I
ran and got hit at the one-yard line and dove for the goal line,
barely crossing into the end zone—where I fumbled. Too late
for the Rams, though. The official's hands had already gone up.
Touchdown. We win by four. The locker room was bedlam.

The rest of the year I played hurt. Among other things,

my foot never stopped bothering me. Nevertheless, four weeks later (after two losses and a tie) we beat the Cowboys before a full house at Tulane Stadium, and I scored two touchdowns and threw for a third. Another huge upset, although we didn't appreciate how huge until later. Tom Landry, the Cowboys' coach, alternated Roger Staubach and Craig Morton at quarterback in that game, but couldn't make it work. The next week he made Staubach his full-time starter and the Cowboys went straight up from there, all the way to the Super Bowl (also in New Orleans), where they beat Miami for the championship.

Winning when you're not supposed to is an exciting way to start a pro career. Big upsets are tremendous confidence builders.

The trouble is, expectations can go out the top. If you don't have the talent to make it keep happening, the disillusionment can be as damaging as the upsets were exhilarating. We were barely mediocre as a team, and we played that way most of the season. Personally, I didn't have a great year. We were behind a lot, and when you're behind you force your throws to make something happen. So I had more interceptions (12) than touchdowns (10). Making it worse, I pulled a thigh muscle against the Cowboys to go with the aching foot—same old vulnerable Archie—and was in and out of the lineup the rest of the way. I probably wasn't on the field for fifty percent of the offensive plays. In some games I only threw three or four passes.

My statistics for that first year were ordinary: 140 completions in 267 attempts for 1,642 yards, plus 172 yards rushing. But I didn't know how ordinary they were until Peyton was in his first season with the Colts and the Indianapolis *Star* ran a weekly statistical comparison showing what we each did in Game 1, Game 2, and so forth. Peyton completed 326 passes in 575 attempts for 3,739 yards and 26 touchdowns. He broke every NFL rookie passing record. I, obviously, didn't. The whole family saw how pathetic I was in some of those games.

On the plus side, I learned a lot, and the Saints as a whole were, once again, encouraged.

And in season two, I took every snap—played every down on offense in every game. Peyton was the only quarterback in the NFL who took every snap in 1998. (Nobody did it in 1999.) I still wasn't consistent, however. Again I had more interceptions than touchdown passes, and at midseason, after a losing effort, I was called into J. D. Roberts's office. One of those chilling "the-coach-wants-to-see-you" summons. I thought, "Uh-oh. Here comes the bench."

But J. D. said, "I don't give a damn if you throw a thousand interceptions. I don't care how the fans react or what the press says. You're my quarterback, and you're going to play every frigging down, no matter what. You're going to have a great career, and it's starting right here!"

It was wonderful for my morale.

Except it didn't change anything.

With the Saints there was always more talk than action. Over the next few years, we had our moments but never really got much better. We were running in place: 2–11–1 in '72, 5–9 in '73, 5–9 in '74, 2–12 in '75. What was the problem? I suppose if you looked at it the way they do now, when money counts for everything and the "winners" always seem to be the ones who spend the most, you would conclude that John Mecom just didn't spend enough. That he didn't make a strong enough commitment.

But it was more than that. As I said, John was a guy in his thirties who liked players so much he even partied with them. I think he'd have spent whatever it took, short of bankruptcy. He just never got the right combinations going. He never had that one sharp guy in the front office, a Tex Schram (of Dallas) type, to give him the settling hand the organization needed. Instead he wound up taking advice from the wrong sources, responding to the wrong suggestions, doing whatever sounded good at the moment.

It's hard to quantify. It's like a business that struggles to break even but lacks the chemistry to do better. I don't think the Saints as a whole ever stopped trying, but maybe when we were desperate to win, everybody got caught up in making decisions just for the sake of making decisions. Everything was done helter-skelter. A lot of firing and hiring. You got the impression management didn't have a clue. At one point, John hired Dick Gordon to be our general manager. Dick had been to the moon. Literally. As an astronaut. But a general manager of a pro football team?

Of course, when the wheels fly off, it's a given that people will first blame the head coach. It's a coach's game, remember. But even the best has to be able to get (and keep) good players and good assistants, and has to have an active, enlightened front office. And with all that, he still needs enough time to get the job done. How much time? Whatever it takes, within reason. When he's making progress it'll be clear enough, and vice versa. But if he doesn't get enough time, it won't happen.

And when you fire the head coach, you almost always have to fire the assistants, and then sometimes you have to hire an interim coach, then the new guy, and when you keep doing it over and over the turmoil becomes a way of life. Not good for team confidence, not good for team continuity. We had eight different offensive coordinators in my twelve years with the Saints. Once, they fired the offensive coordinator in the middle of the season. But worse than that, we had five different *head* coaches during that time. The Saints were firing head coaches at a rate of *one every two and a half years*!

Now, look at the flip side: over roughly that same period, Dallas had Tom Landry as its head coach and Roger Staubach as his quarterback. Landry was also the offensive coordinator for the Cowboys. Staubach never played for anybody else. And in Miami, the same thing. Don Shula was the head coach, Bob Griese the quarterback. Howard Schnellenberger was the offensive coordinator for a good while, but even as that position might have changed hands a couple times, the system under Shula sure didn't. You can't beat that for consistency. Or results. Miami won two Super Bowls in the '70s. So did Dallas.

J. D. Roberts never got much help in New Orleans. Nor much luck. It seemed like every draftee the Saints brought in, every trade they made, rose up and slapped him in the face. High draft choices and players acquired in trades *have* to contribute. That's a given, too. But they'd trade for a guy and he'd show up in New Orleans injured. Couldn't even run. They'd draft a guy and he'd look good a couple days into camp, then go bust. I suppose you could call that ineptness, but we didn't know it at the time. As players, we had our own jobs to worry about.

The next year Ken Shipp left, and I felt bad because he deserved better. I was fortunate to have had him as a coach. Ken never took shortcuts, never tried to cover up, never let you go into a situation unprepared. Some offensive coordinators just say, "Don't worry about that particular defense, throw to this receiver regardless." Ken made you see the whole play, every play, including where the pitfalls were if you were overmatched. He was teaching me for the long haul. But he knew his job was dependent on our making headway in a hurry, and since we didn't, he was expendable. When he got an offer from the Jets, he took it. Which is another constant in this game that gets worse with time: coaches jumping from team to team like, well, players.

To replace him, the Saints brought in John North from Detroit, who had never been an offensive coordinator.

J. D. Roberts was next to go. Ordinarily, management has the good sense to fire a coach immediately after the season, to allow time for the new coach and the team to bond a little, and the deposed coach to maybe find another job (admittedly, a secondary consideration in most cases). Not the Saints. J. D. Roberts got fired during the 1973 exhibition season. You had to know it was coming, though. Comments were made that J. D. didn't have all the tools to be successful. But he'd had a champion's upbringing, playing and coaching under Bud Wilkinson, and I can tell you he'd been good for me, just as Ken Shipp had been. Now they were both gone.

John North was made head coach for the 1973 season and

brought in a friend of his who was coaching at the high school level to handle the defense, Bob Cummings. And darned if the defense didn't get better. We weren't much better offensively, but we won five games under John North that year, and five the next, which was *some* improvement (we had achieved mediocrity!); but once again expectations had exceeded performance.

Actually, the 1974 and '75 seasons were more notable for what happened off the field than on it. In 1974 there was a league-wide player strike over free agency. The players wanted it (naturally), the owners didn't. The fans yawned. The strike started right about the time we were due at training camp in Vero Beach, Florida, and we voted not to go in. Players carried placards: "No Freedom, No Football." But without the players getting nearly as much as they bargained for, the strike ended and everybody was back for the last exhibition game. A subsequent player strike in 1982 was taken a lot more seriously. Then the striking players didn't return until more of their demands were met, again having to do with free agency, and the season had to be shortened to nine games. The fans shook their heads and hinted at mutiny. I think they instinctively know that whatever monetary concessions are made in these things will come out of *their* pockets. They always do.

In both cases, the clubs brought in replacement players— those they could retrieve from draft discards or modified free agency or anybody willing to jump from the Canadian League or the semipros. There were complaints around the NFL about the "quality" of play during and after the strikes, but the truth is that even the most avid fans, bless their hearts, aren't really sophisticated enough to see the differences that *make* a difference. Oh, they can tell that John Smith isn't John Elway, but the subtleties that make a certain pass play work at a certain time, or that make one offensive lineman better than another, would normally escape them. No reflection on fans, that's just the way it is. Football is a complicated game. Typical of New Orleans, however, when they interviewed people outside Tulane Stadium after the first few games in '74, nobody complained about the quality of play. They complained about the price of beer being increased from fifty to seventy-five cents. They raised hell about that.

In 1975, another milestone: the Saints moved into the Louisiana Superdome in downtown New Orleans. A personal triumph for a good friend of mine, Dave Dixon, who led the charge to make it happen. Dave is one of the most unique men I've ever known. He owns an antiques store in the French Quarter, but he's more eager-beaver promoter than anything else, and if he made any money on any of his outside adventures it wasn't because it was a priority. He was the man who thought up the ill-fated U.S. Football League, and with Lamar Hunt started World Team Tennis. But best of all, he was the guy who led the push to get the Saints' NFL franchise in the first place. It was his idea.

The good thing about the Superdome is that Dixon and the others put foresight into the design. It's twenty-five years later now and the stadium is still "current"—nobody complains that it's out-of-date, nobody clamors to tear it down and start over. It still has all the box seats, all the entertainment and food facilities they like to say they "need" for a Super Bowl. Not to mention the assurance that it won't ever rain on the fans who attend or be too hot or cold.

But, of course, it also has artificial turf, and from the aesthetics—it just doesn't look right to us purists—to the hard truths about what it does to players physiologically, fake grass will never get my vote. Nor that of any other player I've ever talked with about it.

The injury factor is undeniable. Almost every study indicates real sod is safer. When Stanford Research Institute measured the threat to football players in the grass versus turf argument some years ago, it found that in seventeen out of seventeen categories, artificial was more injurious. And that it made players more susceptible to *serious* injury. Because under that pretty green toupee are layers of asphalt and concrete that make for dangerous compression effects when players fall heavily or pile onto other players.

I learned to hate it early. I shattered my arm on turf at Ole Miss. I tried to break a fall my senior year, when artifical turf had just been installed, and the arm got hung up on the surface. Friction is a constant problem. I was always nursing bruises and scrapes, both at Oxford and in New Orleans. I used to cringe at the hypocrisy involved. In my college days, artificial turf was used as a recruiting ploy: "Come to our place and play faster on such-and-such!" "Cut your maintenance costs with so-and-so!" "When it rains on such-and-so, your jerseys stay clean!" It took years, but eventually they started counting the bodies in the recovery rooms and realized, hey, how are we saving money if we're paying so much more for medical treatment? How can we say it's helping our team if the team is all broken up over the stuff?

And when somebody says, "Well, my receivers are faster on artificial turf," I have to ask, "But if your receivers are faster on it, isn't everybody else? And is that really a good trade-off?" The only people who could honestly say it's been a true advantage over the years have been the orthopedic surgeons who performed the operations.

Nowadays you see one college after another ripping up the turf and putting in natural grass. In the SEC, not one school still uses it. In the pros, I doubt you'll ever again see turf in an outdoor facility. Alas, they don't seem to have a choice in the domed stadiums. But the pressure is on. The Green Bay Packers insisted contractually that their 1999 preseason game with the Saints be played on natural grass—in the Superdome! The Saints agreed to lay it down over the artificial for that one game.

Which, I guess, will be the next thing. Installing some strain of "indoor" grass, then replacing it when it dies. Which it always does. They tried to make it work in the Houston Astrodome way back when, but no luck. You have to hope science will prevail and develop something along those lines. Meanwhile, the injury potential continues to spread wherever they lay the stuff. I heard the other day that golfers who practice on these mats country clubs are now installing are coming up with a whole new set of complaints—injuries to the elbows, the wrists, the knees. So one more time, ask yourself: if it's not good for golfers, how could it possibly be good for football players?

There was one other more predictable development in 1975: the Saints fired John North. This time they did it *during* the season. Six games in, they made the personnel director, Ernie Hefferle, interim head coach and Ernie finished it out quietly (at 2 wins, 12 losses). But now the organization was getting relentless heat from the fans and the media. Their patience had run out. They wanted to see more than just another face on the sideline. John Mecom responded by playing an ace. He hired Hank Stram, a highly respected name in coaching. Hank had taken the Kansas City Chiefs to the very first Super Bowl (where they'd lost to Vince Lombardi and the Green Bay Packers), and had a reputation as an innovator and an offensive genius.

I knew Hank. I'd met and talked with him a number of times over the years, and he said afterward that a big reason he took the job was me. He'd had Lenny Dawson at Kansas City, and Lenny was older and not as mobile. Hank said he'd be able to do things with me he hadn't been able to do with Lenny: move the pocket around more, do more sprint-out passing, those kind of things.

What Hank didn't know was that another one of my injuries was about to come between us. This one was scary. I'd been nursing a sore right arm since early in the 1974 season and it had steadily gotten worse. I didn't realize how much worse until shortly after the '75 regular season, when the league called to invite me to play in the Pro Bowl as a substitute for an injured quarterback. It was an honor I'd have accepted in a minute, but even as we were talking I could feel the pain shooting through my arm.

I told them I'd call right back. I grabbed a football and took Olivia out into the yard, and for about fifteen minutes tried to throw her passes. No good. No zip, no distance, a lot of discomfort. I went back to the phone and declined the invitation.

Doctors I'd seen said it was some form of tendonitis in the bicep, a chronic inflammation, but they hadn't found a way to alleviate the pain or stem the growing weakness. I began having serious doubts about my football future. So the night before Hank Stram was due in New Orleans for the announcement of his hiring, I called him. I said, "Coach, I think it's only fair that you know. My arm's in bad shape. I don't want you to come in here thinking I'm one hundred percent."

The next morning he had me on a plane to St. Louis to see a specialist. For a week I was examined, by a different doctor every day. During the next couple months, I was examined by specialists in three states, two in California, including one who had worked on Tommy John, the Dodger pitcher. Hank was opening every door in hopes I wouldn't have to be operated on, knowing it would kill the season for me. And wouldn't do him any good either. He had said he would "build the Saints' offense around Manning." You can't build an offense around somebody who isn't there.

It was a dicey situation. Ordinary surgery for such a wear-and-tear injury was not all that promising for people who used their arms in extraordinary ways. The best procedure for an injured accountant isn't necessarily going to work on a quarterback or a pitcher. But it turned out to be my only option. Dr. Ken Saer, the Saints' orthopedic surgeon, performed the operation in March and it was declared a success. But after I'd gone through months of rehab, and enough cortisone to reach the prescribed legal limit, my arm still hurt. When I went to training camp, I couldn't throw the ball fifteen yards. Dr. Saer investigated and found that the injured area had calcified.

He wound up having to operate a second time. I wound up sitting out the entire 1976 season. I was listed "active" on the roster, and Hank even had me dress out a few games, but I never played. The offense that was built around the man who wasn't there staggered through a 4–10 season. But Hank's high-octane presence had inspired fresh enthusiasm, and a belief that things really were getting better. I waited hopefully for 1977. And after that things *did* get better. A lot better, for a while. But Hank wasn't around to enjoy it.

Meanwhile, and in spite of all the bad vibrations surrounding the Saints, the Manning family was sinking roots in New Orleans, even if we weren't entirely aware of it. The roots got a little deeper every year, almost imperceptibly.

At first we were wary. They call New Orleans "The Big Easy," but it's not the easiest place to move into. It has every kind of entertainment imaginable, from the straightest to the kinkiest, and probably more great restaurants per capita than any other city in the free world. And you can't beat it for charm. But it's so laid-back when it comes to lifestyles and casual drinking (probably the reason they called it "The Big Easy" in the first place) that it takes some getting used to. As they say, a fun place to visit, but . . .

So when you first move in, you tend to think, "Do we open our arms or keep 'em extended to fend off?" Then things begin to sift out, and you get more confident about it, and before long you *want* to stay. New Orleans has its problems, but for all of them, one thing is always certain: it's a city you'll never be bored in. Or alone. People love to come to New Orleans, so you are assured that your friends from wherever you came from will be dropping by regularly—for games, for holidays, for the French Quarter, for Mardi Gras.

New friends are a little harder to come by. Established friendships go back and go deep in Cajun country, and New Orleans natives don't worry all that much about making new ones. But they do, of course, and once you get to know them they make terrific friends. They just don't stay up nights thinking about it. In our case, we had the advantage of having some notoriety going in. I was the Saints quarterback from that first season, and the Saints were the only game in town. Even the Jazz when they got started were always a distant second in fan interest. Also, I had been a recognizable face from the recent past—I'd played in the Sugar Bowl, played against LSU, gotten a lot of positive attention.

So Olivia made up her mind early to work a little harder on bonding with the town—going outside the Saints' realm to make other friends and other connections. She got into things that made the place more real to her. She joined the Junior League, she hosted a funny little TV show where she interviewed players' wives, she did charity work. When the kids came along, she got involved in the schools.

Our first New Orleans residence was a penthouse apartment in Metairie, a suburb in Jefferson Parish. It was near the Saints' training facility, but when I look back on it now I think the greater advantage was that it made a statement: I was going to be a part of the city I'd be playing in. That's important, not only for a quarterback's teammates when he's trying to establish unanimity, but for the goodwill of the fans, too. Peyton has done that in Indianapolis with the Colts. He made it clear from the start he intends to live there.

But I have to admit that the decision was also influenced by the mixed feelings a pro athlete's family usually has about "staying put" in a new town. Living in an apartment is like putting one foot in the water, and with that little bit of impermanence we were able to have it both ways. We could plant the flag in Louisiana and enjoy New Orleans year-round without really leaving home. We were nearby enough to drive to it (and stay at the Williams home in Philadelphia or my mother's place in Drew), and it could come to us. Everything but maid service either way.

One of the reasons Olivia quit sitting with the wives at the games was to be with her folks, and with friends visiting regularly from Mississippi, like the Van Derenders. But also, she admitted, "to put up a little barrier" in the fear of getting too close to somebody who'd be gone the next season. Or in the unspoken dread that *we'd* be gone the next season. Or the next day. In most social settings you gravitate to those you're comfortable with, but that can be jarring in pro sports because players and their wives come and go with the tide. Or more accurately, the trade winds. You wake up and the couple you've been hanging with have packed their bags and moved to Oakland. Or been fired and gone home. After a while you get gun-shy.

But as time went by, Olivia began to vacillate. It sort of came out in little announcements. She'd say to her parents, "What do you think we'll do next?" Meaning after football. "Are we going to go back to Mississippi? Maybe New Orleans is going to be home. Maybe we should do both."

Olivia, as the eternal optimist, admits she expected New Orleans to be just like Oxford. The Saints' wives would be like the football players' girlfriends, and we'd all be best friends. Unfortunately, it doesn't work that way on a pro team, even when there's a minimal number of trades and defections. Players come from all over the country, and have a wide range of cultural bents. Sometimes the contrasts are hilarious. When Olivia was sitting with the wives, one of them had a very salty tongue, and little Cooper would spend half his time turned around listening to her soliloquies. When he got home after one particularly educational afternoon, he said to me, "Dad, can I say *bleep bleep*?"—using a familiar pairing of cusswords. Uh, no, Cooper, I don't think so.

Part of Olivia's reluctance to tie too closely with the other wives probably had something to do with the anxious surroundings she sometimes found herself in (and didn't like). When jobs—big-paying ones, at that—are hanging in the balance, distrust and jealousies sometimes bubble to the surface. She first picked up on it when she heard the wives complaining and bickering in the stands—something she had *never* known at Ole Miss.

One player's wife sitting near Olivia in the Superdome regularly made critical comments about me. When I came home one day with the news that the player had been traded, Olivia's eyes narrowed and she snapped, "Good for the Saints!" At her very first game in Tulane Stadium, she witnessed a tense exchange between the starting quarterback's wife and one of the receiver's. The quarterback (not me) had completed a pass to the receiver in question, and the receiver's wife said, "It's about time So-and-so threw him one!" And the quarterback's wife said, "Well, if he could catch the damn ball, maybe So-and-so would throw it to him more!"

The truth is that Olivia never really liked it much in the stands no matter where she sat. She was always comparing it with what she had grown up with. The college game had been fun, the fans forgiving. Up in the stands at Ole Miss, you didn't get those bitter reactions. I know part of that is because we won more often there, but at most colleges they love you regardless. Oh, the crowds boo, all right, especially when it's third and 12 and the coach orders a running play or when he goes for a field goal when the team's down by 14 points; but mostly it falls under the category of good-natured criticism.

Olivia saw the pro crowds this way:

"I didn't associate losing football games with anything that should make me feel less about my husband. Then and now, football is still a game for me, not life and death. But it got so I dreaded going to the Saints games. The boo birds were vicious, and I don't think it was just because we didn't win. Pro fans are different. Partly it's because they drink more. We drank at Ole Miss games when it was cold—we had our little flasks of Scotch that we'd sneak in for the really cold days— but the effect was more friendly than hostile. A bigger reason might be that pro fans bet so much on the games. I mean they really bet.

"So they bet, and get drunk, and get mad. And take it out on the coaches. And take it out on the quarterbacks. Archie did an advertisement for Royal Oldsmobile that ran regularly on the jumbo screen in the Superdome. When the team wasn't doing well, the fans not only booed Archie, they booed the ad!"

She's right, of course. There *is* a difference between pro fans and college fans, and it's palpable, and even a little frightening. I think resentment has become a big factor. Pro fans are up there in their $75 seats, drinking their $5 beers and eating their $5 hot dogs and counting up the damages to their pocketbooks, and they see guys on the field making more in one game than they make in a year dropping passes and throwing interceptions and fumbling the ball away, and they resent it.

They resent it, too, because they know what we're doing isn't quantum physics. They know it's something we've been doing, mostly for fun, for the majority of our lives. And maybe without even thinking about it, they resent the fickleness of the relationship. They know that when the star player they've invested their time and money in performs well, he'll immediately start talking about going somewhere else for a lot more money if his contract isn't rewritten to include *another* big pay raise.

So they're left to root for players who they feel don't really care *where* they play, don't really care how much the fans are made to suffer on their behalf. There's a crisis in the NFL right now and it has to do with allegiance—players rewarding their fans' support with an equal amount of loyalty. Players caring as much as they expect you to care. The Bart Starrs, Bob Grieses, Roger Staubachs, and, more recently, John Elways and Dan Marinos, who spend an entire career in one place, for one set of fans, are getting rarer and rarer.

So unless they've been fed—by watching exciting players and exciting games, and at least a nourishing number of victories—the fans will turn on you. They'll take their frustration out on the players.

But don't think fans are entirely blameless in all this. The betting factor plays into their hostility. Betting is a way of buying in, and who else is there to take it out on when the team loses or doesn't cover the point spread?

Pro football is one of the biggest gambling tools in the history of man. Everybody acknowledges it, and much of it is perfectly legal. Go to Las Vegas and see it live and in color, with whole buildings devoted to "sports gambling." Bets placed right on the nose of teams and players. Nowadays, just about every big city in America has these "sports bars" that practically advertise the reason for their being: a place to go to get down on a game or two (or three or five or ten). The media sucker in. Boy, do they ever. They report on the "spread" and devote space and airtime to touts. The "national line" is printed in every newspaper, and if anybody doubts the line is a gambling tool, ask yourself this: when a team is favored by "three and a half points," what does that mean? Has any team ever won a game by "three and a half" points?

All that's another subject, of course, but gambling's odor is there in ever increasing amounts, and I think you'd be a fool to believe it's a benign influence. Or that one day it won't explode into another major scandal. One that could make the Black Sox case look like a Boy Scout prank. I hope and pray that never happens, but who are we kidding when we look the other way when players—and coaches and owners—are revealed to have violated gambling laws? Sure, those are isolated cases, but not isolated enough. What do we think is the root cause of scandals past? Sports betting is a multibillion-dollar business, and while I admit some fans just wouldn't be interested if they didn't have a bet down, it's also a multibillion-dollar threat. Think about it.

Our area of Metairie eventually got nicknamed "Fat City" for all the clubs and fancy restaurants it spawned, but by then we were accumulating the reasons why adult couples get involved in schools in the first place, and had moved into a house on Seventh Street in the Garden District downtown.

Cooper was born in March of '74, right after my third season with the Saints. We immediately started looking for a house where we could be closer in without sacrificing ambiance. We put it on an option basis: if we were going to live in New Orleans, we'd live *in* New Orleans, whatever the cost (within reason); then if we chose to move back to Mississippi, we'd at least be able to say we gave it our best shot. The Garden District answered all requirements, a beautiful area with antebellum homes so steeped in history they draw tour buses. We moved in a few months after Cooper arrived.

Now, *that* was an experience, Cooper's birth. He weighed

twelve pounds, three ounces, and was as rough a delivery for Olivia as that sounds. The obstetrician was an Ole Miss guy, Dr. Buddy Webster, and I think it bothered him later that he hadn't insisted on a cesarean. I know in the recovery-room nursery where they had the babies in their little cribs, they put Cooper between two six-pounders and he looked like Gulliver among the Lilliputians. Like he could have gotten up and walked right out of there.

Olivia was so exhausted, she stayed in the hospital a week with Cooper. In those days they catered to you more than they do now. One of the owners of the Commander's Palace restaurant, Dick Brennan, who had seen how big she'd gotten in her pregnancy when we were in his place a couple weeks before, sent a six-course dinner for two to her room, complete with a bottle of his best wine. I wore a coat and tie for the occasion.

The next day the pediatrician, Dr. Brown Mason, came in and said, "I see by your chart you didn't take anything for pain yesterday."

Olivia said, "Well, I drank half a bottle of wine last night."

Dr. Mason, a New Orleans legend, raised his eyebrows. "In *Baptist* Hospital?"

When Peyton came along almost exactly two years later, Olivia was forewarned that it would be another big baby, another tough delivery. Correct on both counts. After it was over, she asked Dr. Mason how much Peyton weighed. He said, "Oh, not nearly as much as Cooper. Only twelve pounds, one ounce."

When everybody stopped snickering, he said, "But, of course, we weighed him *after* he was circumcised."

I can't tell you how much fun it was having Cooper in my life, having a child to spoil. It was March, so it was easy for me to be home and involved. One of the perks pro athletes enjoy in seasonal sports is that there's so much downtime in the off-season. And it's even better for NFL players, because during the season (meaning after the rigors of training camp, where you're pretty much confined twenty-four hours a day, seven days a week) you have enough openings in your weekly routine to work in about as much family time as you want.

My off-season schedule, if you could call it that, was mostly taken up doing promotional work, playing in golf tournaments, and working out. In other words, I had a lot of time for the kids. I took advantage. I must have pushed Cooper a thousand miles around our neighborhood in his stroller those first couple of years. I liked to say I was doing Olivia a favor, but mainly it was something I enjoyed—being with my son, showing him off to our neighbors. Like Rhett Butler did with his little girl in *Gone With the Wind*.

And when Peyton came along, the same thing. I made the two of them part of *my* life as well as insinuating myself into theirs. I even took them to football practice. Some pro teams let you do that, bring your kid in on Saturday morning before a Sunday game. Players usually just watch film on Saturdays or have a walk-through of their plays. It's an easy, relaxed session, with the game plan already in place. So the Saints would lay out doughnuts and milk for the kids, and the kids would play together on the field or even interact with the team afterward.

I had Cooper out there when he was two years old, and that might have been pushing it a little, but nobody complained. Certainly not Cooper. I have a picture of him when he was around four, with his little coat and tie on, going with me to the annual team banquet. A couple years later I took him and Peyton to a football camp in Maryland where I did a quarterback clinic every year, and I remember Peyton being so tired on the plane home that he made a big scene. We were settled in bulkhead seats, with Peyton by an emergency exit door, and the stewardess asked me to change with him to comply with safety regulations. When I woke Peyton to move him, you never heard such squawking. Cooper acted like he didn't know us.

To make matters worse, the flight was overbooked. Loaded to the gills. And while the plane was still at the gate, an announcement came over the public address that anybody willing to take a later flight would be given a new ticket and a $100 bonus. Cooper immediately grabbed his little bag and started down the aisle, ready to cash in. I said no way. It would take a lot bigger bribe than that to make me wait around for another flight.

I have to say that I never thought of any of this as "making up" for things I might have missed with my own dad. I just loved being with my kids, that's all. Whenever I went anywhere, did anything, I wanted them to go with me. Still do. If I've got a business trip to Los Angeles or Miami or Chicago or someplace, and one of them is available, I invite him along. Peyton is like that now. He gets invited to something and calls and says, "Hey, wanna go to the Masters?" "Wanna go the Super Bowl?" And then do I go? Are you kidding?

With Cooper (and wife Ellen) living in New Orleans, sometimes it's just a matter of one of us dropping by and saying, "Got an hour to spare?" Or, "Let's go to lunch. Your treat." (Of course, if it's dinner we're talking about, Olivia and Ellen will gladly make the sacrifice and come along.)

I call Cooper every day at his office to see how he's doing. As I said, Peyton and I talked sometimes twice a day when he was at Tennessee, him calling me or me calling him, and I'd probably be doing it now when he's with the Colts if it wouldn't seem so intrusive. Eli? Ah, that's another story (as we shall see). Eli is of a "different era," being five years younger than Peyton, and is more casual about those things. Or shy, Olivia says, the way I was at his age. Now when Eli's at Ole Miss, I think if we left it for him to call us, we'd go weeks without talking. A different type kid. Less communicative. More laid-back. "Easy."

Yes, I wish Buddy Manning had been alive to enjoy some of this with his grandkids. The boys have been blessed with a wonderful grandfather in Olivia's dad, and they've given him a lot of joy. But I often wish that my dad had gotten his chance with them, too. He hadn't been much of a traveler most of his life. I think once he retired he would have worked on it, and gotten a big kick out of what has happened, and been right there with Olivia, Sis, and me to see it.

Anyway, Cooper and Peyton were going to the Saints games regularly by the time they were four or five, and it wasn't long before win-or-lose became a factor in their lives, too. Once, when Cooper was just three, we got beat by the youngest and worst team in the NFL, Tampa Bay. It was, in fact, Tampa Bay's first victory after twenty-six losses in a row. And I was awful. I've tried to forget the details, but I do remember that I threw four interceptions. I was so bad that the opposing coach, John McKay, "credited" me with his team's victory.

I couldn't imagine a worst scenario than to have to be with people afterward, but we were driving some friends back to their hotel in New Orleans, Cooper sitting on his mama's lap, and somebody asked, "Well, who do you play next week?"

"The Atlanta Falcons."

And Cooper sorta snarled and said, "Yeah, and we'll beat the hell out of 'em, too!"

Olivia looked at him and then at me as if to say, "Where'd *that* come from?"

Mars would be my guess.

5

Of all the doors opened to Archie Manning by his career in professional football, none provided more insight into the world at large than the experience—and then, in gathering amounts, the pleasure—of playing with black athletes. For a son of the Mississippi Delta, it was an ongoing education, not always easy, but always enlightening. . . .

I'm Old South. I love it, period, exclamation point. I respect the grace and the charm of it, and the familial bonding that it has always represented. But that doesn't mean that beneath this bland exterior beats the heart of a bigoted white man with a plantation mentality. The stereotyping is repulsive to me, both ways. All black men aren't noble, all white men aren't swine. And vice versa. It bugs me when the South is depicted even now as an unyieldingly prejudiced place. (How do you identify a wicked bigot in a modern-day movie? Easy. The white guy with the Southern accent.) The South isn't and never has been that twisted or that simple, just as life overall isn't.

I grew up in the 1950s and early '60s in Drew, Mississippi, and that meant a small, insular farming town, predominantly white, mostly Christian, with a history of having accepted segregation as "normal." With the demographics much as they were a hundred years ago, there were plenty of black people living on farms around Drew and serving on them as laborers. My uncle Andy-Frank had two or three black families at the Manning place. They were my first experience with blacks. And yes, they were extremely poor, with hand-me-down clothes and the meagerest of housing.

But so were the white families who worked there.

And, of course, Uncle Frank himself wasn't that much better off. I mean, there weren't a lot of amenities at the old homestead. Indoor plumbing was a luxury. The basketball goal he put up for me was one of those flimsy peach baskets that you punch out the bottom of and nail to a tree. When I went there to visit or spend a weekend, the black kids would sometimes play basketball with me, or we'd throw an old tattered baseball around, and it all seemed perfectly natural. We got along fine. No big deal. My father had a couple of blacks working for him at Case, too, and if there was any resentment on either side, you couldn't sense it.

But I did learn firsthand how close and warm black-white relationships could be in that environment. When we were doing well enough to hire a black maid occasionally, I got a look from inside *our* house. The interplay, as best I could see, was never patronizing or marked by any lack of mutual respect (Sis wouldn't have allowed it). After my daddy died and we were able to get my mom financially stabilized, she had a steady black maid, Emmer Jean Evans, and you can't imagine how strong their friendship was. How much they cared and did for each other. Like sisters. You'd have had to be there to see it. Emmer Jean worked for her until *she* died, and I don't think Sis has gotten over it yet.

In my adolescence, there were no blacks in local government, none on the police force. Segregation was only beginning to unravel. There was an elementary school, a junior high, and a senior high for whites, and the same for blacks. In other words, "separate but equal," except anybody with eyes could see they weren't equal. But change was happening. The one incident I remember as a forerunner involved a group of white college kids who came to town one summer to organize Drew's blacks into exercising their voting rights. Drew didn't look too favorably on being invaded, likening it to carpetbagging, and the college kids were longhairs we called "beatniks" in those days, but as controversies go it really wasn't much. No fights, no arrests.

I didn't trouble myself over it at all at that point. I was shy and quiet and didn't fully appreciate what it all meant: that the South, used to subdividing the races in the aftermath of slavery, was going to have to change; that the government was going to push the civil rights agenda no matter what the mind-sets had been for generations. Obviously, for the *Deep* South, it would take getting used to, no matter how right and inevitable it was. And sure enough, in my senior year, we had blacks at Drew High—four, to be exact. From one family.

I didn't have any problems with that, either. None.

But four years later when I was finishing up at Ole Miss, the oldest girl in that family did something that still hurts. To my knowledge nobody had given her a hard time, neither the teachers nor her fellow students, and what little I knew of her I liked. I thought she was nice. Quiet (understandably), but nice. The Drew schools were much more integrated four years later when the town—and the state—had that special day for me after my senior season at Ole Miss, and the organizers asked a mostly black band to play for the ceremony. The band refused. The director said this girl told him I had been ugly to her our senior year.

There was no truth in it. I was class president, I was valedictorian, and I considered myself a leader, and that would have been the polar opposite of what I would have done. That entire year we had had nothing close to an "incident" at Drew High. There were no KKK demonstrations, no scenes, no clashes. This girl didn't need defending over anything. I admit I have no absolute way of knowing if anybody ever said anything mean or derogatory to her, but *I* damn sure didn't.

I didn't respond to the charge when it surfaced because I didn't want to make a big deal out of it and ruin my special day, but it bothered me, all right. A lot.

During my four years at Ole Miss, we had a growing number of blacks in the student body, and occasional walkons trying out for football, but none of them were good enough to make the team. My sophomore year, Kentucky had black players when it came to Jackson to play and there was some concern of what might happen, but nothing did. Tennessee had a black player named Lester McClain who was very good, and Houston had a number of blacks, almost a majority. But again, no problems.

My own feelings at that point were that integration had arrived, so let's just get on with it. For too many generations in the South, the black male was thought of as the guy who just naturally would be doing the day labor and the cotton picking and the street cleaning and the shoe shining. For me there was nothing traumatic about opening up the system to accommodate loftier expectations. I don't recall my parents ever sitting me down to talk about it one way or the other, and if my sister and I had any hang-ups over it, they were never expressed. But my Christian sensibilities were clear-cut: God doesn't discriminate, why should we?

More interesting to me over the years is how the black athletes have emerged in such numbers. Advancing, in a short time as history goes, from being thought of as "inferior" to being the dominating presence in sports such as basketball and football, where they have flocked to the opportunities and made a terrific impact. Indeed, to being thought of as "superior" in those sports. What had to be gratifying for them during this emergence was that they not only could compete as equals, but could in just a couple generations aspire to be "another Willie Mays" or "another Jim Brown," with good reason to think they had a level playing field to do it on.

I first played *with* blacks right after my senior year at Ole Miss when I was chosen for the Hula Bowl in Honolulu. The new reality was stark, at least in my first encounter. Training at all-star games is never tough, and I had rushed in right after practice one day to take a quick shower before a function I was scheduled to attend. I had soap in my eyes, standing there under the water, and when I cleared them, right in front of me was the blackest man I'd ever seen. A great big linebacker named Charlie Weaver from Southern Cal. Charlie was a first-round pick of the Lions, and I competed against him, sometimes helmet-to-helmet, for years afterward. A heckuva player. But there he was, full view, and I have to say it startled me. The thought of showering with blacks—integration down to the bare essentials—had never occurred to me.

I always tried to make friends at all-star games and at gatherings like the Playboy All-America weekend in Chicago, and one friend I made during that period was a black wide receiver named Elmo Wright. I had played against Elmo three times when he was at Houston, and I liked him. We were together on one of those occasions when another black player joined us and said to me, "You know, I really thought you being from Mississippi would be a problem, but you're a pretty good guy."

I said, "What did you expect, I'd be wearing a sheet over my head at practice?"

We both laughed at the image, but I admit that when I first came to the Saints I had my concerns about the implications of just that kind of thinking. I was *more* concerned about being singled out as the first-round draft choice—I didn't want to come on as a prima donna—and I spent half my time trying to hide that big white Lincoln Continental I was driving. But I also wondered how black players might think of the rookie white guy from Ole Miss with the newfound "wealth."

I needn't have worried. Any hang-ups I had were wiped away by a defensive end from Southern University named Richard Neal. Neal was the number two draft pick of the Saints, and a real leader. And black. We hit it off right away. And he must have anticipated my feelings because he actually came to me. Richard liked to talk, and we talked. He told me to forget about race, that it wouldn't be a problem, that we were a team and were going to work together to win games.

The first week Olivia and I were back in New Orleans after the Saints broke camp, Richard and his wife, Phyllis, invited us to dinner, to the house they lived in with their two young kids. For both Olivia and me it was the first time ever to eat at a black family's table. And the Neals couldn't have been more hospitable. I even remember what we had: roast beef. And turkey. And ham. A spread you'd expect only at Thanksgiving, offered up as just another weeknight meal.

Besides loving Phyllis, Richard also loved Chivas Regal, and that night we had a couple drinks beforehand, then they served cold duck with the meal. From an apparently inexhaustible supply. Our glasses were never empty. The next morning when I got up to go to practice, my mouth felt like it had been welded shut.

There's a very sad ending to that story, I hate to say. Richard went on to play for the Jets and had a good career. But shortly after he retired, without any warning, he died of a massive heart attack. Here and healthy, then gone, just like that. I shudder to think what the loss did to his family. A special human being, Richard Neal.

For sure, such positive channeling helped me through the land mines of intramural "race relations" that year. But I like to think Olivia and I went into it with the right attitude, too. Rookies tend to hang together anyway, and since a number of the Saints' draft choices were black, we made it a point to carry it over to the families. One weekend when the Saints were playing on the road, Olivia invited all the rookies' wives to our Metairie apartment for dinner. She told them to come at seven o'clock. But when it got to be seven-thirty, there were only white wives there, and she began to worry. What had she said? Then they all showed up at once, and everybody had a great time. Olivia, too, but mostly out of relief that she'd pulled it off. She was a rookie, too. Only twenty-two at the time.

I think you could say without exaggeration that the marbling of prominent professional and college teams through those years was a great thing for race relations in the South, and even in America as a whole. In fact, when I'm asked now to talk about teamwork in my speeches, I try to mention the capacity of a good football team to work it out when it comes to blacks and whites pulling together. Oh, I know the argument. That the tendency is for blacks to hang with blacks and whites with whites. Birds of a feather. There's truth in that, and I'm not sure anything can be done about it since it's a matter of choice. But in the locker rooms and on the fields, you *know* when you're together as a team, skin color be damned. It's cathartic. An almost magical feeling.

It's also true, however, that racial animosities still simmer beneath the surface, and sometimes run deep. I had one incident at training camp back then that gave me some insight on how deep, and how dumb.

It was in 1974, when we were training in Vero Beach, Florida. The team was fully integrated by then, and most of the receivers were black—seven out of ten, as I recall. I didn't dislike any of them, but one was a knucklehead. He had the talent; he could have been a great player. But he couldn't lay off the drugs. One morning after practice he comes up to me and says, "Archie, the receivers want to have a little meeting with you and Bobby Scott." Bobby was my backup quarterback.

I said, "Fine."

We met at the designated time, and when everybody was there I said, "Okay, guys, what's going on?"

And this one receiver, whom I'll call X, gets up and says, "We all been talking and we think you're throwing more passes to the white guys."

I saw red. My reaction was instantaneous—I blew up. I don't get fighting mad about many things, but I wanted to fight him right there. Some of the guys were wide-eyed. Bobby Scott said he didn't think I had it in me. But I was so mad because I was so right and felt so wronged.

I said, "You're full of it, X. I don't have those feelings, and I won't stand being accused of it by you or anybody else. What you're saying is wrong in every way possible. You want me to show you the films? You wanna know what *they* say? I'll tell you. That I'm back there trying to read defenses and avoid the rush and doing what a quarterback is supposed to do on pass plays: throw to the guys who are open. If you think you can prove otherwise, get the film out."

It was over in a couple minutes. And every single black

receiver except the complainant and one other came to me afterward and said they didn't know beforehand why the meeting had been called. Turned out it was just those two guys, the wide receiver and a tight end, both of whom got cut the next year. Funny, but I really was pulling for "X" to do well. Hoping he'd straighten out and contribute. He had the ability. But he had one very large hang-up: race.

To be sure, group mentalities tend to kick in under stress, and I don't say whites or anybody from an ethnic or religious minority wouldn't be subject to the same kind of paranoia. I *will* say it always bothered me when the players clustered together by skin color, especially in training camp when you'd go to chow and they'd divide up like they were quarantined. So I made it a point whenever I could without it being too obvious to take my tray and make the rounds, sitting with one group and then another. At team meetings, I tried to always sit with different people, black and white. I was the quarterback. The team captain. Supposedly the leader. I had a strong obligation, I felt, to make it all come together. To make *them* come together.

Peyton is that way now with the Colts. He positively will *not* allow himself to be typecast as anything but a team man. Because he is definitely that. To the bone.

Again, though, if I were black I know I would have looked at these things differently over the years. Blacks were the ones hurt most by segregation, the ones made to feel inferior. It's understandable they would be alert for signs of prejudice and then be more apt to hang with guys in whose presence they would be more comfortable. From the broader perspective, though, I think there's enough reason now to strive for a let's-just-get-on-with-it rationale. I'm white, you're black, so what? A pragmatic approach. I say that while admitting that it took whites time, too, to adjust to the larger picture in the South. That even the most avowed integrationist would agree that you can't always get from A to Z *right now.* That you have to go through B, C, D, et cetera, et cetera, to reach the level of empathy needed.

I've kept a letter from a young black player sent to me during that time that I think tells how a true mutual effort (team play) can break down the stereotyping. He recalled a time when he was at a Saints game with his father and noticed that the father kept cheering me. He said, "How can you applaud that man? He's from Mississippi, a state that has done so much to hurt black people." His father replied, "I not only applaud him, I stand up when I do it. Because he gives his all, every time." Maybe the first step toward real integration is appreciation. Maybe it has always been.

I feel now that I was probably too passive about these things over the years. I never liked stirring hornets' nests. But in the end I came away with friends of every shape, size, and color, and I know if I ever leave New Orleans, a lot of the people I'd want to hug and say good-bye to would be black. And I think they'd hug me back. The "black community," if you will, has been wonderful to me. No, they're not all people I see every day, but I've known many of them twenty years or more and I consider them blessings in my life.

For my boys, race has never been much of a concern either way. Certainly never an issue. It's been a more enlightened (or at least more accepting) time for them. When they see things that are racially charged, or maybe racist-driven, at either extreme, and it makes no sense to them, they complain. Then I can only say, "Well, that's the way it is." Or better, "That's the way it *was*." But I don't think you'll ever see anything close to prejudice come out of their lives or out of their mouths.

I remember when Peyton was being recruited by Tennessee, which at the same time was recruiting a black offensive tackle from Marrero, Louisiana, named Jarvis Reado. A great kid, Jarvis, as we found in getting to know him over the years. When Peyton committed to the Vols and called Coach Fulmer (and then his grandparents, and then his high school coaches), his *next* call was to Jarvis Reado. It was six-thirty in the morning, and Jarvis had his answering machine on. Peyton said, "Jarvis, get your big black ass out of bed and get moving. I'm going to Tennessee and you're going with me!" Jarvis did, too. To their mutual gratification.

That's the way it should always be between teammates, regardless of color. If you can't have fun with one another, if you have to walk on eggs, if you have to constantly watch what you say in fear of being misinterpreted, it's an unhealthy association. When you're in a football locker room, or any other team environment, and you can needle a guy and get needled back without offense, you know it's working. You know it's okay. The funniest people I've known in my professional life have been blacks who got on me for one thing or another and always cracked me up doing it. Tony Galbreath, a fullback with the Saints, was a world-class needler. We never stopped ragging each other.

The irony for the Saints during that period was that although we had no divisions over race, we couldn't seem to get anything else together. Not even with a quality coach like Hank Stram to show us the way. Of course, Hank wasn't around long enough to show us much of anything. For which I can only blame the Saints.

From a strictly personal perspective, the question for 1977 was whether or not I could come back from the trauma of sitting out an entire season. Relatively speaking, I did, being pain free from the previous injuries. But of course, not from *new* injuries. Jeff Merrow of Atlanta broke my jaw on one borderline hit (no penalty was called), and along about midseason I sprained an ankle—there are just too many body parts that can betray you in football—and the sprain was severe enough for me to be hobbled the rest of the way and to miss three games. And that year we won only three.

It didn't bother Hank so much, because he was building for the future. That had been his announced intention, his "five-year plan": to build carefully through the draft and through trades, with the understanding that enough money would be spent to make it happen. He brought in Dick Nolan from San Francisco as an assistant, which tells you something about the commitment. Nolan had been head coach of the 49ers and made a big name for himself in the NFL. A first-class addition. Everything Hank Stram did was first class. He had no qualms about spending money—for good players, good coaches, good appearances. He said that was the way you do it if you're a winner, and he wanted everybody to get on that track with him.

And in the off-season, the Saints put him on a track right out of town. They fired him.

I was in Palm Springs at a golf tournament when it happened, and I was crushed. I'd played ten games under Hank Stram, and despite the record, thought we were in sync at last. Hank was a fiery, energetic guy who could wake up the dead with his style, and he was waking us up. We didn't have all the linemen we needed, and we'd lost a few players to injury, but I knew he was going to be great to play for because he was so smart about offense. He also believed that quality didn't come cheap. John Mecom evidently didn't agree. The bottom line became the bottom line. I would never knock John, because he was always generous to me, but I think he should have found a way to accommodate Hank Stram.

At that point, a kind of anxious pall settled over the house on Seventh Street. I'd now been in the league seven years, and the team I was on had gone absolutely nowhere. Was it time to think the unthinkable? Get out while I still had some marketable time left? Danny Abramowicz had been traded after the '73 season but still lived in New Orleans, and I heard it from him regularly. "You gotta get outta here. Go someplace where you'll have a chance. You're getting killed for no good reason."

Frank Crosthwait said it in more polite terms: "Are you sure staying with the Saints is what you really want to do?" But the way he said it made me feel like I'd agreed to man an oar on a slave ship.

All right, then, what to do? Stay or go? It's hardly an uncommon dilemma in pro sports nowadays, where money is so plentiful and loyalty so scarce, and your first impulse is to be aggressive. Go to the general manager and say, "I want to be traded!" But in those days you couldn't add, ". . . to the Giants, or the Dolphins, or the Cowboys." You were obliged to take pot luck. I had to think, "If I ask and get traded, what then? Teams looking for starting quarterbacks might be worse off than we are, else why would they need a new quarterback?" I could be going from the frying pan to the fire.

And other things gave me pause. Thanks to Hank, the Saints now had Chuck Muncie at running back and Tony Galbraith at fullback, and the promise of a first-rate running game. Tony was one of the best athletes I'd ever played with. We'd also added a tight end named Henry Childs who was definitely a cut above. And I really thought the offensive line was better. Dick Nolan was named to replace Stram as head coach, and he'd brought in Conrad Dobler and Ike Harris from St. Louis and drafted Wes Chandler. Nolan's reputation was made as a defensive coach, but he hired Ed Hughes, his brother-in-law, as his offensive coordinator, and Hughes was a level-headed guy who taught good stuff. He'd briefly served as head coach of the Houston Oilers.

So I weighed all that, together with our growing love for New Orleans, and our growing family, and that anachronistic sense of loyalty, and said, "How can I leave all this?" Answer: I couldn't.

And wouldn't you know it? We did get better. We moved the ball better than we ever had in '78, scored a lot more points, and even won seven games. We were, in fact, competitive in almost every game right to the end. We beat the Vikings, the Rams, the Giants. We beat the 49ers twice. We even beat Tampa Bay (polite applause, please). And by far I had my best season: 3,416 yards passing on 291 completions in 471 attempts, 17 touchdowns (and one fewer interceptions, I'm happy to add).

And—*and*—I was chosen the NFC's Most Valuable Player. And then was voted to play for the NFC All-Stars in the Pro Bowl.

The only problem we seemed to have was adapting to Dick Nolan's "flex" defense, which is complicated and takes time to learn. So while he worked on that, Ed Hughes ran what was clearly a much-improved offense. Another example of how head coaches have to adjust to the needs at hand. Dick Nolan is a quiet, contemplative guy, the exact opposite of Hank Stram, and I had my best years in pro football under him, but not one day in my life did I ever talk X's and O's with him. Not even on the sidelines when a big decision had to be made. Ed and I would be going back and forth, trying to decide what might work, and Dick would just look at us and say, "Well, what do you want to do?"

Ed Hughes's offense was fun, and figured to get a lot more so.

And in 1979 we made it all the way to .500: eight victories, eight defeats. The offense ran up more points (370) than any Saints team before it—almost 100 more than the year before. Muncie ran for more than a thousand yards, and Galbraith wasn't far behind him.

And I made the Pro Bowl again, with statistics almost as good as the year before. We finished second in the division, and in the off-season were generally regarded as the favorites to win it outright in 1980. Perhaps even make the Super Bowl. Just the sound of it seemed dreamlike: the Super Bowl! The summit of pro football. Rarefied air indeed.

Then a funny thing happened. And I'm still not sure how much impact it had on the disaster that followed, or if it had any impact at all. It certainly had nothing to do directly with how we played in 1980. We deserve all the credit for that. But as another unsettling influence, it couldn't have been more untimely for the atmosphere around a franchise that had already gone through more than enough trauma.

John Mecom hired Steve Rosenbloom, the son of the former owner of the Rams, Carroll Rosenbloom, to an undefined executive position. I really didn't know the particulars of Steve's disenchantment in Los Angeles, only that his daddy had died and his stepmother, Georgia Frontiere, was in charge and everything was a mess. But Steve made himself "available" and John hired him, and the question everybody asked was, to what purpose? There didn't seem to be one. Every front office job was filled, and with the team seemingly moving in the right direction, what would the Saints do with Steve Rosenbloom? Or perhaps more to the point, vice versa? You can't blame Steve, of course, but I knew that Dick Nolan and the coaches were wondering about it with some uneasiness. Like "What is *he* doing here?"

And the much-anticipated 1980 season started with a bang—the kind you associate with air rushing from a flattened tire. We lost to San Francisco by 3 points in a heartbreaker at the Superdome, then got beat in Chicago, then lost to Buffalo at home. And just like that it became a habit. We went through a nightmare series of missteps and misfortunes, where we played well but still lost. Where almost every game was close and tough, but every outcome the same. It's a cliché, but the awful truth: We couldn't win for losing.

We lost on last-minute scores. We lost in overtime. We went down to Miami and blocked a field goal with time running out, then worked our way back to the Miami goal where on the last play of the game I threw what appeared to be the winning touchdown pass, only for an official to call *offensive* interference. No touchdown. No instant replay to prove the decision wrong (it might not have been, but we'll never know). Game's over.

The NFL seldom had seen anything quite so pitiful. I, personally, have never been so miserable. And it totally wore away our resolve. We lost fourteen in a row before finally beating the Jets by a point in New York, then lost again to finish 1–15.

That season I passed for more yards than ever (3,716), and for more touchdowns (23), but the figures might just as well be catalogued under desperation. The running game fizzled. Nolan and Ed Hughes tried nine different combinations at running back, and still had the least productive ground

offense in the league. The defense, meanwhile, gave a breathtaking impression of an open window, week after week,
allowing an all-time record 487 points.

In the end it was a season marked by a total team disinte-
gration. A total breakdown of cohesion. A total breakdown of
spirit. And then, after the fact, revelations of a darker influence and a worse nightmare.

Cocaine had raised its ugly head in the NFL. And taking
into account New Orleans's tendencies toward over-the-edge
lifestyles, it was a sure place for it to find expression. Don
Reese, a former Dolphin and Saints player, came out the next
year in *Sports Illustrated* telling how prevalent cocaine use
was in the NFL, and implicated a number of Saints players
who had been traded away after the Miami game, for reasons
open to conjecture.

Me, I knew nothing about it. Not until after the fact. I
suppose I was too straight, too naive, too removed from the
element involved, but I just didn't know. Drugs are obviously
not my style. Ignorance, of course, doesn't stop a cancer. The
drug problem had gotten worse and worse, with the consequences spilling onto the field.

Much more obvious and telling was the effect all this had
on Dick Nolan. As the season wore on, you could see the
pain in his face, the strain in everything he did. His eyes were
always red from lack of sleep. It was like watching a man die.

On a Monday night in New Orleans, we got creamed by
the Los Angeles Rams for our twelfth straight loss, and it was
so humiliating I think the Rams' all-pro defensive linemen,
Freddy Dryer and Jack Youngblood, let up on me. I could feel
them holding back when they hit me, as if to sympathize. I'm
sure they'd never admit it, though. Sympathy is not the most
admired trait in football, especially in the NFL.

That night the Saints put Dick Nolan out of his misery by
dismissing him, and made Dick Stanfel, one of his assistants,
the head coach. Stanfel didn't really want the job; he was a
line coach to the core (and became one again the next year,
and still is today), and was also Dick Nolan's best friend. He

asked me before his first team meeting what the hell he should say. I told him I didn't know (although "Help!" flashed across my mind). He decided on a full frontal attack, and with his gravelly voice ripped into the Saints players for "burying the best man you'll ever know," meaning Dick Nolan.

I found out later that when Stanfel took over, Steve Rosenbloom, by then designated as "general manager," told him to bench me and play the backup, Guy Benjamin. Stanfel refused. Probably because I had a history of dealing with "interim" head coaches and could empathize. He was now my fourth, which has to be a record—one that should never be duplicated. Most players go through ten- and fifteen-year careers without ever hearing the words *interim coach*. Why is that better? Because interim coaches are the equivalent of substitute teachers, unlikely to get the allegiance they deserve. Substitute *lame duck* and you have the picture.

But it's funny. Or maybe *weird* would be the better word. A lot of times under duress teams will rally around a new guy as if he were a life raft, and then get enough adrenaline going to win games they wouldn't have on talent alone. Sometimes, too, they flat-out get better coaching. I'd say it was mostly adrenaline, but that very weekend we played the heavily favored Minnesota Vikings to a standstill. With time running out we scored a touchdown on a goalline play that would have won it, but an offensive lineman had jumped offside (a cardinal sin on a play where linemen shouldn't be moving forward hardly at all); we were penalized, missed a field goal, and lost again. Oh, well.

The following week we had the 49ers down 35–7 in the first half in San Francisco and blew that one, too. In overtime, 38–35. Joe Montana had a great second half for the 49ers. Bill Walsh, the 49ers coach, had a funny story about it afterward. He said, "When you're in the dressing room at halftime with your team behind 35 to 7 to the worst team in the league, what do you tell 'em? Frankly, I don't know. I didn't say anything to them. Nothing."

On the field at New York the next Sunday, Richard Todd

of the Jets came over to talk to me, practically oozing sympathy. I like Richard a lot, ever since he played against Ole Miss when he was at Alabama. But when he said consoling stuff—like "I know it's been tough, but you guys'll be better next year. Hang in there. You'll beat somebody one of these days."—instead of being consoled, I bristled.

I said, "Richard, old buddy, we're going to whip your ass today."

And we did, by a point, 21–20. Our only victory of the year.

I've never had the thrill of celebrating after a Super Bowl victory, or even being around a team that did. But if it's any more exhilarating than our celebration after that game, it must be fantastic. You'd have thought we won five games, not one. Or the Irish Sweepstakes.

Without really knowing it, and without fully accepting it, I was now on the hairy edge of a final reckoning with pro football. Bum Phillips was about to become the new head coach of the Saints, which in the end would not be good for me. Or for the Saints, you'd have to say, if you go strictly by the record: Bum's teams never got above .500 either. But there were personal factors that had taken hold that would not only soften the ultimate blow, but make my impending football "afterlife" by far the more rewarding. (Obviously, I'm not talking about money here.) In short, the happiest days were yet to come.

Olivia, naturally, was at the center of this transition, just as she had been through every other up and down since Ole Miss. And though she quit going to the games during that painful 1980 season (being pregnant with Eli was the official reason, but it was the oppressive atmosphere and oral abuse in the Superdome that finally wore her out), the grandparents were around to escort Cooper and Peyton and keep the Manning support team operational. And, of course, by then the boys were old enough to be an integral part of whatever I was doing, on or off the field.

I had always vowed never to push the kids into any sport, much less football. And I didn't, not in the way you think of as typical of sports-obsessed parents. (You know, the well-intentioned screaming, swearing, politicking yahoos at youth league games.) But from the time they could walk, I am not ashamed to say, I "exposed" them to sports, the more the merrier, just in case they might find the enjoyment I once knew. There was, however, one deviation from my games as a child on the sandlots and streets of Drew, Mississippi: My kids started in the house.

When we moved to Seventh Street in the Garden District, we didn't have much furniture, but we did have a big, carpeted, all-but-empty living room, shaped like a football field, and Cooper and I, and then Peyton, would play "knee" sports there. Which is to say, if it was football, I'd get on my knees and they'd try to run around me or throw over me or take me down. We'd use a miniature rubber football, and play by the hour, one-on-one at first, then two-on-one, and then when they had friends over, maybe three- or four-on-one.

We didn't have a yard the way we do now on First Street, so when we needed to get outside we'd borrow a neighbor's, or go to a park on Octavia Street near the Newman school where there was grassy space opposite the swings. Cooper's joy in this was evident from the get-go. As the first child and first grandchild, he had no inhibitions and immediately loved being center stage. His enthusiasm was utterly contagious. If he liked something, Peyton liked it. Until they got older and more competitive, Peyton followed him around like a puppy.

Cooper had a way, though, of pushing you to the limit. From the time he was old enough to have renegade thoughts (meaning about age three), he was a handful. He'd do almost anything for a nickel or a dime—tell jokes, do a dance, take a dare—and what made it so hard to discipline him was that he was so darned funny. I'd try to hide my grin by shaking my head, but he said later he could always see it in my eyes. One time I had to go outside to let it out and he caught me there, laughing my head off. Which was just the kind of thing that made it easier for him to take liberties. Like calling me "Archie" whenever he thought he could get away with it.

Actually, when he was a toddler his formal name for me was "Archibald Watermelon," origin unknown. Olivia smiled every time he said it. I agreed it was funny, but it was also bizarre. Where'd he get it? Why "Watermelon?" Then one day he up and quit, never to say it again, and today even he can't tell you why he stopped or how it ever got started in the first place. Archibald Watermelon disappeared without a trace.

Cooper's natural athleticism marked everything he tried, and early on I really didn't expect that of Peyton. Physically, Peyton was a little butterball by comparison. But the older he got, the tougher he got, and the better coordinated. And alas, the more like me: injury prone. While Cooper was keeping us in stitches his way, the pediatricians were keeping Peyton in stitches in theirs. He was always getting something sewn up.

One time with Olivia he fell out of the back of a slow-moving station wagon onto some gravel and had to have a gash in his head worked on. That night I picked pieces of gravel out of his scalp with tweezers. Another time I had him at a workout and he fell headfirst into some barbells in the training room and *really* opened it up. We had to rush him to the emergency room. What made that trip so memorable was that Peyton refused to cry. He said, "It doesn't hurt," and shook his head emphatically. But you knew he had to be in a lot of pain. It was a trait that carried over. When he's hurting now, Peyton just won't let it show. He refuses to give the other side the satisfaction.

One of the convictions Olivia and I had about raising them was that the boys would be well-rounded. That they would be involved in all kinds of activities. Sports if they wanted, the band if they wanted, piano lessons, guitar lessons, whatever, just as long as they were "doing." My only hard rule was that they had to finish whatever they started. But sometimes that didn't always work out either. We got Cooper involved in the Cub Scouts when he was in grade school and he liked it, but he had a chance to be the manager of the junior high football team and opted out. I objected, but the mother who was his Scout leader said she'd seen his interests shifting and I was wasting my time.

So the boys went from sport to sport, just the way I'd done (surprise, surprise): football in the fall, then basketball, then baseball in the spring and summer. Each tried soccer for a season but backed off when they realized it overlapped basketball. Our Christmas giving was mostly a question of what new equipment they wanted. What new uniforms, new gloves, new bats, new balls. My marching orders from Olivia always sounded the same: "Get these shoes . . . Get this jersey . . . Get the new football with the SEC logo."

When she started looking for our present home, Olivia would bring me preliminary reports on her findings: the closet space in the house, the size and number of bedrooms, the height of the ceilings, how big the garage was. And I'd say, "Is there room in the yard to play football? Is there room to throw the baseball? Is there a place where we can put up a basketball net?"

I was having the time of my life.

Meanwhile, from almost the beginning of their preschool days, Cooper and Peyton were locker room regulars at the Saints practices. Carefree Cooper had no trouble breaking the ice. He went right into the training room and conned one of the assistants into taping him up "just like a player." Thereafter he and Peyton got their ankles and wrists taped before practice, as if they were going to play, and when the sauna or the whirlpool wasn't occupied, they'd occupy it. After games, Cooper thought nothing of going on the field or outside the visitors' locker room to strike up a conversation with members of opposing teams, like Roger Staubach or Dan Fouts or Lynn Swann. He particularly liked Lance Alworth, even though Lance had retired.

But it really wasn't fawning over players that counted most for Cooper and Peyton, it was the sheer fun of it all. I'd let 'em come into the dressing room ("if you behave") after a game, and they'd hang through the postgame interviews just long enough to scrape enough used tape off the floor to wad into a ball they could take outside and throw. A lot of times the lights would be off in the Superdome when I'd come out, and they'd still be on the field, throwing and running around in the dark.

Star athletes were more like props to them. People they could insinuate into their lives. When Peyton was four, I took the family to Honolulu for the Pro Bowl I'd been chosen to play in after the 1979 season, and one afternoon he turned up missing. We were frantic. When we finally located him, it turned out he had been out sailing on a catamaran—with Walter Payton. Dan Reeves was on Tom Landry's staff that coached our team in that game, and for years afterward every time I saw him he'd ask me if Peyton had sailed home yet.

Now, when Cooper is contemplating children of his own (with Ellen, of course), he remembers those special days:

"Archie didn't hire baby-sitters when he was going anywhere, he just carried me along. I don't think I was much out of the crib before he was taking me places, sometimes where I probably wasn't supposed to go. I'd hunt with him and his hunting pals, the good old boys, and listen to 'em cuss. He got the team to let me sit on the bench for a game, which was against the rules, but who cared? I hung out in the locker rooms. I thought Chuck Muncie and Wes Chandler were my buddies.

"As much as we enjoyed going to them, Dad's games didn't dominate our lives. The next day he'd be right back on the floor in the living room, playing 'knee football.' Sometimes on Mondays when he was still hurting or just worn out, he'd lie facedown on the carpet and have us compete to see who could give him the best massage. I'd rub his back, then Peyton would, and Arch would say, 'Uh, that was too close to call. You'll have to go into overtime.'

"As we got older, we'd have 'spend-the-night' parties, where seven or eight of our friends would come and we'd play together all day for two days, with as little sleep as possible in between. The 'game' didn't matter. Football or hide-and-seek or kick-the-can or basketball, just anything. Dad would take videos. He had one of those big clunky original video cameras that made him look like a Hollywood producer, and he never stopped shooting. He was a video nut.

"The only thing he didn't like was me fighting with Peyton. It would make Archie mad when we fought, which we did. Often. Kid fights, with no real damage, but still fights. Usually starting with me calling Peyton a wimp or something. Archie would say, 'You ought to be best friends. You don't know how lucky you are, having a brother.' He hadn't had a brother. He tried to make us appreciate the fact that we did. And we do now. Yeah, and then, too. I admit it.

"What I think Mom appreciated most, though, was that he never took his losses out on anybody. He had way more than his share, and a lot of them were heartbreaking, but he never let them get him down. Yes, when the booing got really bad at the Superdome, Peyton and I wanted to boo, too. Just for the hell of it. And we wanted to wear the bags over our heads. But through all that, I never remember him bringing his defeats home with him. Not ever."

As it turned out, I soon wouldn't be close enough to bring them home at all. One more season in New Orleans and I'd be gone to another city, to another team, with the end of my career suddenly looming large on the horizon.

How radically things had changed. Olivia was pregnant with Eli coming off that 8–8 encouragement in 1979, with the due date the first week in January 1981, and we were thinking (well, hoping) we might have a scheduling conflict with the playoffs that everybody was predicting we'd be in. Olivia said, "Too bad. I probably won't get to go with you because I'll be delivering." One-and-fifteen took care of the conflict.

Bum Phillips replaced Stanfel, as advertised, and once again football people I respected advised me to cut and run. To find a better place to end my career. Bum was a Bear

Bryant disciple, with a country-boy manner and a reputation for preferring the run over the pass. Friends said I'd die a thousand deaths trying to adjust. "The only time Bum Phillips passes is on third down," they said. "With Bum, the air force is just for show. He wants to win with tanks." He'd done just that in Houston with Earl Campbell, the great Texas running back.

Naturally, I didn't listen. Or listened but didn't heed the warning. It was a big mistake.

In retrospect I have to concede I liked Bum Phillips, to a point (the point where he traded me). And the one season I played for him gave me a lot of material for my speeches. His pregame pep talks were like pop art, and never predictable. One time he went on at length and great detail on "what it's going to take today for us to beat the Falcons." The trouble was, we were playing the Buccaneers. The upside was that Bum wasn't a hard-ass. His style was to play hard, have fun, and let the winning happen. And since I still believed it *would* happen, one of these centuries, I wanted to be there when it did to enjoy the vindication.

But there were more compelling reasons to stay. John Mecom was one factor. He was my owner-cheerleader, always saying reassuring things like "The only problem with Archie is that everyone else around here can't measure up to the standards he sets." High praise. And what Bum Phillips didn't know coming in was that Mecom was about to sign me to the biggest contract in the NFL, one that would insure my retirement whether I remained a Saint or not. So the money factor—what the world has now come to expect as dominant in a professional athlete's thinking—was finally playing in.

Ah, but most of all it was the contentment factor. Olivia and I had come to love New Orleans, and all the friends we'd made. After eleven years, we were root-bound. Olivia was involved in the community. Our kids were thriving in the schools. I had about five off-season jobs, including doing dealer development for Royal Oldsmobile and radio and television spots. I had a deal with an insurance company, and another with a radio station. I did promotional work for BellSouth Mobility and was on the board of a half-dozen charities.

In the final analysis, none of that could save me. Only one thing counted, and it was as unambiguous as a sock on the nose: Bum Phillips didn't want me. In his system, it really didn't matter who the quarterback was, and the thought of changing to a pass-oriented offense was anathema to him. For me the situation was reversed. Bum's offense was conservative. Run-oriented. Passing only as a diversion, or when absolutely necessary. As a team, we threw 125 fewer passes in 1981 than we had in '80. I threw *260* fewer, having to sit out a couple games with injuries. His approach to the game was harder to adjust to than I thought.

But we did have one exciting week that year, the week we went to Houston to play Bum Phillips's old team, the Oilers. Bum was a legendary figure in Texas, and people there didn't like it when he got fired. The pregame hype was something you would expect only at a playoff game, or maybe a World Wrestling Federation Tag Team Extravaganza. The Oilers had struggled since Bum left, and the media were enjoying giving his successor a rough transition. Houston papers and TV stations sent crews of reporters—to New Orleans! To cover *our* preparations. Bum acted like he was above it all. He kept telling us, "Don't pay any attention to all this stuff. It's just another game. No hard feelings either way."

Well, it was just another game as far as the standings were concerned, but it was also a zoo. And a lot of fun. I've always told my boys that big games are what football is really all about. That you get more kick out of playing in a big one, win or lose, than you ever get beating some hapless underdog by 50 points. Of course, in my pro career I'd often had to *make* games big in my mind. To force myself to think of them that way for incentive's sake. But this one caught our fancy, and the urge to win it reinvigorated the Saints team.

We stayed at the Warwick in Houston, one of John Mecom's hotels, and that morning at the pregame meal—

which is when the head coach gets in his last licks—Bum bared his soul. He told about facing a team he'd worked so hard to build, and how the organization took it out on him when they faltered, et cetera, et cetera.

And finally he said, "Fellas, I been telling you all week this is just another game. *Bull ... shit!* This ain't just another game! This is life or death! My life—or your death."

We yucked it up, and then went out and beat the Oilers, 27–24. It was one of four games we won that year.

And after one game of the 1982 season, Bum Phillips traded me.

To Houston.

Could it have gotten any more ironic?

Bum telegraphed the final blow. During training camp, the Oilers cut Kenny Stabler and the Saints picked him up. Stabler had been Bum's quarterback when the Oilers made a run for the Super Bowl a couple years before, and in the opening game of the 1982 season, at the last minute, Bum started him over me. I didn't get in but for a few plays.

Five days later the Saints traded me to Houston for an offensive tackle named Leon Gray, which tells you where they thought I was in my career. Gray was on the *down*side of his, to put it politely. In effect, Bum was saying he'd take anything to get rid of me. It happens all the time in pro football. A coach is faced with a potential "quarterback controversy." He resolves it by getting rid of one of the quarterbacks—i.e., the one who doesn't figure in his plans. It was an easy way of taking the pressure off Stabler, who might not be so comfortable if I was still hanging around.

I could be wrong, but I don't think it had anything to do with Bum disliking me. I think he just had a quick-fix agenda, and didn't have a lot of patience at that stage of his career. I read later that what he was hoping for was an immediate trip to the playoffs so that he could retire and turn the team over to his son, Wade. He had no interest in changing or obliging others. He traded away our best receiver, Wes Chandler, who could catch anything, and when I asked him about it, Bum said, "I just don't like that boy's attitude."

It was hinted that Bum also wanted me gone because I had a lock on the endorsements in town, and he liked to do endorsements. I did have an edge there. I had been a definable, dependable commodity for a long time in a city that wasn't big on endorsements for pro athletes in the first place. A lot of businesses paid in trade-offs—cut a commercial and get a car; do a promotion and get a television set. Nowadays it's a lot better. I make more money as a nonplayer than I ever did when I played. One deal with a bank alone pays $100,000 a year. (Peyton, the hotter property, cut a similar deal with a company that pays $350,000.) But if Bum was envious he never gave me any indication. We got along fine. I just wasn't the quarterback he wanted. I only wish I'd known sooner.

Leaving the Saints broke my heart. I'd never been cut from anything in my life, never discarded in any way. It was rough enough on my ego, but the worst part was I just didn't want to leave. I thought I had two or three good years left, and I wanted to finish them *there*, on *that* team. But in such a touchy situation a pro athlete can't say, "Oh, please, Bum, let me stay." Not because of pride, but because in football you simply can't be where you're not wanted. It wouldn't work.

In the end I came out way ahead financially. I had gotten my salary up to $370,000 after winning the MVP award in 1978, and that was more than Roger Staubach was getting, more than Terry Bradshaw, more than Bob Griese. Bradshaw couldn't believe it. He was winning Super Bowls and making $200,000, I was with a team going nowhere and making almost twice as much. He needled me about it whenever he saw me.

I have to believe, though, that part of my favored status had to do with John Mecom's appreciation for what I did for the Saints *off* the field. John lived in Houston, and I in New Orleans, and I could be there when he couldn't—making appearances, attending banquets, being a "spokesman." John would call at the last minute and say, "There's a shindig at the Performing Arts Center tonight and we need someone there. Could you do it?" Nine times out of ten I'd say, "Sure." I think when he paid me, he had that in mind. I was his emissary. By the beginning of the 1980s, I'd spoken at just about every high school in Louisiana, and at least as many in Mississippi. And I'd been given the NFL Players Association's Justice Byron (Whizzer) White award for good works, which for me was as big as winning the MVP trophy.

All things considered, I have nothing but good feelings for John Mecom. With me he was always straight, always generous. Sure, I wish he'd hired better people to make the team better, but it didn't happen, and I don't think it was for lack of trying. In the end, his last expression of appreciation was the kindest: the new contract I got just before the '81 season. A contract that probably *did* put me on the bad side of Bum Phillips. I heard later that he and Pat Peppler, his assistant in charge of player negotiations, were livid over the terms.

It happened in the off-season with a year left on my old contract. John and I crossed paths out of the office. One word led to another, and the next thing I knew he had Frank Crosthwait and me out on his daddy's yacht along with his acting general manager, Fred Williams, to cut a new deal. I wound up with something I would never have dreamed possible when I was a rookie: five years, $600,000 a year, with the money guaranteed an extra year ahead if I passed my physical. Meaning, when I passed for the '81 season, the contract was also guaranteed for '82, and so forth.

John never said anything to Bum or Pat (not that he had to); they found out after the fact. But if you look at it strictly from Bum's perspective, you could appreciate his discomfort if he really had a mind to trade me. It meant less money to spread around on other players he might have valued more. Which, of course, is the big hang-up for franchises today when they have to accommodate *really* huge salaries—*and* the salary cap. By today's standards, the money I got was peanuts, but they were working with a lot tighter budgets and a lot less capital in the NFL in 1981.

Would it have happened the way it did if John Mecom had told Bum his intentions beforehand and then Bum had told him *his* intentions? I don't know. I like to think John would have insisted. Either way, it wasn't so good for Bum. But I sure didn't cry in my pillow over it.

So with my guarantees in place, I went to Houston as a full-fledged mercenary, playing for the buck, and *really* got to know why mankind created lawyers. The Saints had to pay me $600,000 for the '82 season; the Oilers made the trade on the basis that they'd pay half (splitting salaries for traded players wasn't frowned on then). It sounded silly for one player to be paid by two teams, but I didn't care as long as I got it. But two years later when I got traded to Minnesota, it went from the ridiculous to the sublime. Minnesota was willing to pay me only $150,000 and insisted that Houston contribute $150,000, or half of Houston's half of what New Orleans still owed me (are you following this?). New Orleans would have to pay the rest: $300,000.

Which meant that at that point I had *three* teams paying me. Which *was* a big problem for the league because it just didn't look right (I'll say), and a problem for the teams because the two I'd left weren't all that excited about holding up their ends of the bargain. Evidently there was some bad blood between them. The Saints didn't like the Oilers, for whatever reason; the Oilers didn't like the Saints (and didn't seem to care much for the Vikings, either), and around it went. Each was out to stick it to the other.

Frank Crosthwait eventually called the NFL commissioner, Pete Rozelle, and threatened a lawsuit if it didn't get resolved. "They're not paying," he said. "This is absurd."

It *was* absurd. One week when I was with the Vikings we were playing the Oilers—when the Oilers still owed me money! Which meant that I was being paid by both teams on the same field in the same game. Crazy. It went round and round like that for months. Quietly, though. Without fanfare. The media were never told.

Rozelle finally ruled that I had to be paid by one team,

period. Minnesota got the nod, being the team I was with at the time. I still don't know who paid what percentage or how much, but they met the guarantees. When you're resigned to the fact that for all intents and purposes you are now playing for pay instead of fun, that's what matters most.

6

Given the limits of human physiology, a pro football player knows going in that his career will likely be over before he is confronted with his first gray hair. Some cope with this imperative better than others and move easily into a "second life," no matter how abrupt the termination of the first. Some resist to the end and slouch into the future under a canopy of bitterness. Either way, it doesn't change the dynamics. Those who have mastered the transition with peace of mind say the secret (besides holding on to as much of all that boodle as possible) is to have something else to go to. Archie Manning didn't even have to think about it. His NFL career stretched fourteen years—the average is less than five—and his thinking had long before gone from the World of Me to the World of Us. Cooper, Peyton, and Eli were growing up and would soon be occupying center stage. A very pleasant transition was coming fast. But, of course, Archie still had to get through the hand-wringing of that one painful, inevitable good-bye.

What made the move from New Orleans and the Saints to Houston and the Oilers even more depressing was convincing myself to do it alone. Olivia and I had just bought our dream house on First Street in the Garden District, our final commitment to being permanent New Orleans-ians, if there's such a word. She was into some major restorations on the house, and the kids were already in school, when I took off for Houston that second week of the preseason.

It was a Friday. On Saturday I met the Oilers coaches and players and was issued a playbook.

And on Sunday I dressed out as the backup quarterback and almost got put in the game. Eddie Biles, the Houston coach who had replaced Bum Phillips, gestured for me on the sidelines, then changed his mind. *That* would have been a first. An NFL quarterback quarterbacking a team without knowing any of the plays.

The very next day all the players in the league went out on strike—the infamous 1982 "Players Rebellion."

As usual, the issues revolved around free agency ("No Freedom, No Football"). The sound and the fury, part two. I had been a reluctant participant in 1974, agreeing in principle with some of the demands but not so sure about insisting on retirement concessions and a "percent of gross receipts," which players nevertheless eventually got. But I was a lot younger, concerned more about finding ways to win games, and I spent most of the strike trying to hold the team together for when we *did* come back in.

What I remember most about either strike was that the first put me in direct conflict for the only time with John Mecom, the Saints' owner. He'd seen me on the picket line and said, "We've had a difficult time developing a leader, including Mr. Manning. I've been very disappointed by his actions the last couple weeks." Mecom was the kind of guy who'd say something like that and the next day invite Olivia and me to dinner, or invite our parents to stay in his New Orleans apartment when they came to town. But since at that moment I was trying to *mend* fences, I got my back up. I said, "If Mr. Mecom wants to get into a debate about leaders, he's been the leader of this team for seven years. If I'm to blame for the past three, who's to blame for the first four?"

I actually came closer to pulling out when the late World Football League started about that time and three Miami Dolphin stars—Larry Csonka, Jim Kiick, and Paul Warfield—all went to the Memphis team. A wholesale defection was predicted, and the Memphis owner made me an offer through

Ed Keating of IMG calling for more money than he'd paid Csonka. It tempted me, because Memphis is right up the road from where I was raised. Frank Crosthwait alerted Mecom, and there were some strained feelings for a while, but I really didn't want to leave the NFL for something so iffy. Keating and Crosthwait worked it out. Mecom redid my contract and extended it, and harmony was restored.

We stayed out for seven weeks in '82, which at least gave me a chance to study the Oilers' plays. Eventually I took residence in the garage apartment of a doctor friend, in a nice suburban Houston neighborhood . . . and contracted the worst case of homesickness ever visited on an adult American male. Or so it seemed.

I overcame it the way a seasoned New Yorker would. I commuted.

Houston is a short hop by plane from New Orleans, and Southwest Airlines had fifteen flights a day, $29 each way. I took to the air. I flew home every chance I got.

Sometimes I flew home just for supper. Practice would end around four, I'd shower and zip to the airport for a five-thirty flight, eat with the family in New Orleans, share a couple hours of catch-up, then make the ten-thirty back to Houston. That's how much I missed Olivia and the boys. And how much I learned to appreciate the discretionary funds you have when you make a little more than you need. At such times, I was absolutely unashamed to be an "overpaid professional athlete."

When the strike ended and we started playing again, I'd also bring the family to Houston. Sometimes the boys came one at a time, for four or five days, and I'd take them to practice, to meetings, and tried to stay current with *their* activities. Olivia actually enjoyed one element of the separation. Years later, she would reminisce about the marathon telephone conversations we had when I was in Houston and Minnesota. How much fun they were—"better than when we were home together," she said, "because there were no distractions, no interruptions. How often do a husband and wife really get to just sit down and talk?" Our long-distance bills were whoppers. We'd talk by the hour, about anything and everything, like we couldn't bear to hang up. Like we were courting again.

The strike lasted deep into the fall and the season had to be cut to nine games. I was the starting Oilers quarterback in the fourth, and from then on. Not that it helped much. We won one of the nine and averaged just 15 points a game. And on Christmas Day, with the end of the season at hand, I tore a hamstring running. I mean, ripped it. A serious, painful injury. Eighteen years have come and gone and I still have pain there.

Fortunately, the nominal healing process had run its course before the '83 season and I was Biles's starter again. But I knew very well by then we were not a good offensive team and not likely to be, even with Earl Campbell still at running back. Campbell, Hall of Fame–bound, had been terrific for a long time, but he'd taken a fearful beating. Our mutual frustration played out like a burlesque routine: he'd get mauled running the ball on first and second down, and I'd get mauled passing it on third (and occasionally fourth). I took one sack after another. The Oilers' offensive line was a sieve.

After seeing three games from mostly the prone position, I was desperate. I told Earl, "I gotta take the linemen to dinner. Try to make everybody realize we're in this together."

I set it up with a friend who owned the Ruth's Chris Steak House in Houston, Bob Ruby. I ate there a lot because Bob knew I hated eating alone and he'd sometimes join me. It was the perfect place to entertain the line (along with Campbell and a couple others) because Ruth's Chris restaurants made a statement: not only the best steaks, but the most expensive. I figured they'd appreciate the gesture, and Bob would give me a break on the bill.

I wound up hosting eleven guys. And with my blessings, they really chowed down. The Michelob tab alone was more than $300. My pal Bob charged me full price for everything.

Or at least it seemed that way. The total bill came to four fig-ures. But that was okay with me. I'd do anything to get some blocking. We had thirteen games to play. I was thinking about survival.

And that Sunday against the Raiders I got sacked four times.

And we lost again.

And on the following Tuesday, I got traded to the Minnesota Vikings for the rest of the '83 season.

Eddie Biles didn't perform the coup de grâce in person the way he should have. He did it by telephone. I'd been at a quarterback meeting that very day but nobody had said any-thing, and afterward I went to a rodeo with a friend. When I got home about 10 P.M., the phone was ringing. It was Biles. He sounded irritated. "Where the hell have you been?"

I said, "Wait a minute. I think I'm over thirty, and this is my day off. I live in this apartment, not at the stadium, and I don't have to tell you where I've been."

And with that he told me where I was going.

Earl Campbell used to laugh about it, in a sick kind of way. He said he was in his kitchen, feeding his toy bulldog, Peggy, when he got news of the trade. He turned to his wife and said, "Do you believe this? Archie and Ghost just got traded to the Vikings!" And he said with that, little Peggy grunted and fell over dead. To this day he kids me about killing his faithful dog. I keep telling him I'll buy him a new one, one of these days.

"Ghost" was Dave Casper, a veteran tight end who got his nickname—appropriately, I always thought—from the cartoon character, Casper the Friendly Ghost. Dave was glad to be part of the trade. He despised Biles. He was nearing the end of his career, too, but he was still a fine player, with unique credentials: two-thirds greatness and one-third free spirit. Unquestionably a character. I'll never forget the first day I saw him after I came to the Oilers. We were in the mid-dle of a light workout—shorts, shoes, helmets—and Dave pulls up in the parking lot, hops out of his car, and runs over to join us. No shoes, no helmet, just shorts and a T-shirt. On the third play, I call his number, and as he runs downfield, barefoot, I loft a floater that he catches on the dead run.

And he keeps running. And running. And running, all the way off the field to where there's a Dempsey-Dumpster—no telling what's inside, broken glass, torn metal—and he dives in, headfirst. Then he pops out, runs back, flips the ball to the center, runs back off the field, gets in his car, and drives off. That was Casper.

It's probably a law that "convenient" isn't an allowable option when you get traded. This time the word came just after I'd switched addresses from my friend's garage to a new apartment that Olivia had come to Houston to decorate. She'd finished outfitting the place just that week: new furniture, appliances, plates, silver, everything. What she didn't buy we rented. And I was so disgusted when I got traded, I said the hell with it, left it all right there, and flew to Minneapolis. My friend packed up everything before the lease ran out and kept it in his garage for two years before we shipped it home to New Orleans.

To avoid suffering a similar fate, I elected to make the Radisson Hotel my home in Minneapolis. There I could come and go as I pleased and be where there were people. But my view from any angle at that point was bound to be the same: downhill. The Vikings brought me in as a starter but with unspoken term limits. Their ace, Tommy Kramer, had just blown out his knee. He would miss the rest of the season, but after that. . . ? The first backup, Steve Dils, and a rookie named Wade Wilson didn't figure to replace Kramer when he was healthy again. At age thirty-five, neither did I. If I went beyond the year, I had to think it would be as a substitute.

I knew some of the cast of characters in Minnesota. I'd played in the Pro Bowl for the Vikings' head coach, Bud Grant, and his offensive coordinator, Jerry Burns. The team had been outstanding under Grant, making the Super Bowl four times (without ever winning it, unfortunately). Grant was another Hall-of-Famer-to-be, and I have to admit I was really looking forward to hearing his first pregame pep talk. It came three days later, when we went to Green Bay to play the Packers.

For me, just being on the Green Bay field was a thrill, with all the history it evoked—Lombardi, Hornung, Bart Starr, Max McGee, Jimmy Taylor, and Willie Davis. A whole galaxy of superstars. I'd never played at Lambeau Field. Never even seen it. And now I'm on it with the Vikings, big winners, too, and with Bud Grant, another great coach. What would he say before the game? What nuggets of inspiration to send us storming after the Packers?

The locker room quieted as Grant came in, hard-eyed and unsmiling. Everybody edged forward on their stools. In a calm, measured voice, he said, "Okay. The American flag will be on your right. I want you to stand up straight during the National Anthem, and don't be chewing any gum! Let's go."

(In all fairness to Bud, I have to say that I realized later his pep talks—when he was inclined to give them—were usually served with the pregame meal. Quietly.)

The Minnesota offense was the most complicated I'd ever seen. So complicated, in fact, that the team really needed a long-term Viking like Kramer to make it go. They had so many plays, they ran out of numbers to call them by. They were using names, like the "Ahmad Rashad Special" and the "Sammy White Extra." The staff had been together so long that the offense was a mass of cross-wiring. For example, in all my years coping with different systems, the even-numbered plays always went to the right, the odd to the left. Here in my last stop, my twenty-sixth year of organized football, odd was going to be to the *right*.

Jerry Burns gave me two weeks to learn the system. I spent just about all my free time cramming and watching film. And I learned it.

But by now I was harboring a new set of anxieties. A new, more personal fear.

I wasn't feeling well when I got to Minneapolis, and I

wasn't getting any better. My practices were labored. I wasn't accurate with my passes and couldn't seem to get any zip on the ball. My arm was sore for no apparent reason, and when I ran or extended myself in any way, my breathing came in gasps, like an asthmatic's. When I lifted weights, I felt weak and shaky. Practice sprints were more like mile runs. If I tried to run a little extra, I felt like I was dying.

I never had so many symptoms at one time. But symptomatic of what?

As a matter of course, the Vikings were supposed to have given me a complete physical when we came in, but they hadn't. They'd sent a Lear jet to get Casper and me on that Wednesday morning, and we went straight into meetings, then to the dressing room to get outfitted. Bud Grant came through when Casper and I were suiting up and the trainer said, "They're supposed to get physicals, aren't they?" Grant said, "They look okay to me." And we went directly to practice.

A week went by, and the symptoms persisted. I kept telling myself it was just a matter of being out of shape. But I remembered that in my last week in Houston I'd also told the weight coach I felt weak. I'd never been so tired, and I wasn't sleeping well. I'd get drowsy when I needed to be the most alert.

Then one day I was in a meeting taking notes and I looked down—and my hand was shaking! Like I had some kind of palsy. I was horrified.

I went to the Minnesota trainer, Fred Zamboletti. I said, "Fred, something's not right."

He said, "Don't worry. We'll get you that physical you should have had. We'll clear this up right away."

But they couldn't clear it up right away. When the blood tests came back, the doctor called me in with the bad news. I had a "thyroid problem." He read from a medical manual about what happens when your thyroid is diseased and the illness goes undetected. How weak you get. How your eyes bulge. He showed me pictures of victims. They looked like those cartoon characters who have been so frightened by something their eyes popped out. Except they weren't funny.

The doctor told me to take a few days off and he'd get back to me with a plan. But the next day I was in the Vikings' office—with no real home to go to, I was always hanging around—and ran into the owner of the team, Max Winter. Max was the dearest little man and the sweetest owner you could ever hope for. He was getting up in years, so he knew a lot more than I did about the body's frailties.

He said, "How'd you like to go to the Mayo Clinic and get this thing settled once and for all?"

I said, "Boy, would I."

"Good. I get my physicals there every year. I can have you in, examined, and out quicker than Ronald Reagan could get in."

I drove to Mayo the next day. It turned out I had what is known as Graves' disease, a hyperthyroid condition that can be very serious if not treated in time and with the proper medication, but controllable if it is.

After a couple of false starts, they wound up administering radioactive iodine. By that time I'd lost fifteen pounds and was shaking like crazy. But I was on the right track, and in good hands. One of the doctors at Mayo was an old-timer who had treated the Bears' great quarterbacks of the '40s and '50s, Sid Luckman and Johnny Lujack.

I rallied but realized soon enough that there was not going to be a miracle cure. I spent most of the season on injured reserve—went to meetings, kept up mentally, but didn't really practice or play. Except once, when Dils was hurt briefly. I went in, called an audible at the line of scrimmage, handed the ball to a running back, and we made a first down. I then ran off the field and Dils went back on. My '83 season in a nutshell.

I went home to New Orleans full of doubts, and fully aware that I looked like a cadaver to anybody who hadn't seen me in a while. I'd heard a version of that diagnosis earlier from Olivia when the Vikings came to New Orleans for a game and I stayed through the weekend. She threw a little party for me, and later everybody told her how awful I looked. The popular guess (whispered, of course) was that I probably had cancer.

Yes, I would have to say at that point the homesickness contributed. It's tough on the psyche when you're alone and sick at the same time. All I did was stand around at practice, sit around at meetings, go back to the hotel and read or watch television, and hope for an occasional invitation to dinner from one of my married friends. Not much to buoy the spirits. Nevertheless, when I went home for the off-season, I was still thinking about playing again. I figured I was finally with a good organization, with good players and coaches. The Vikings had started well in '83, but faded in November and finished 8–8; but that was still equal to my all-time best with the Saints. I thought if we were competitive enough to make the playoffs in '84, I wanted to be there.

But my recovery dragged. One morning in New Orleans I looked in the mirror and my eyes were bulging. Not as bad as I'd seen in the medical book, but bad enough to scare me. I called the doctor. He said to stop worrying. "What we're doing will work. You've got to let it take its course."

So I did, and sure enough began feeling better. Regaining some confidence. Looking almost normal. I went back to working out.

And lo and behold, Bud Grant quit. With no warning, and none of the usual will-he-or-won't-he debates on the talk shows. He just up and resigned as Vikings head coach, agreed to a meaningless job in the front office—meaningless in that it didn't seem to require his presence—and went fishing. Bud had always been an avid outdoorsman, and the speculation was that at that stage of his life he would rather hunt and fish than expend all the energy it would take to get the Vikings back to the Super Bowl. Both sides professed regrets but no hard feelings.

But then another surprise. Management gave the job to a young assistant coach on the staff named Les Steckel— bright, smart, gung-ho, but an insult to the older coaches.

They'd been together for years and weren't at all pleased that the Vikings had passed over Jerry Burns.

Nevertheless, I went to the pre-training-camp workouts Les Steckel ordered up, not only to help myself through the transition but to get a better picture of where I stood physically. It wasn't a pretty sight. And I suddenly realized the spot I might be in: I was now eyeball-to-bulging-eyeball with the very real possibility that I could lose over a million dollars if I didn't pass the mandatory physical before training camp.

Sure, I wanted to beat out Tommy Kramer and be the starter. Sure, I wanted to play for a winning team at last. But this was the practical, consider-your-contract side of my brain taking over, which is what happens when you've become a mercenary. To assure my family the $600,000 I would get for the 1984 season and the $600,000 for '85, I had to pass that one physical. That's the way the carryover clause worked. If I passed, I would get the same money in '85 without being tested again, as the last phase of my original five-year deal with John Mecom. After that, I'd have to renegotiate, if there was anything to renegotiate.

What seemed like something we'd carved out in the Stone Age now glowed like an insurance policy. Players just naturally think and plan that way all the time nowadays; their agents plot their careers inch by inch so as to nail down every dime they can. And why not? Knowing how expendable "talent" is, and with hardly any sense of allegiance on either side, they'd be fools not to get as many guarantees as possible.

I needn't have worried, though. The physical at the beginning of training camp is more a health test than a fitness test, and my thyroid problem was under control. Except for some residual aches and pains, so were my various other ailments and breakdowns. The old bones held together and I passed, insuring the contract through '85. Three cheers. The suspense was over.

But not the agony. Les Steckel had some, well, original ideas about training camp, and this one started with a one-day "Iron Man Contest" that was made more for television than conditioning. In fact, they even sold tickets. It wasn't football training at all, it was a military exercise. Les was an ex-marine, and acted the part. He had the players paired off by positions—linemen against linemen, backs against backs, et cetera—and lifting great weights competitively, running cross-country marathons, hand-swinging rung-to-rung across a suspended ladder—a smorgasbord of body-testers you'd never see (or need) in football.

The results attested to the folly of it, as Les himself admitted later. At least two starters came up with badly pulled hamstrings that took them out of early games, and others suffered various sprains and strains and pulls. We all would have been better off working on our football skills and expanding our knowledge of the Viking offense or defense. I got through it okay, and even won a set of golf clubs in our group's competition. But then when regular training started, Les imposed a daily rope-climbing requirement that just the thought of still makes me cringe. I mean, what does climbing ropes have to do with quarterbacking? Tommy Kramer was smart: He refused to do it.

But I can answer the question from personal experience: I frayed the tendons in my elbow climbing that rope, and played hurt the rest of the year.

Not that I played much. I never came close to beating out Kramer. But I did start one game—against the Bears, the best defensive team in the league. Maybe one of the best defensive teams in the *history* of the league. (Does the name Mike Singletary mean anything to you? How about Wilber Marshall? Or William "The Refrigerator" Perry?) And they just clobbered me. Sacked me eleven times, made me hurry my throws, then whacked me after I'd thrown. I mean I got pummeled. And the passes I *did* put on target were mostly dropped. We were pathetic.

I roomed that year with Jan Stenerud, the veteran place-kicker, and both of us were older than Les Steckel. As the team stumbled along, Les would seek us out for "conversation," like we were confidants. He'd ask our opinions, and we'd give them, but more as theory than suggestion. Jan and I regretted later that we didn't tell him at the beginning to please take it easy on his elders. Team spirit crashed and rumors flew that Les wouldn't be with us a second year.

One day late in the season, I was sitting by Wade Wilson at the offensive team's pregame meeting, and Steckel, his voice rising defiantly, said, "I just want you all to know that *I'm* going to be here, no matter what." The words beleaguered football coaches always say just before the switch is thrown.

I sighed and dropped my head, and Wade Wilson picked up on it. As we walked out, he said, "What's up?"

I said, "Les is gone. You can take it to the bank."

Even with Kramer at quarterback, the Vikings won only three of sixteen games that season, and Les Steckel got fired immediately afterward. He hasn't been a head coach since. Last I heard he was the offensive coordinator for the Tampa Bay Buccaneers.

The word *retirement* should then have flashed across my mind in bold letters, but I was still resisting. The fun was mostly gone, and the indicators were unanimously negative: I was slower and older, and was a backup quarterback on a team that was going nowhere in the foreseeable future. But I left myself one opening. I had to make an appearance at training camp in '85 to get my guarantee, and I was afraid that was all it might be, an appearance. But if I got there and did well . . . ?

The one positive about Minnesota that '84 season was having Olivia and the kids there to share it with me. We rented a furnished house in Lake Minnetonka right outside Minneapolis, and in September enrolled the kids in public school—Cooper in the fifth grade, Peyton in the third, Eli in a nursery school. From my perspective, it was practically perfect. I had no local commitments. The phone didn't ring as much. I could devote whatever spare time I had to the family.

And in my contentment I must have been more vulnerable

to their "requests," because that fall I broke a long-standing rule that the boys could not play organized football until they were in the seventh or eighth grade. I can pinpoint the exact moment of the sea change. Cooper came home one day and said, "Dad, guess what? They've got a fifth-grade football team, and I'm going to be the quarterback!" I mean, how could I refuse?

Actually, I did refuse. I wasn't *that* vulnerable. I said, "No, you don't want to do that," holding to my conviction that parents make a mistake channeling kids into full-fledged, fully equipped, eleven-men-to-a-side, blood-and-guts football before they've had a chance to enjoy all the wonderful aspects of the game as played at the sandlot level. Kids eight, ten, twelve years old should be playing five or six men to a side in the sandlots, away from prying eyes and "organization." Where they don't spend five afternoons a week practicing for that one game on Saturday when more than half of them won't even touch the ball unless it's fumbled.

I think the predominance of super-organized youth league football is one of the reasons white kids aren't playing the game in the numbers they used to and are moving on to other things. The game at the lowest levels has lost much of its spark. Hundreds of high schools have canceled the sport. Statistics nationally show an alarming dropout rate that has reached epidemic proportions. I'm not surprised. You hardly ever see kids playing it in the side yard anymore, or playing touch football in the street the way we did. It's almost as if it has been reprogrammed to provide roster fillers for the colleges and the pros. Just one big farm system, turning out tackles and guards and linebackers and cornerbacks. The modern equivalent of gladiators.

Of course, you don't see white boys "hanging out" at the park in numbers anymore, either. They don't gravitate there after school and stay till dark, or live there on the weekends the way my generation did—honing skills, developing competitive edges. Ask Larry Bird what made him so good and he'll tell you all those hours he spent at the playground in

Indiana. Nowadays, white kids show up in carpools, for those parent-dominated little leagues where everything is structured, time-limited, and safe.

That's the operational word: *safe*. And not just because mamas are more concerned about their little boys breaking something. We've drawn inward and become wary of uncontrolled play, perhaps for good reason considering the dangers we now live with. But go to a park in a mostly black neighborhood and see the crowds. From morning to night they're there, playing and learning, and making the difference. I know I wouldn't have been as good an athlete as I was, or become as good a professional, if I hadn't put in the time in somebody's backyard or some vacant lot or at the playgrounds and schoolyards of Drew. Black kids do that. I go to work and see them out in the street, throwing the football, and I say to myself, "Good for you."

Cooper had that kind of desire. And he was fearless. He badgered me and badgered me about that fifth-grade team, and when I finally checked it out, I withdrew my objections. The league was coached by teachers who cared more about the kids having fun than being drilled on techniques. They promised a lot of play and a minimal amount of practice. A powerful argument. Cooper played. Peyton volunteered and was named the team manager.

But I also saw in Minnesota that I had lost Eli a little. I had been living somewhere else other than home during the football seasons in Houston and Minneapolis, and though he was just a tyke and I knew there was still time, we hadn't approached that bond I'd been able to seal with Peyton and Cooper. I hadn't "strollered" the neighborhood with him like I'd done them. Hadn't talked to him as often, father to son. Child-rearing experts tell you the first three years are pivotal, and I just didn't have the intimacy with Eli that I'd have liked.

The awareness hurt most when I'd come home in January and he'd act like he hardly knew me. I believe now, as Olivia does, that it was a matter of him being more like me at that age, but he had become a quiet, almost shy little boy and hard to know. So I had hopes that having them all there in Minnesota for those months would help close that gap a little.

Of course, all that was strictly from my perspective. Olivia didn't share my enthusiasm for Minnesota once the cold weather set in. And she soon tired of people telling her she "talked funny." The South still dominates her speech, so I suppose if you thought Scarlett O'Hara (as played by Vivian Leigh) talked funny, you'd think Olivia does. She wasn't insulted, she has too good a sense of humor for that, she just got tired of being reminded. She'd take the kids through a McDonald's and be at the window picking up her stuff and the help would crowd around and ask her to "talk" for them.

I would think that contributed to her wishing we could all just go home for good. She was in her fourteenth year of being a player's wife, and she wasn't interested in doing the "pro football wives thing" anymore. Hanging out with other wives, having "wives' clubs," arranging for get-togethers, those kinds of things. She had served her time. She just wanted to last out the season and go home. She just wanted to be Olivia. And, of course, Mama.

But she would concede we had some good times in Minnetonka. Don Hasselbeck, a well-traveled tight end from Colorado, joined the Vikings after I came, and the Hasselback family also included three boys. We meshed, which allowed the women and boys to do things together while Don and I commiserated over the Vikings' failings. When I was sacked for the eleventh time by the Bears, a picture in the papers around the country showed me spread-eagled on the field, my chin split open and my eyes crossed—a comic but grotesque reminder of the blocking I wasn't getting.

The next day the owner of the Rendezvous restaurant in Memphis, where Peyton thinks I spent half my college life, FedExed us a huge box of dry ribs, the Rendezvous specialty. I was so banged up I couldn't practice, and we had the Hasselbacks over early to feed on the ribs. It took hours. Don later got released (he was used to it by then) and his family moved to Boston, where the first two Hasselback boys eventually played quarterback for Boston College and the oldest went on to Green Bay, where he's now a backup quarterback for the Packers. The second son is starting for Boston College now. Shades of the Mannings.

But all of this I saw while sharing my waking hours with the Vikings. You have to appreciate it from Olivia's perspective, where Minnesota to her was just another venue for total immersion, familywise. Hers was the longer, broader view:

"When Archie was living at the Radisson in '83, I came up for a weekend and had such a good time, I wound up staying a week. Then I took the boys up, and they had a ball playing football in the hotel hallways. One of their shoes they used as a football is probably still there somewhere. So I was glad to go up for '84, and into the house in Minnetonka. Archie needed us there, if for no other reason than he wanted to get closer to Eli. When he'd make visits home from Houston, and then Minneapolis, it killed him when Eli ignored him. Just killed him.

"In time we understood. Eli was one of those kids who is very reluctant to show feelings, for anybody or anything. It was sad at times, but funny, too. Somewhere along the way he made a rule that you could only kiss him on Sunday nights. Our family has always been big on hugs and kisses, but Eli wasn't interested. I mean not at all. Then he finally gave in a little and agreed to Sundays. One kiss, that's all, good night, good-bye, see you at breakfast.

"Of course, now when we see him with his friends he talks nonstop, and they don't think he's shy at all. He's just 'Easy' to them, and witty. I've seen things he has written, and it looks like he might be developing Cooper's sense of humor, heaven help us. And he dances like crazy. Wild stuff Archie calls 'vulgar,' but he laughs when he says it. Eli's not Cooper, though. He has this tight little group, with girlfriends included, and he doesn't care whether he adds any more or not. A typical New Orleans attitude, which wouldn't fit with

Cooper, who's always looking for new friends, always looking to expand his horizons.

"Cooper can find things to like in almost anything, and he liked Minnesota. But I don't think Peyton was all that crazy about it. He was a hold-back kind of kid then, a little insecure, a little afraid of messing up. He'd show me his schoolwork and say, 'Maybe you oughta call the teacher and ask her if this is right.' I had helped him once with his math and he got all the problems wrong, and got really mad at me over it, and never asked for my help again. For the rest of his school life, he'd come home and go right up to his room to do his homework. Wouldn't come down until he was finished. Cooper you had to shove up the stairs. He charmed his way through school.

"Stubbornness was a major part of Peyton's makeup even then. With Archie gone so much, even when he played for New Orleans, I'd take the boys on vacation trips—to Mississippi, to Martha's Vineyard, to Nantucket. They were fun to travel with. Rough-and-tumble, but still fun. And one summer when Peyton was three, I took them and my mother to Mount Eagle, Tennessee, along with a college friend, Ann Ross, and her family. A nice little town, Mount Eagle, but it was too cold to go swimming, and it rained every day—I thought I was going to mildew—and we were pretty much confined to the house we had rented.

"And Peyton got jealous of the time I spent with Ann. Then he got rude. A classic Oedipus reaction. I had to give him time-outs almost by the hour, sending him to his room for one thing or another. I'd never had a problem with him until then, and I was dumbfounded, because no matter how much he was punished, he kept it up. He didn't want anything to do with Ann's little boy. He said, 'He plays with trucks. I play football.'

"Then one day while we were there, Cooper fell off a bike and cut his head and I had to take him to the emergency room in Sewannee. Peyton stayed with Ann and the others. My last words were 'Be good.' But as soon as I was out the door he told Ann exactly what he thought. He said, 'You're not a good cooker. You're not a good driver. And I don't like you anyway.' We laughed about it then, and still do, this emphatic little three-year-old, but it was the weirdest two weeks of my life.

"The thing is, even then Peyton was determined. About everything. I remember him in kindergarten when the class got up to do the motions of 'Row, Row, Row Your Boat.' Peyton did the grandest, most obvious arm-flailing 'rows' you ever saw. I laughed, but I wanted to cry. What is going on with this child? When it carried over to later years, though, it was actually fun to see. When he was in the eighth grade, the teacher got him to do the tango for a play called The Boyfriend.

"By then he was so wrapped up in sports that it was a major intrusion, but he consented. He let us dress him in a red ruffled shirt, with tight pants, yellow cummerbund, high-top patent leather shoes, and he and this girl did the tango. I mean really did it, a hundred and fifty percent. If they'd had an eighth-grade highlight film, Peyton's tango would have made it.

"All that is part of being competitive, I know. Like Archie. But it's also just wanting to do something well. Peyton was never satisfied just getting by. He wanted to do everything to the utmost. And he had ways about him that were downright beautiful. I mean, you'd almost have to force money on him: 'You need any money, Peyton?' 'No.' Ask Cooper the same question, any hour of any day, and he'd say, 'Sure do.' Cooper always had a pocketful of money. And when you gave Peyton more than he needed, he'd always bring home the change and fork it over. Cooper you had to ask.

"From the time he knew right from wrong, Peyton was the kind of kid you could rely on. His third-grade teacher told me she used him as her 'rock of order.' She'd say, 'Peyton, they're acting up,' and he'd make everybody in the class simmer down. To this day, when he's home he goes around and checks the locks on our doors before he goes to bed. And he's a neatnik, like Archie. You never had to ask him to pick up the toys or fluff the pillows, he just did it. Same way now. If he comes home and sees something out of place, he puts it up.

"Everything considered, I think the boys would have been fine in Minnesota if it wasn't for the fact that we knew there was something else waiting. I mean, I sure knew it. We rented the house in Minnetonka through December, which would indicate at least a little doubt. And we'd paid for the year at Newman in New Orleans to protect the boys' enrollment there, so we had an out if it didn't work. So we moved into the Minnetonka house, which was in the Ten Thousand Lakes area, with ducks all over the place, and we got through most of the season fine, and when Thanksgiving eve came it was cool and crisp and beautiful.

"Now, bear in mind that the kids had never seen snow. I had, but in small doses, and was never all that crazy about it. But this wasn't Mississippi, this was Minnesota. Nothing about a winter in Mississippi would prepare you for a winter in Minnesota. One day the boys came home with instructions on how to wait for the bus on a freezing day. How to get a snowplow to bring you from your house, and how to dig a tunnel in the snow and curl up inside if it got really bad. I thought, 'Excuse me?'

"I kept my eye on those ducks. I'd say to Archie, 'What's going to happen to the ducks when it snows and the water freezes? Where will they go?'

"And that night, Thanksgiving eve, it snowed. Really snowed. Fourteen inches of snow, with all the numbing cold that usually goes with it. Naturally, Archie couldn't wait to get the kids up the next morning to see it. 'Get up, get up! It snowed!' And it was pretty, all right. But it wasn't all that pretty when you had to trudge through it, or shovel it off your walk, or dig your car out, and everything turned brownish gray.

"Then I realized the ducks were gone. I said, 'Archie, what happened to the ducks?'

"He said, 'I dunno. I guess they went south.'

"And I thought, 'Sounds like a good idea to me.'"

They left for New Orleans soon after that storm. Olivia packed everybody up and flew home. She'd seen the future and decided against it. She put the kids back in school at Newman, and they all picked up right where they left off. Except I spent the last month of the season there by myself in the house, pretty much convinced that none of us would be around to experience another winter in Minnesota.

We made it official, as far as the four of them were concerned, after I got back home. We used to have what we called "board meetings" on family matters, sometimes at breakfast (I always insisted we eat breakfast together), but usually on a Sunday night. We'd rehash the week, plan for the next, talk about it, pray about it. A family isn't a democracy, but at a Manning board meeting everybody at least had their say. Cooper always cracked jokes. For me the meetings were important because once you have kids, you should grant the fact that your life is no longer just yours; that your responsibility now is to the whole family. And if you *don't* think that way, chances are you'll be a lousy parent.

I had worked hard on my schedule to be home as much as possible, even when I played in New Orleans, where I had a thing about never being gone more than two nights in a row for away games. I concede that I probably wasn't as needed as much as I thought, and maybe was a little stricter when I was around than I should have been, but Olivia was the saving grace. If I was the iron fist, she was the velvet glove.

Funny how you learn those things about yourself. A couple weeks after I went to Houston on that first trade, Olivia had to take Cooper to the pediatrician, Dr. Mason, for a checkup. Dr. Mason said, "I guess you really miss your dad, eh, Cooper?"

And Cooper replied, "Yeah . . . but you know, he's real strict."

We discussed the Minnesota decision at our board meeting in January. Olivia made her pitch: If I wanted to play another year, fine, she'd support it, but she thought it best that she and the kids stay in New Orleans so as not to interrupt their schooling again. I agreed. The vote was unanimous.

When I went back in the summer for training camp, it wasn't nearly as depressing as it had been, because no matter how I looked at it, the end was in sight. One more year at the most. I went into the '85 training camp still open to the idea I might make one last stand. Unlike Custer, I had a couple of reasons to be positive. Bud Grant had changed his mind about fishing his life away and was back as head coach. And Tommy Kramer hadn't been effective in '84. He didn't look like the sure thing he seemed to be when I first came to the Vikings. I thought if I did play, I might even start.

On the other hand, the truism hadn't changed any: The older you get in football, the harder it is to get in shape. My elbow was still bothering me, and I had remnant aches from the torn hamstring, plus the shadow of the thyroid problem. Nevertheless, I made it through training and into the preseason, and played the second half in a game at Miami where I took us on a two-minute drive late in the fourth quarter to the winning touchdown.

But in the process I tweaked my hamstring, which meant I now had two things to cover up: my elbow and my leg. I got treatment for both—with pain pills, with cortisone shots, even with DSMO, the stuff they use on horses.

Then just before the end of the preseason schedule, Bud Grant called me into his office. I'd gotten so I really liked Bud. A quiet, stoic, almost forbidding guy on the surface, but the type veteran players love because he loved veterans, even to the point of keeping some of them around too long. We had no trouble communicating. One player told me he'd been there six years, "and I've seen Bud talk to you more in a week than he's talked to me the whole time."

Except this meeting hadn't been called to exchange recipes.

Bud opened with the kind of observation any pro player in any sport isn't exactly dying to hear about himself: "You know, Archie, you're not very fast anymore."

I said, "Well, I have a little hamstring problem . . . "

"Yeah, I noticed. I could tell you were trying to cover it up. But how about your elbow?"

Uh-oh. "Well, we're through two-a-days now, and I won't have to practice as much, so I think I could . . . "

"You know, Archie, there's four of you now at quarterback."

I knew, all right. The lineup included Kramer and Wade Wilson, still there from before, and now Steve Bono, a rookie from UCLA. He said, "What do you think of Bono?"

"He looks like a prospect."

"I agree."

Then, at last, the reason for the conversation: "You ever think of retiring?"

In spite of myself, I grinned. "Not until now."

It was crazy. At that very moment, the thought of retiring actually excited me. I was ready without having realized it, and I think Bud Grant must have sensed it. I think he knew I had no desire to be a backup, or third string, or even be on injured reserve, not with all the physical baggage I was carrying. And certainly not to be stuck in that position for four months without Olivia and the kids. I was ready.

And now, just like that, I had an out, and was excited about the prospects of (could I say it at last?) leaving football.

I said to Bud, "Shall I retire or are you going to cut me?"

"No, you've been a great player. This would be your fifteenth year in the league. I think you should retire."

I was just about to say, "What about the money?" when he said, "Don't worry about your contract. It's a done deal. You'll get fully paid."

I was then not only excited but relieved.

I thought, What a difference time makes. I had a sudden, vivid reminder of the day the Saints traded me, and *how* the Saints traded me. The painful contrast of one scene played against the other.

I remembered how I'd cried that day in New Orleans. How after a hurried press conference I quickly went to my car because I knew I couldn't stay around and talk to the players, I was too shaken up. There were three guys with the Saints I felt close to besides players: the trainer, Dean Kleinschmidt, who'd been there my entire eleven years (I was best man at his wedding); the equipment manager, Dan Simmons; and Dan's assistant, Silky Powell, who weighed 350 pounds. I worked out so much I was always around those three. I've since told my boys that two of their very best friends in football would invariably be the trainer and the equipment manager. Sure enough, when Peyton was at Tennessee one of *his* best friends was the equipment manager, Roger Frazier.

Anyway, I'd gone to the parking lot without my football shoes, which you always keep, and Silky brought them out in a bag and cried all over me. Kleinschmidt and Simmons were there, too, and it was all very emotional. I got in my car and cried all the way home, packed my bags, and went to Houston. I wasn't all that calm inside when I got traded to Minnesota either, but it was nothing like that day leaving New Orleans. I hated going, and I hated the way they did it.

I was reminded again in the spring of 2000 when the Saints fired Dean Kleinschmidt after thirty-one years of faithful service (he'd started there as a rookie himself and had always worked without a contract). They did it with the same lack of class. A different owner, a different coach, a different general manager, but an even worse disregard for his contributions all those years. Just: "You're out, Dean. See you around." It was ruthless. And classless.

But with this final curtain in Minnesota, I went out smiling. I called Olivia with the good news. I called my mom and sister, and everybody I felt the need to alert. I called Frank Crosthwait and shocked the hell out of him. On the phone when he's surprised by something, Frank goes into these long silences, which can bug you to death, and he went into one, just as he did later when I told him Peyton was going to Tennessee instead of Ole Miss. When he does it I always want to say, "Frank, I hate it when you do that!" But I didn't. He finally came to and wished me well.

The next day we had a little get-together with the Minnesota media, and the announcement was made. I said my good-byes, and that was it. Kind of anticlimactic as career enders, but it got the job done. I flew home.

To a new and happier life, as it turned out. With no more frustrations over lost football games in which *I* was the quarterback, no more anguishing over what was coming next or what might have been. For those who had the stomach to examine those fourteen years and concluded that it couldn't possibly have been worth it, I'd have to say, "Oh, yes, it was." Even with so little to show for it, I'm glad I lasted as long as I did.

Playing pro football was something I had dreamed of among all those dreams of glory as a kid back in Drew. The football part came true. And the time spent didn't add to the frustration, it helped get me through it. If my career had ended in 1976, when I was suffering so much with my arm and wondering if the next operation would be the last, I would have been unhappy to have quit. I heard people say, "He'll never come back now," and I knew I'd taken my health for granted and was on the edge of losing it. I said to myself then, "Boy, if I ever *do* get to play again, I'm going to make the most of it."

And I got to play again. And I made the most of it, within the limits of what one person can do in a team sport. I worked hard, and I thank God for every game. Nobody wanted to win more than I did, but I can say in all honesty that even the *lack* of winning didn't ruin it for me. When I saw the bitterness in other players who had been cut or traded for the last time, I made up my mind that would never be me. I said to myself, "Be glad you're still here, and remember that it's still just a game, even with all the money and the pressure, and there are a lot of people in this world who never had the privilege."

I'd see the bitter ones, even five or ten years after they'd been out of the game, still hurting, still mad at coaches, still mad at owners, still talking about "those rotten sons of bitches" and then openly rooting against their old teams.

And I would tell Olivia, "What an awful way to start a second life."

Because that's what it should be, a second life. A chance maybe even to take advantage of what you learned in college, if you can imagine, and whatever else you've picked up along the way—which often includes a lot of benefits that have accrued that you seldom even think about. It's a valuable thing to walk down the street and have people know you, people who are glad to speak to you, or just to see you—in restaurants, on the street, in church. And yes, in businesses. It truly is another life in that regard, and you should be appreciative.

Would I love to have played in a Super Bowl? Hell, I'd love to have played on just one winning team. Just one. In that I probably get more positive feedback than I deserved. I still think about where and how I might have contributed more to those teams that weren't very good, maybe made them better. I don't think I was a really good quarterback a lot of times, despite the MVP awards and making the Pro Bowl a couple times. In terms of real achievement, it was mostly an unfulfilling career.

That's not intended to sound overly humble. I think I proved myself in the NFL, despite the teams' records. I have a picture on my wall—Lenny Dawkins, Kenny Anderson, Neil Lomax, Steve Bartkowski, Earl Morrall, Sonny Jurgensen, Roger Staubach, Bert Jones, and me—and I have to say, none of them made me feel inferior. I never thought I was better, but I knew I fit in with those fine players. On the other hand, I remember the times I'd be in the company of Staubach or Terry Bradshaw or Bob Griese, and they'd be talking about this championship game or that, this Super Bowl or that, and I'd have nothing to add, and I'd realize again how little I had to show for it all.

It's ironic but true, however, that some of the players you most remember in team sports didn't win championships. In football, so much is dependent on the players around you. And when you have constant change—coaches coming and going, systems being retooled over and over again—you tend to live in no-man's-land of arrested development. You get into bad habits, or let things slide. It's not hard to pinpoint. If you get a new head coach every couple years or so, or a new offensive coordinator, your progress will suffer. Most of the time they won't have the patience to bother with mechanics, and your bad habits will get set in stone.

If I knew then what I know now, I think I would have made some changes. I came in as a sprint-out passer, so I know I would have concentrated more on being a better drop-back passer. I'm not saying I didn't have coaches who could have corrected that, or even emphasized it. I just didn't have them very long. And, of course, there were all those injuries, and I sure can't blame anyone for them.

Ah, but would I have acted on the chances to leave the Saints earlier? To play for a better team, maybe even a contender? Roger Staubach once said, "If Archie Manning had played for Dallas, he'd be in the Hall of Fame now." I appreciated it, but to this day, knowing all that I know, I'm still not sure I would have done it. And I really don't feel any bitterness because of it. Those things happen.

I repeated the line often to myself those last few years: "Never look back. Never." And I haven't. When I finally left the Vikings, it was an upper instead of a downer, a plus instead of a minus. Good-bye football, hello rest of my life. And hello Cooper, Peyton, and Eli, and the football I would enjoy through them. A whole new world.

7

Archie Manning felt no compulsion to press football on his sons. That they embraced it anyway didn't surprise him; they had always been interested, and he certainly hadn't discouraged that interest. When they started playing the game at the "organized" levels he was supportive because they were having so much fun, but at that point he smothered all impulses to push them further. He questioned the wisdom of putting them in a position where their ambitions would be saddled with the reputation (and the perceived expectations) of a famous father. Moreover, he knew that the odds are prohibitive that even a good high school player will make it into college ball, much less beyond that. So when they were of an age when a course had to be set for their future, he and Olivia chose one that was more apt to bank the fire than stoke it. Instead of a "jock" school, Cooper and Peyton (and finally Eli) were put in one that was better known for its academics. As it turned out, that didn't deflect them, either. . . .

Sure, I wanted the boys to play football in high school, for all the reasons high school football is so wonderful, but not with any ulterior motives. I wanted them where they could get the enjoyment without compromising their education, and where future play (in college) would be considered only if and when it made sense. I hadn't been around high school teams for so long that I had no idea where mine fit in, *if* they fit in. All I could see was they were athletic, and determined. But how good? I wasn't going to worry about it either way.

Newman—the Isidore Newman private school in uptown New Orleans not far from the Garden District—was our choice. It was practically a given. Newman was already an integral part of the circle of friends we'd made and the groups we hung with, and was a known academic commodity. It had been a strong presence in the city for a long time (the year the school opened and its number on Jefferson Street are one and the same: 1903). Newman offered all grades through twelfth, a superior faculty, and great physical facilities on nine acres. Total enrollment was limited to about 1,000 students, keeping the tuition high and the waiting list long, a sure way to sustain quality. And as Olivia liked to point out, it was the first private school in New Orleans to go coed.

Yes, and Newman also offered sixty *(sixty!)* sports teams from the seventh through twelfth grades. Sports of all kinds for all kinds of kids, with participation being the only object, not future occupation. It worked beautifully: Eighty percent of the eligible students at Newman, male and female, played on one or more of the teams. And when it came to football, they still had all the great traditions—the pep rallies, the letter jackets, the dances (does anybody ever call them "hops" anymore?), the "hanging out" after games.

But Newman was not a place top athletes were likely to go, not if their hope—or their parents' hope—was a college scholarship. College scouts seldom came around. The level of play was good, Division IIA, but not the best. If parents wanted exposure, they were more likely to send their kids to John Curtis in nearby River Ridge, another private (Christian) school but *very* big into football. At last count, John Curtis had won sixteen state championships and had a reputation for putting players on college teams (Reggie Dupard at SMU, Mike Stonebreaker at Notre Dame, Chris Howard at Michigan, et cetera). Newman had no such reputation.

Which was fine with us. We didn't send our boys there to change anything. That was their idea.

People ask me, "So when did you see it? When did you say to yourself, 'Peyton's got it. He's going to be great.'? How old? What grade?" The answer is, I didn't see it at all before he and Cooper were well into their teens. I wasn't looking for it. I refused to judge their play that way. Besides that, I had a mind block about being a pushy "sports father." My dad was the same way. I heard a man tell him once, "Archie's going to be a superstar," and Buddy said, "I just want him to be normal. The rest of it will take care of itself." The sensible, considerate approach. Over the years I've had fathers even ask if their *preteens* were "pro material." I was always tempted to say, "Hey, your boy's twelve years old. Why even think about it now? Let him enjoy himself. *You* enjoy *your*self." I didn't, but I think that's unhealthy.

Yes, I made videos of my kids playing sports from their earliest attempts . . . and Olivia and I bought them all kinds of sports equipment . . . and I played with them by the hour whenever I could. But none of it was diabolical. Or unusual. I videoed just about everything they did short of taking a bath. I still tape every Christmas morning. We all gather around and open presents and eat breakfast snacks while Olivia gripes about being photographed in her nightclothes, and the tradition lives because nobody wants it to die. Peyton always wears a Philadelphia Eagles sweatshirt I gave him fifteen-plus years ago when I went to the Pro Bowl. At the time, it touched the floor. Now when he's six-six, 230 pounds, he can barely get in it. He wears it anyway.

As for buying them uniforms and sports stuff every Christmas, it's what they wanted. I tried fishing gear, but they weren't interested in fishing. And any parent will tell you that most of the time you buy a kid something, he plays with it for thirty minutes, sticks it in the closet, and goes on to something else. It wasn't football I was pushing, it was involvement. The bottom line is that if they'd chosen basketball or golf or tennis for their one big sport, or if they'd quit sports entirely and elected to play the piano, I'd have said, "Godspeed." As long as it was an "extracurricular activity." As long as it helped round out their lives.

But as far as their aiming to be professional athletes, I

wasn't just against it, I was afraid of it. Afraid I'd do some-thing or say something to give them the impression I expected it. I've known too many former players who allowed themselves to get caught up in making their boys "good enough for the pros." The disillusionment when it doesn't happen—which it doesn't ninety-nine times out of a hundred—can result in deep-seated resentment, and even estrangement. Fathers and sons no longer talking. I was pleased when my boys went out for teams at Newman, but it wouldn't have bothered me if they'd never played sports past high school.

So I was a self-determined lousy judge. And the truth is that at those earliest formative stages, about the only thing *anybody* can see is whether a kid looks good at whatever sport he's doing, or that he clearly loves to play. The standouts are usually the early developers who've got hair on their legs at age ten and run faster and are a head taller than anybody else their age. But even then you can't be sure. Growth patterns shift, and that same kid wakes up at seventeen, three inches shorter than his buddies and not so dominant anymore.

Every now and then, though, I got an inkling. Vince Gibson is a good friend of mine. He'd coached under Doug Dickey at Tennessee and been the head coach at Kansas State, Louisville, and Tulane. He was living in New Orleans when he saw Peyton play as a sophomore. Newman used to book one game a year in the Superdome, and Vince was on hand the night when Peyton threw I don't know how many interceptions, but also for enough yards and touchdowns to win the game. His determination practically shouted at you. Vince came to me afterward and said, "You're gonna have to beat 'em off your doorstep with a stick." Meaning college scouts.

Vince is out of coaching now, but he'd been in it thirty years, and that was really the first time I was prompted to say to myself, "Gosh, maybe . . . "

I never told anyone about it except Olivia. I certainly never told Peyton. And I don't know if I entirely believed it myself. I put it out of my mind—or back far enough where it wouldn't get in the way.

Actually, I saw Cooper's ability first. Not just because he was older, but of the two he was the better athlete growing up. Or at least the more versatile. He was playing everything going into high school—football, basketball, baseball, a little track. It all seemed to come easy for him. His football skills were such that in another era, he would have been a natural single-wing tailback.

Peyton, on the other hand, was a natural *quarterback*. Built that way, thought that way, and always willing to out-work everybody else to make it happen. He learned quickly. He learned how to drop back to pass—the three-step drop, the five-step drop—when he was four or five, imitating me or the quarterbacks he'd seen or been around. Cooper used to egg him on: "C'mon, Peyton, show us your five-step drop!" A lot of things about quarterbacking he picked up in the car. He was an information nut when it came to football skills. I'd be driving and thinking about getting from one place to another, and he'd be asking one *question* after another. "When did you learn such-and-such? . . . When did you do so-and-so? . . . What was your thinking when you did this-and-that? . . . "

And, of course, he had this thing about catching Cooper. Which wasn't easy. A two-year age difference is nothing when you're in your twenties, but when you're five and the other guy's seven, or eleven and thirteen, or even fifteen and seventeen, it's a chasm. Given Peyton's mental toughness, getting beat by Cooper (and then being needled relentlessly by him afterward) had to make him better if for no other rea-son than it fed his desire to get even. Peyton never stopped trying, frustrations be damned. Beating his brother was more than just a challenge, it was a crusade.

Sometimes they'd be playing one-on-one basketball in the yard and I'd take Cooper aside and say, "Coop, you know you don't have to beat him 20 to 2 *every* time." Then one day when they were older and the gap had narrowed, Cooper let up a little and before he could turn it around, Peyton had him beat, 20–18. At the finish, there were a lot of flying elbows and body checks, mostly from Peyton. Which was typical. At whatever sport he played, Peyton was a bruiser. (Cooper used to call him "Python.") And this time *Peyton* rubbed it in. Cooper gave me a look and said, "Don't ask me to do that anymore. It's too hard on the ego."

I think down deep Peyton worshiped Cooper. And Cooper always looked after Peyton, including him in games with his friends and making sure he got picked on whichever team Cooper was on. It had to be a big factor in Peyton's development. But they really didn't become pals until later when they played together as starters on the Newman football team that one season. Until then, they were just normal male siblings, yelling at each other and scrapping and threatening mayhem with sticks and shovels. No real damage was ever done. Olivia, the great pacifist, resolved most of their fights. I think her terms must have been more lenient because they tended not to get into them when I was around.

I have no idea what made the difference in their personalities—Peyton so focused and dedicated, Cooper such a free spirit. The closer I got, the less I really understood, and I got very close. I'm a firm believer that the first two tenets of effective child-rearing boil down to "spend a lot of time with your children" and "cherish them," because, one, they need you when they're growing, and, two, they're going to be up and gone before you realize it. So I spent the time, and listened, and counseled and cajoled; and the only thing I came away convinced of is something you'll never read in the parenting books: Your children will all be different, in one significant way or another.

Cooper had that wonderful Dennis the Menace aura you knew would surface anytime you were exposed to him for more than five minutes. Peyton was the opposite: tough-minded from the start, and dead serious, and eager to jump in and get done whatever needed doing. And finally, Eli, so laid-back and reserved that half the time you weren't even sure he was in the house. A different breed of cat entirely.

All that just happened, gene pools be damned. God has a sense of humor.

Cooper's influence on Peyton was palpable. He liked sports in all their forms, and Peyton was a willing disciple. They were participants, students, trivia buffs. Cooper collected pro football cards and dragged us to all the card shows. He knew who Otto Graham was when he was ten years old and Graham was sixty—and he knew that sixty was not only Graham's age but also his jersey number. For trips in the car, Cooper made up a game he called "Ten Questions," where one of us would think of an athlete and give the others ten questions to guess who it was. We played the same game using uniform numbers. Either way, Cooper usually won.

But here's the funny part. In most other things, Peyton showed no desire to be like Cooper at all. Peyton was studious to the extreme. Cooper charmed his way through school. When Peyton went upstairs to do his homework, Cooper offered a million excuses to put his off. Teachers loved him anyway. On his report cards they'd write, "Cooper is a delight to have in class . . . Grade: C." (How could you yell at him for that?) Or "Cooper is a dynamo . . . B–." Getting him to study was like getting him to volunteer for rabies shots. He advanced on schedule anyway, and later actually made good grades in college. He said it was probably because we weren't there to nag him.

Cooper was the logical choice to plant the flag at Newman, having never been shy about establishing his presence. Quite the opposite. Once when I was at the Saints training camp in Vero Beach, President Reagan was shown on the news making a talk at the Neshoba County Fair near where Olivia grew up in Mississippi. She took the kids to the fair every year, so I was paying close attention. When the cameraman panned the podium where the dignitaries were sitting, my eyes dropped down so that I could see through their legs. And there was Cooper, mugging for the camera. He was maybe six at the time. It didn't matter. He'd made up his mind to be on television.

What marked Cooper best, though, was that he never met a tradition or a status quo that could intimidate him. If anybody could tailor Newman to his own designs, Cooper could. When we got back from Minnetonka, Newman had a sixth-grade football team that Cooper joined, and after that he never missed a beat. Except when he got to his sophomore season in high school and checked the depth chart, he realized that if he still wanted to play quarterback, and all went according to the line of ascent, he wouldn't start on the Newman varsity until his senior year. There were two upperclassmen ahead of him.

He chose not to wait. He told his coaches he would serve instead as a wide receiver. He said he always thought of himself as more the Lance Alworth type anyway.

But he didn't stop there. He then talked the coaches into going to a three-receiver offense, which Newman had never used. (No, I didn't say a word. He didn't even mention it until he had closed the deal.) Naturally, supersalesman Cooper became the third receiver. And was the guy who made the key catches, game after game. He had a knack for it. The other two caught more passes, but Cooper would invariably catch the one that made the crucial first down or the one that won the game.

He also had a knack for living on the edge. I used to see him practice his end zone dances, à la Billy (White Shoes) Johnson, even though they were forbidden by the Newman coaches and frowned on by his conservative dad. Sure enough, one night he caught a long touchdown pass and a defensive back gave him an afterthought late hit in the end zone. Cooper got up grinning (he had, after all, just scored) and did an in-your-face pirouette around the defensive back. When he trotted off the field, obviously pleased with himself, the head coach, Tony Reginelli, said, "Manning, you do that again and you can find yourself a spot on the bench." (He didn't do it again. He was a free spirit, but not a dumb one.)

Cooper got a taste of higher-level quarterbacking that sophomore season, but it was bittersweet and turned him off the position for good. He still shakes his head over it. He says

it showed him the difference between quarterback and anything else. In Newman's fifth game, the first two quarterbacks went down with injuries, and Cooper was sent in with
the ball on Newman's one-yard line. We have a picture somewhere showing him going into the huddle, his eyes big as
saucers. The coaches called a play-action pass, and Cooper
managed to calm himself enough to throw it to a wide-open
receiver who took it the rest of the way for a touchdown.
Imagine the thrill. A 99-yard touchdown pass on your first
play. How many quarterbacks ever did that?

But for the rest of the game Cooper struggled, and the
next week he threw five interceptions and told me afterward
he hated every minute of it. "I was crying to myself in the
huddle. I kept thinking, 'What can I do to get this game over
with?'" He played out the season as the starting quarterback
but without enough success to change his mind about a permanent change in position. He was convinced the receiver in
him had a larger voice. He said, "I don't ever want to play
quarterback again."

But he wasn't defeated, only detoured. If anything, he was
now even more sure of what he wanted to do. He said he
wanted to play college football. My first reaction was to try
to scare him out of it. I really didn't think he could. He was
tall and skinny, and not very fast. But I remembered from all
those times we played together that he *always* caught the
ball. And in those games that he made so many clutch receptions for Newman, he often did it when there seemed no
chance—leaping, tumbling, standing on his head. Just as he
had making "Amazing Catches" in the yard (or into the pool).
He had great hands.

So I told him, "If you want to play college football, you're
going to have to bust your tail because the odds are against
you. You're going to need to pump iron four days a week to
get stronger. You're going to have to work on your speed. And
when it's time to practice with the team, you'll need to be
the first guy on the field, and the last guy off. You'll have to
catch as many balls as you can, as often as you can, whenever

you can get somebody to throw to you. And if you can't get them to throw to you by asking, beg."

In other words, I told him he had to be as unlike the sky-larking, fun-loving, homework-shirking Cooper as he possibly could be.

It didn't scare him at all. In fact, he did everything I said, not because I said it but because he wanted to. I saw how dedicated he was when I told him he'd get cracked in half by burly college linebackers if he didn't do something about his skinny body. He immediately started drinking supplemental milk shakes. Except he couldn't stand the stuff. He'd hold his nose and try to get it down without tasting it, but he gagged on every swallow. He said it was like drinking sawdust. I had to laugh. He said, "Tell you what, instead of letting the linebackers hit me, what if I just run out of bounds?"

He gave up one of his sports, baseball, during that period to concentrate on football in the spring, and sure enough, as a junior he was the best receiver Newman had and made the All-State team. A great honor, considering everything. Now he *really* lobbied for college ball. So I tried to direct him along what I thought was the logical path. I said, "The guys who have the most fun in college are the guys playing in Division II and Division III, where there's not so much pressure." He wouldn't buy it. Cooper never worried about limitations. And he was soon getting vindicating letters from major colleges, feeling him out. Just a few, but enough to satisfy his ego.

Meanwhile, Peyton was closing fast. But he was also coming from a long way back. The sixth-grade team had been dropped just before he got to that level at Newman, and he about died. He still hadn't played organized football yet. But it only bothered me that it bothered him. I thought he needed more time before getting into too-structured an environment. At that stage, he wasn't bigger or faster or stronger than his peers, or anything close to it. In fact, he was slow-footed. And when he made the seventh-grade team and was the starter, he still wasn't throwing eye-catching 30-yard frozen ropes. No one should have expected him to. I sure didn't.

But he had something that made a huge difference right from the start: He was efficient. Let me emphasize that, because for such a modest-sounding word it's important: He was *efficient* doing what quarterbacks do, especially in his leadership skills. His junior high coaches picked up on it. Instead of throwing four or five passes a game, which teams are more likely to do at that stage because passing and catching abilities are just kicking in, Peyton's coaches would have him throw fifteen or eighteen. And sometimes they'd try "sophisticated" stuff—throwing deep or throwing to the tight end across the middle or on crossing patterns. Peyton had a good arm, he had decent motion, he was accurate. And unlike me at that stage, he knew how to drop back to pass. Cooper said, "What the heck did you expect? He's been doing it all his life."

The things that really stood out were how much he knew and how forceful he was handling his teammates. Even in the seventh grade you could see him talking to 'em and yelling at 'em, getting them to respond to what he wanted. It had a galvanizing effect. When he started on the junior varsity team as a ninth-grader at Newman, the coaches did things you would never expect at that level. They said there was no mystery to that either. It was because of Peyton's knowledge of the game.

I tried to be there for both of them as much as I could during that period. A cardinal rule we had in their upbringing was one that had been impressed on me by *my* father: If you start something, finish it. Especially when it involves a group effort and others are counting on you. Cooper had made a commitment, and Peyton was following in line, so I encouraged them when they needed it and tried to help whenever I could. I went to the practice field a lot during Cooper's junior and senior years. Not to cast a shadow (I made it a point to assure the Newman coaches I wasn't there to scrutinize), but because Cooper wanted me. So as not to be too conspicuous, we borrowed a key to the gate so we could use the practice field after hours.

The boys couldn't get enough. I never had to say, "Get your shoes, get some balls, let's go practice." At the appointed time, they were ready and waiting. And we'd go out, me throwing and Cooper catching (sometimes me throwing as hard as I could and Cooper *still* catching), then Peyton throwing and Cooper catching, then me working with Peyton on his techniques. Sometimes other Newman players would join in. It was like those serendipitous jazz sessions in the French Quarter.

What came next was a huge bonus for Olivia and me. Into his senior season, Cooper was clearly Newman's star receiver. And apparently to the surprise of no one, sophomore Peyton was named the starting Newman quarterback. He had caught up with his big brother at last. The beneficiaries were numerous. Isidore Newman High was about to have a season that would take it to a place in football where it had never been. Archie and Olivia Manning were about to have the happiest football season of their lives. And Cooper and Peyton Manning were about to give nepotism a good name.

Well, mostly.

Peyton Manning played on the same football team with his brother Cooper only one season, though when it was over they had legitimate reasons to believe they'd be doing it again soon enough (in college for sure, then . . . ?). That particular dream would end quickly, and sadly. But it did not take the shine off that one special season. For the Mannings, it was like an affirmation, a happy testament to cause and effect when a family really does "play" together. Something worth examining over and over, like an heirloom. For Peyton it was also a coming-out party. . . .

I doubt I could adequately explain how much fun that year was. I can tell you that it was the *most* fun I ever had playing football, but even that doesn't cover it. For me football was always fun, from the games on the rug to the games in the yard to the "Amazing Catches" to the videotaping to the Christmas uniforms, and even to right now, when I'm playing at the top level and *still* having fun. But 1991 was like no other.

I know, I know. I'm intense, I hate to lose, I stew over my

failures. But that would be true if I were a piccolo player or cleaning windows for a living. Believe me, I know the difference. Football grabbed me early, and held on, and thanks to Dad there was never any pressure except the pressure I put on myself. The fun always came first. And thanks to Cooper, I was never anything but tuned in and turned on.

And for that one season, it was more than just me, it was "us." A family affair, from Mom and Dad in the stands, cheering us on, to Cooper on the field with me for every play. The further removed I am from it in time, the more it seems to mean to me. Because I was playing for and with the people who have meant the most to my football. Dad was my role model, the place to go for knowledge about the game. I couldn't have had a better example to follow, on or off the field. Cooper was my goad, and though he was a pain in the butt a lot of the time, he is now my very best friend. I mean, could anyone have had it any better?

All those learning experiences in the yard and in the playgrounds came to a head that 1991 season. And it turned out to be as much a breakthrough for Newman as it was for me. Cooper and his group of seniors were like Bolsheviks. They wanted to change things, mainly Newman's laissez-faire attitude toward football, and they did. Cooper was the captain, and he challenged the Newman administration about letting the players get more committed to the program, more involved in preparations. More success-oriented.

Newman had never sanctioned "off-season" practices, where players could come in on their own to lift weights, run, work out. Which was one of the reasons Newman's football teams seldom won more than five or six games a year. A lot of kids played—participation wasn't the problem—but the approach to getting *ready* to play was lackadaisical. That wasn't necessarily typical of Newman athletics either. Other varsity teams were much more challenged. Basketball and baseball, for example, were very demanding on the kids, and had a lot more to show for it—a whole string of winning seasons and several state championships.

Billy Fitzgerald—"Billy-Fitz," the adults called him—coached both those teams, and I wound up locking horns with him in a big way in basketball (guess who lost, and guess who *still* played on Billy's baseball team), but he was great. The basketball teams won state championships back to back when Cooper was a starter his junior and senior years. They were four white guys and one black, a terrific player named Randy Livingston, and they beat all-black teams consistently that last year, which should tell you that white guys *can* jump when they have a mind to. I played with Cooper on that team, but I didn't start.

So Cooper's group of reactionaries said to the football team, "We want you here every day to lift weights, and we're going to throw three or four nights a week." And he got a bunch of them to work together on techniques and play recognition and pass routes. The players didn't seem to mind. I know I didn't. I thrived on it. We were on our own, though. The coaches had nothing to do with it. I don't *know* what they were thinking. But one night at a school board meeting Dad said one of the board members complained about "too much emphasis on athletics." He said he didn't want Newman to become a "jock school." (Parents are very protective of Newman's image.)

Newman will never be a jock school, of course, and though I sometimes feel football could still use more emphasis, I think—I *know*—it (the school) prepared me well for college. But for that year and then the next two, when we were able to sustain what Cooper's group had set in motion, we were very good. We won thirty-four games and lost only five those three years, and Newman football really did get bigger. The team hasn't lost more than three games any one season since.

"Manning to Manning" was the talk of the town in 1991. That's not my assessment, that's from the feedback in the media. One New Orleans paper put Cooper, Dad, and me on the cover of its preseason football magazine. But I don't think anybody realized how eagerly Cooper and I took to the idea. We had a ball. Newman prided itself on a balanced pass-run

Archie's father, Elisha Archie "Buddy" Manning, in an imposing three-point stance. In his high school yearbook they wrote, "When the fights broke out, Buddy was there."

Archie hands the ball off to teammate Steve Clark at Drew High School. "I was quarterback from the sixth grade on. For me, the challenge of playing quarterback was as thrilling as it was daunting."

Archie in college at Ole Miss. "Seven other freshman quarterbacks came in with me in 1967, and I was fortunate enough to be a starter for the varsity team in my sophomore year."

On January 21, 1971, Archie and Olivia Williams of Philadelphia, Mississippi, were married. Archie says: "It was on a Thursday night, during a whirlwind period in my life where within a month's time I'd gone from the Gator Bowl to the Hula Bowl to the NFL draft. And we had our final exams."

Archie drops back for a pass for the New Orleans Saints. "When the media started calling the Saints 'Ain'ts,' and the fans started wearing brown paper bags over their heads, Cooper and Peyton wanted to wear the bags, too."

Peyton joins brother Cooper as the Manning family grows. Archie says: "I made the two of them part of my life as well as insinuating myself into theirs. I even took them to football practice."

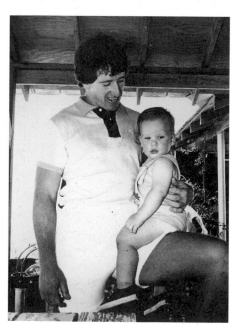

Archie bounces Peyton on his lap. Archie says: "When Cooper was born, he was 12 pounds, 3 ounces. Peyton was lighter—only 12 pounds, 1 ounce."

Archie with Peyton and Cooper. Peyton says: "Outside of my mom and dad, Cooper has been the best thing that ever happened to me in life. He gave me the path to follow into football and encouraged me all the way."

Eli rounds out the family as Peyton *(left)* and Cooper *(right)* look on. Archie says: "One of the convictions Olivia and I had about raising them was that the boys would be well rounded. That they would be involved in all kinds of activities. My only hard rule was that they had to finish what they started."

Peyton (#11) on his seventh-grade football team. "People ask me, 'So when did you see it? When did you say to yourself, "Peyton's got it. He's going to be great"? What grade?' The answer is, I didn't see it at all before he and Cooper were well into their teens."

The boys at the beach . . .

. . . and at a ranch in Jackson Hole.

Archie is inducted as the first player in the Saints Hall of Fame.

Lynn Swann interviews Archie and Olivia at Peyton's first game with Tennessee.

Olivia and Archie with Peyton during Parents' Day at Tennessee. Peyton says: "I approach life on an order of four: first my faith, then my family, my education, and my athletics."

Peyton is flanked by two football legends, Johnny Unitas and Earl Morrall.

Peyton accepting the Scholar Athlete Award at the College Hall of Fame banquet in 1997.

Eli in full uniform in his freshman year at Ole Miss.

Peyton visits current Ole Miss head coach David Cutliff and Archie's coach, the legendary Johnny Vaught. Peyton says: "I have no doubt I'd have gone to Ole Miss if Cooper hadn't gotten sick. I really wanted to extend what we had in high school, and the thought of our doing it where our dad played was practically irresistible."

Peyton accepting the James Sullivan Memorial Award for Top Amateur Athlete in 1998.

Hall of Famers Bob Griese and Roger Staubach join Archie and Peyton.

Peyton in form with the Indianapolis Colts.

offense, and I threw only a couple hundred passes that year. But at least half of them were to Cooper.

If he'd had his way, all 200 would have been. Every time we huddled up, he'd say, "Try blank-blank," naming a play. "I'm wide open." The other receivers heard him lobbying, but he could have cared less. They were his friends, his class-mates, and they'd get mad as hell at him, but he didn't care. He wanted to catch every pass. I was trying to parcel them around, and in practice I did it pretty well, but in games there was no doubt who I'd be throwing to on third down.

And if I *didn't* throw to him, Cooper would come back screaming. "What are you doing? I'm free as the wind over there! I can beat that guy all day!"

There's just no getting around it. He was a royal pain.

But, boy, was it fun. Unbeknownst to the coaches, Cooper and I worked out our own set of signals for that sea-son. We didn't tell anybody except Dad. If I touched my nose, it was a come-back pass (to Cooper, naturally). Tap my hel-met and it was a curl. It wasn't exactly fair to the other receivers, I admit, but they didn't know, and it was working, and we were winning, so we kept doing it. And I can say it now because I know it's true. For a quarterback there's noth-ing like having your brother as your primary receiver. You're on the same genetic wavelength. You know each other's every move. And you've been living in the same house together all your lives. How could you beat that?

We went undefeated until the last game of the regular sea-son, then went all the way to the semifinals in the state tour-nament. Mom and Dad were at all fourteen games. They'd come real early to set up, first in the parking lot with a tail-gate party if it was feasible, then to seats up high in the mid-dle sections with their friends. Usually Dad took videos. They never stopped telling us how much they were enjoying it. Dad had refused a request by a television station to do a special on Cooper when he was a sophomore, saying it would be better if he deserved it first. But now with Cooper a deserving senior, they wanted to do one on him *and* me. Dad had to agree because it wouldn't have been fair to Cooper not to. He said he guessed "a little extra publicity" wouldn't hurt.

Cooper was now about six-four, 185 pounds, and a true college prospect. Not a lightning bolt, but plenty fast enough, and could he ever catch the ball. Even when he was a marked man. In the second round of the state playoffs, Port Barre, a perennial playoff team from North Louisiana, double-teamed Cooper the whole game and he still caught 12 passes. Right before the half it was 14–all. On a play where he was supposed to run a 10-yard hook, I said, "If they're in bump-and-run, go deep." That's not really football terminology, but that's what happened. Cooper burned the defender and caught a 60-yarder for a touchdown. After that it was no contest.

We lost to Haynesville in the semifinals, but equalled Newman's best finish ever in football. Late in the game, when it was still in the balance, we were in a two-minute drill, driving for what could have been the winning touchdown, and I threw an interception to end it. I'd completed the same pass to the tight end a few plays before, but this time the linebacker raised up out of nowhere and intercepted. Cooper chirped, "Blame it on the sophomore!" But he came over to me right afterward and put his arm around me. "Don't worry about it, Peyt. It was a great year."

The season was over, and so was our football partnership. We had no inkling at that moment, but we would never play together again. One season of "real" life was about to lead into another, when in crisis our athletic paths would split but my lifelong tormentor would be my biggest booster. And *his* lifelong torment would become his number one fan. But to appreciate how far and from where we'd come, you have to see it from Cooper's perspective as well. In his big, broad strokes:

"I think I already knew back then that I wasn't going to hit the jackpot. I don't regret that, or any of what happened next. I think I was lucky, if you want to know the truth. I've got everything I need or want, a good job, a wonderful wife, a great family, and I say my prayers thanking God for that every night of my life. I'm just glad Peyton made it for what *he* wanted.

"Things happen for different reasons. People are different. Peyton's levelheaded, like Dad. He's not a spender. He's a jeans-and-tennis-shoes guy. He wears baseball caps. He doesn't have anything to spend it on. When he got all that money to sign with the Colts, I had to go out and buy him some sports coats and shoes, with his money, of course, so he would look the part. I said, 'I bought you a couple presents.'

"But if it had been me, I'd have taken the money and said, 'Oh, my knee hurts,' and retired immediately. I'd still drive the same car, live in the same place. Just not worry about it. It wouldn't change me toward people, I'd just live differently. Every day I'd take my friends to lunch, then make fun of them for having to go back to work. Then I'd go play nine holes, get a massage, come back home, b.s. with Ellen, and put my kids (when we get some) to bed. I could pull that off. If I won the lottery, that's what I'd do.

"Not Peyton, as everybody can see. Peyton's got it all now, or just about, and nobody deserves it more. And nobody will handle it more responsibly. He's working like hell to be a great player. He has *always* worked like hell to be a great player. I couldn't always appreciate that. In fact, I didn't appreciate Peyton hardly at all when we were growing up. I mean I *loved* him, but . . .

"Peyton and I had a different relationship as kids, because *we* were so different. We were always butting heads. He was kind of a tattletale, a study guy, a mama's boy—and a daddy's boy, too, for that matter. While I was . . . well, not. Not to all of the above.

"He was so neat, and I was a slob. If we got into an argument, I'd get even by messing up his room. I'd pull the covers off his bed, take his phone off the hook, mess up his pictures.

"It came from a combination of things. Dad for one. Archie and I had a good relationship, but he was a lot more serious, like Peyton, especially at those times when I wasn't. When he realized he was always going to be himself and I was going to be myself, he'd say, 'There's ol' Cooper, he's the crazy one,' which was sort of like telling me it was okay to be crazy. From then on we had a better understanding. We became pals, Archie and me, and are today. I think he decided to like me for what I was. And I could appreciate him more for what he is.

"Same way with Peyton. We butted heads even when I was into high school and dating. I taught him a few things then by example, though I don't think he used everything I taught him. If you wanted to stay out late in the Manning house, you called home and specifically asked for Mom. Mom was the girl who'd had a much more relaxed upbringing. She was the one who drove a new car every year in college, and knew how to be liberal without being soft. So if you called from someplace along about the time you were supposed to be home for curfew to ask if you could spend the night at a friend's house, and Dad answered, you'd say, 'Is Mom there?' If you wanted a little extra time, a little extra freedom, talk to Mom.

"Peyton got so he could do it, too. Sometimes he'd call home and if Dad answered, he'd hang up and try again later. Eli is doing that now, or was until he went to college. If he wanted anything, he went through Mom. It's not that Dad is so strict. He just has a set of rules he feels need to be followed, and he would be the one to enforce them. That's the way Peyton will be. He already was back then, and when I stretched 'em a little, I'd get it from him, too. I'd come in at twelve o'clock instead of eleven, and Dad would get on me, and so would Peyton! I'd say, 'What are you *doing*?' Already he's like a father figure to Eli. Me, I'm more like his fraternity brother.

"That last season made everything right, though. We were closer then than ever. Not just closer in maturity—we were getting old!—but in everything. And when I got sick, we really became close."

All of it's true. (Especially the part about him being a slob.) I was always picking things up or putting things back or cleaning any messes off my desk. I get that from my dad. He's the ultimate neatness freak. When there's a piece of trash in the pool, he immediately scoops it out. He can't stand to see it there. When it's time to clean up and go home after the tailgate party, *he's* the one who goes around picking up the debris in the parking lot. He's a big listmaker. He wants his schedule kept up-to-date, not to the minute but at least to the hour. I do that. I like things to go smoothly.

I was a lot easier to raise than Cooper because I wasn't even close to being as reckless. I would never have streaked across the campus the way he did at Ole Miss when he lost that bet. Not in a million years. I wouldn't have made the bet in the first place. He was always wheeling and dealing. I thought more about the consequences. Nowadays I get these interviews where they ask, "Have you *ever* done anything wrong?"

Well, of course I have.

"But what? Tell us the bad stuff."

And I say, "Well, I was raised by my parents to make smart decisions. I never beat up anybody. I never got arrested. So if that's the kind of thing you're looking for, you won't find it. But I'm not perfect and don't pretend to be. I just don't like to cause trouble. My dad was the same way."

From as long as I can remember, I worked hard to do well, not only because I was competitive that way but because I worried about what people would think if I didn't. What teachers would say if I flunked a math test or something. Cooper could be cavalier about his studies, I couldn't. But here's what people miss: It was never easy for me. I had to work to get good grades. I had to work to be a good football player. None of it came easy.

Except for throwing the ball, I was not a "natural" in anything. Most kids aren't. I see that at our camp every summer, the Manning Passing Academy. How a few of them will just naturally throw well. I'll put a ball on the ground and tell them, "Pick it up and throw it to me," and you can tell just the way they do it, the motion they use and all, if they can throw. When they have to wind up, you know they've been programmed. Like robots.

Everything else I had to work on. My strength, my footwork . . . my *speed*. Dad didn't pass down the great speed he had as an athlete, not to any of us. He ran a 4.6 for 40 yards out of college, and he could high-jump, and it was all so, well, God-given. Even when I was in college I'd be looking for new ways to run faster, to the point where for a while I wore some innovative strength shoes with weighted platforms on the bottom. It helped, but I never got mistaken for a speed demon.

And I never got timed in the forty either, because I kept finessing it. Whenever they'd try to time me, I'd fake a hamstring. I'd say, "I'll do it next time." My senior year at Tennessee, when I thought I was finally ready to face the clock, I had a knee injury. A real one. And when the pro scouts said, "You don't need to run if you don't feel like it, just throw a few," I said, "Fine." I sure wasn't going to volunteer.

I actually was pretty fast up to about the fifth grade, even to the point of winning foot races with the other kids. But then I started growing straight up, and then I got tendonitis, and my feet hurt, and I slowed down. From about the sixth grade to the ninth I couldn't run a lick. I think because we have height on both sides of the family, I was destined to be bigger than my dad, and it turned out that way. And I probably have a little stronger arm than he had. But he was the runner I'd never be. Of course, part of that was because he was running for his life a lot. I've had better blocking.

The whole business about "time in the forty" is overdone anyway. A quarterback has to be nimble or he'll get killed, but he never gets down in a four-point stance and pushes off like they make you do for those speed trials. I was aware, though, that I needed to at least look good running. I used to work on my form just so I wouldn't be an eyesore going downfield on a busted play. But when all is said and done, I'm a quarterback, not Jesse Owens. The important thing is to have good footwork on my drops and then be able to move to get away from the rush. That's really all a quarterback needs.

I'm glad now that Dad didn't let me play "real" football until the seventh grade, because when I did, I was hungry. I might not have loved it as much if I'd started earlier, because like he always said, once you get into organized football, the game shrinks. I played quarterback from the start, and though I was originally listed as a safety on defense that first year, I have never played a down of defense in my life. Never played a down on special teams. I think that's bad, if for no other reason than you should at least know something about the positions you have to face. It's true of any sport.

Now, when I'm always looking for an edge, I'd like to know without having to ask secondary coaches what the safety would naturally do on this formation or that or what the cornerback will be thinking and what it might take to sucker him out of a play. My dad started at safety on the freshman team at Ole Miss and had something like six interceptions that year. I think that was a big advantage, and it made the game more fun for him, too. I mean, would basketball be as enjoyable if you never got to shoot? Or baseball if you never got to bat?

Anyway, like Cooper, I played all the other sports in the organized leagues, and particularly liked baseball (his best "second" sport was basketball), but football was always number one. And that probably had more to do with Cooper than anything or anyone else. As sure as he followed my dad into football, I followed him. What he did, I did. Or wanted to do. Not to diminish Dad's influence, but Cooper was right in my line of vision. His world was the real world for me, not something Dad had done in the past.

At that point, I'd probably have followed him anywhere. And I'm not kidding when I say it. If he'd opted for baseball out of high school, I might be trying to make a big league team right now instead of starting in the National Football League.

From childhood we were competitive to the extreme. We'd fight, I think mainly so that he could get the satisfaction of making me cry, especially when his friends were around and he could show off. It was like a comedy routine. He'd wrestle me down and let me know who was boss, and I'd get up and come back for more. Because through it all he kept encouraging me, too. Egging me on. When we got older and realized the damage we could do, we confined our disagreements to arguing.

Then came 1991, and all that pleasure and achievement, and at the end we were actually talking about playing together in college. Where we would have a *choice* and still do it. (Talk about how times were a'changing.) And that prospect was not only growing, but it even looked like we might be heading for a grand reunion at Mississippi, Dad's old and beloved school—if I could hold up my end of the bargain two years down the road. Dad said he wasn't sure Ole Miss could handle it.

Recruiting Cooper was easy, because he loved the fun of it. Typically, he had friends at every school he visited. And what he didn't have, he made. He just wished more schools had been after him so he could socialize more.

At Virginia, a couple of redshirt freshmen were assigned to show him around, and one of the nights he was there they went into a fraternity house where nothing was happening and Cooper said, "Hey, let's go to ——." And he took his "hosts" to another house on campus where things were hopping and everybody practically mobbed him at the door. The freshman players said, "We're going to sign you for sure!"

Dad found out later a number of other schools would have recruited Cooper except that they thought he might be too slow. Not because he *was* too slow, but because Dad had told him to be accurate with his statistics on the recruiting forms he got in the mail. He said most recruits lie about their weight (if that might be a factor) and lie about their time in the forty, so coaches almost automatically tack on two-tenths of a second or more. He said, "Be honest, because they won't believe you if you put down 4.4."

So Cooper put down 4.65, and he got recruited and got the offers from the five. And eight or nine months later he and Dad ran into a coach from one of the schools in Texas Cooper was interested in, and the coach said, "Oh sure, I remember Cooper. We liked him."

Cooper said, "Then why didn't you recruit me?"

And the coach said, "Well, you had your forty time as 4.65, and we figured you'd lied about it and that you were probably a 4.9."

Cooper looked at Dad and said, "Thanks a lot."

It really didn't matter all that much, though. He was tickled to be going to Ole Miss.

But a small shadow had crept onto the picture. And like a spot on an X ray, it would bring frightening repercussions. Nothing in our family has ever been so devastating. I know Dad has always said that he hadn't had those kinds of awful feelings since his father's suicide.

Cooper missed a couple passes that senior season that I knew he should have caught. Dad said the same thing. I remember being so surprised—right into his hands and out again. Then in one game he was the holder for a field goal try, and when the snap was bad, he grabbed the ball and raised up to throw a pass downfield. The ball fluttered out of his hands like a shot quail.

Cooper said afterward that it surprised him, too. He made a joke out of it. And I didn't know enough to do anything but laugh it off. But it was a sign something was wrong.

He wound up getting recruited by five schools—first Ole Miss, with Billy Brewer coaching; then Texas, which really excited him, getting an offer from another major conference; Tulane, Texas El Paso, and Virginia. A couple other scouts came around, but with nothing definite. His final three choices were the same as Eli's would be nine years later: Texas, Virginia, and Ole Miss. But Texas reneged when the coach got fired, and eventually Virginia backed away—without showing much class, I thought.

It was just as well. Coach Brewer seemed to like him more than anybody and supplied the most pressure. So with all the other natural inducements going for him, Cooper signed with Ole Miss.

Then during the high school basketball season, when Newman won another state championship, Cooper complained about losing the spin on his shots. You could see it from the stands, Dad said. They were going up like knuckleballs. Cooper complained, too, about sweaty palms. By the end of the season, we both could tell the difference in his shooting, like it wasn't coming from the same guy. It had changed dramatically. At that point, he began complaining about numbness.

So Dad took him to the Saints' orthopedic surgeon in New Orleans. The club did an MRI and operated on his elbow for a "nerve condition." By July, though the feeling in his hand wasn't back, they cleared him to play in the Louisiana High School All-Star game. I wasn't privy to all that was happening, because nobody seemed to know for sure what it might be, but Cooper was great in the game. He made two catches where he went up and absolutely snatched the ball away from defenders.

With so much excitement going on around him, I don't think Cooper knew to even notice anything more at that point, and he went on to Ole Miss. We all rationalized that the feeling in his hand wasn't back because of the trauma from the surgery. The doctors at Ole Miss more or less passed on it because they knew Dad, they knew the surgeon in New Orleans, they knew what had been done.

Dad and I drove up to Oxford for the second game of Cooper's freshman season. Coach Brewer had planned to redshirt him but then announced he was going to let him dress out for the game, and Dad decided we ought to be on hand. In football you can never tell. A receiver could go down and Cooper could be in there in a flash. Little did we know.

We drove up early Saturday morning—six hours one way—with plans to drive back immediately afterward because Dad had to announce a Saints game on Sunday. As it turned out, Cooper didn't play. But this young doctor at Ole Miss, Dr. Ed Field, who was new to the physicians' staff that year, took Dad aside and said, "Mr. Manning, I'd like you to call me on Monday so we can talk. I don't feel right about Cooper's arm."

He said that the team doctors had checked Cooper a couple of times and that "we don't like what we see." He said they were concerned enough that they'd actually pulled him off the practice field one afternoon.

Dad said a chill shot through him that was so strong it made him flinch.

We hadn't seen Cooper for a few weeks, and when we got together with him after the game, he had his head shaved, like they always do with freshman players, and that alone made him look a little emaciated. But there was something else, too. And afterward when we compared notes, Dad and I had the same observation. Cooper's right arm didn't look right. When we shook his hand, it felt like something was missing. Like the muscle was shriveled or something. In the time he'd been there, it had clearly gotten worse. Cooper complained that some of the numbness had moved into his right side.

Dad tried to stay optimistic. He said he thought it might just be atrophy from the surgery. But when he talked with Dr. Field on Monday, the doctor's recommendation was stark: Cooper needed to see a specialist as soon as possible. He named one in Dallas who he thought would be the best qualified.

Dad met Cooper in Dallas and stayed with him through all the procedures. The doctors there ran every test they knew to run, checked everything out, and reached the same grim diagnosis. Cooper had stenosis, a constricting and narrowing of the spinal cord that can cause paralysis and even death if not treated. But treatment would only arrest the condition, not reverse it. Either way, he was damaged for life.

They said Cooper was lucky. That he was fortunate they had caught the stenosis when they did. And lucky, too, that he hadn't been badly injured in the high school all-star game, given the extent of the illness and the stage it had reached. But that if he persisted in playing, he would risk being paralyzed for life. As we would learn later, their findings were no reflection on the doctors in New Orleans and those who had first examined him in Oxford. They just missed it. It happens.

But Dad didn't just leave it at that. He took Cooper to see doctors he knew at the Mayo Clinic and was referred to others there. They visited medical centers in Memphis and Los Angeles and a couple other places. But the diagnosis and the prognosis never changed. Dad was particularly depressed by what he was told at Mayo, especially when they recommended radical surgery that involved drilling a hole in Cooper's head.

The upside was that it had been caught in time to do something. The downside was that it had been there, getting worse, and nobody even knew it. One of the physicians in Dallas said Cooper should not have played football as long as he had. "If I'd seen this boy when he was in the eighth grade, I'd never have let him play in high school." He said one hit to a vulnerable area at any point during the years since and Cooper would have wound up in a wheelchair.

I didn't know all this then, only that something was wrong. I had my worst day throwing the ball trying to impress Cooper when we were all still waiting for the test results from Dallas. He'd gone back to Oxford from Texas, then come home to see me play, alert to a possible problem but nothing more, and he came to our game over at Fisher High in Lafitte. The weather was as bad as I was, and I was awful: 8 for 32 for 35 yards. It never stopped raining. As a result, we had an epidemic of dropped balls, and we lost by a baseball score, 8–3. Embarrassing.

That night when I got back home, Dad took me aside and gave me the news. That he was going to have to tell Cooper he needed an operation and would never play football again. He was crying when he told me. He gave me the option of being there when they told Cooper. I said, "No, it's going to be too hard on him as it is. I don't want him to worry about me. It's bad enough without him having to look at my sad face." I said I'd just go get something to eat and be home later.

There were a lot of tears that night. Cooper obviously knew he was in serious trouble but until that moment didn't know the bottom line. I think in one respect it bothered me more than it did him. He knew then there was nothing he could do about it—it was like contracting a disease, not an injury where he maybe got careless or got hit in the neck. It was a condition he was born with. Something he couldn't have changed.

But what I saw were all those years of being so close, playing together with the hope of playing again at a higher level, and then maybe even higher. All that was officially over and done.

When I got home, Cooper was in bed, asleep. We talked about it the next day, but I think we were both still in shock. And I was in denial. Cooper seemed to be a lot more at peace with it than I was. On Monday, he and Dad were packed and ready to drive back to Ole Miss when I got up. As they were leaving, Cooper gave me a letter he'd started the night he got the news. He told me to read it later.

Early that summer, in June, a neurosurgeon at Tulane, Dr. Donald Richardson, whom Cooper had gotten to meet and "approve," performed the surgery. ("Dr. Richardson's my man," Cooper said; he liked him right off.) I had a baseball game the day it was scheduled and Dad told me to go ahead and play in that. But in the second or third inning, the Newman coach, Billy Fitzgerald, came over to me and said, "Peyton, you need to go with my wife, Peggy. Your mom called. She wants you at the hospital."

I went in my cleats. When I got there, Mom and Dad were in a little anteroom with a chaplain. Mom's eyes were red with tears. Three hours after the surgery they had found a blood clot. They had to go back in. There was a very real threat of paralysis.

That's when it finally sunk in. I'd been griping to myself about losing the chance to play football with Cooper longer, and here he was facing paralysis. Or worse.

We prayed. We prayed a lot. Eli was there, and he was crying and praying, and I remember seeing my dad cry again, too. He doesn't, not very often, but then he couldn't seem to stop. It was just so scary.

The blood-clot surgery took two more hours. Then finally Dr. Richardson came out with the news. The blood clot had been removed, and there was no paralysis. More room had been created around Cooper's spinal cord through a procedure called a laminectomy, where the surgeon goes in through the back of the neck. Dr. Richardson said Cooper's spinal cord in that area was almost flat, but that Cooper would be okay. He'd have some permanent limitations with his right arm and hand, and there'd be no more heavy-duty athletics, and he'd have to be careful, but he'd be able to live an otherwise normal life.

I realize now, as anybody would who gave it a minute's thought, that a lot of people have worse things happen in life. That there are greater tragedies and crises. I mean, I can't imagine being in my dad's shoes when he found *his* dad after the suicide.

But that day changed my thinking about football. I always loved the game, and will always love it, and it's still very important to me. But what happened to Cooper shifted my priorities. I had always said that I approached life based on an order of four: first my faith, then my family, my education, and my athletics. But I think I was saying it because Dad always said it and I thought it sounded good. From then on, I meant it. Because what happened to Cooper really can happen to anybody, at any time. And it won't be football you turn to when it does.

The doctors checked my neck later and found that it isn't completely normal either, but that it presented no foreseeable danger. I play now with the same intensity, giving my all on every down, but with the sense that every down might very well be my last and that I might as well make the most of it.

Outside of my mom and dad, Cooper has been the best thing that ever happened to me in life. He gave me the path to follow into football and encouraged me all the way. Then he gave me an object lesson that was profound, through an experience I wouldn't wish on anybody. No dream world this time, only hard reality. I tell people that all the time. "Click!" and it was over for Cooper.

For him to have handled it the way he has, with such a wonderful spirit and attitude, and making so many friends along the way even when he was going through rehab, is a lesson for us all. With the advantage of hindsight, I like to think I could have handled it, too. I've already had more good things happen to me in football than ninety percent of the people who ever played it, so if it all were to end tomorrow I'd still be way ahead. But I know down deep I couldn't have. I hate to admit it, but unlike Cooper, I'd have felt sorry for myself, and people would have known it because I'd have wanted them to feel sorry for me, too.

Like I say all the time, Cooper is now my biggest fan, and I am his. He says, "Peyton helps me get serious, and I keep him loose. Life's a trade-off, and that's ours."

I still have the letter he gave me that morning when he was getting ready to drive back to Oxford. I read it all the time. It's something I cherish. It told how much he appreciated our times together, and how he would be happy from then on just to be some small part of *my* football. He said he would be there for me whenever I might need him.

He said, "I'll be playing my dreams through you."

He said, "I love you, Peyt."

8

Archie Manning knew from childhood where he wanted to play his college sports—up the road in Oxford, at Ole Miss. It was his dream. What he didn't know, until almost the last minute, is which sport he would "major" in there. Since it had to be one that would pay his way, football was it. Archie's son Peyton knew from childhood which sport he wanted to play in college. It was always *football. But when it came to deciding at which college he wanted to play, his options turned out to be almost unlimited; and though Mississippi was one, and everybody expected him to take it, he wound up going elsewhere. The decision was reached painstakingly. And pain—a lot of it—was the stunning after-effect on his father. . . .*

I have no doubt I'd have gone to Ole Miss if Cooper hadn't gotten sick. I really wanted to extend what we had in high school, and the thought of our doing it where our dad played, in a setting I had idealized for years, was practically irresistible. But Cooper's illness took the shine off. It didn't lessen my desire to play football. Not at all. If anything, it made me more determined to play every down and every game as if there wouldn't be another down or another game. But it made me think more about priorities and where they might lead.

Cooper had a hand in that, too, unwittingly. I became very close to him during that period, with what he was going through. I still pray about it every day of my life. From his surgery one year and a second operation a few years later to now, when he's on the mend and married and getting on with *his* life, I know down deep it's still frightening for him. Every time he looks in the mirror he sees the result of that fork in the road. But what he has that I envy, and that grows on me with each passing year (thank God, because I certainly didn't change overnight), is a settled understanding of what life is really all about.

I'm sure Cooper still has the fire in his belly, because football does that to you. When you've been separated from something you love without fulfillment, you miss it all the more. But by controlling that fire and by adapting to the realities (and by needling me every chance he gets), Cooper gives off a better spirit for everything else—what else he can do with his life and how the people around him might benefit.

I get asked all the time why I give myself so freely, from talking to young people—about whatever it is they want me to talk about—to spending so much time signing autographs. Easy. First, I learned from the master. When it came to autographs, Dad used to say, "It takes ten seconds to smile and sign your name. That's all it takes to make a fan happy. Don't be like the jerks who brush people off." Second, fans deserve your courtesy. They pay good money to see you play. But more than that, those who look up to you for whatever reason ought to get something positive in return, especially if they are limited themselves, like in a hospital or a wheelchair or confined to a bed. In other words, it's the right thing to do, so do the right thing.

As important as football is—and now it's my job and *very* important—I would probably have been a different person in high school and college if I'd had Cooper's experience when I was younger. I know I'd never have been a meathead saying, "Football is the only thing, nothing else matters." As it was, the learning process has taken time, but I'm learning. I called a buddy of mine from high school the other day. Surprised him on his birthday, right out of the blue. I hadn't spoken with him in years. I think he appreciated that I took the time to call, but *I'm* the one who got the biggest kick. That's more important to me now, too. Letting people who matter know that they do.

The numbers who visited Cooper in the hospital were amazing. True friends who really cared. Cooper and Eli have a ton of them. I think back to my high school days, when I made a jerk out of myself ordering *my* friends around, undoubtedly alienating some of them, and I think, "I wish I'd shown a little more Cooper in my actions." Now when I scream at somebody in a game (not *if* I scream at them, *when* I scream, because I really can't change the part of me that wants to make everybody do better) at least I pat 'em on the butt afterward.

At Newman those last two years, I was always hard on my teammates. Always demanding and outspoken when it came to commitment. Dad says I had that "focus," that persistence that borders on zealotry that sticks out sometimes in athletes, from before I was ten years old. He only coached me once back then, in basketball, and remembers it as more of a sentence than an assignment. He wasn't keen on coaching anyway, and when they held the "draft" he picked all his friends' sons, just as they'd asked him to. Most of them weren't very good athletes, so the team was awful. I think we won two games out of twelve.

And I badgered him the whole season about his personnel decisions: "Dad, I don't believe you *did* that!" At the finish, he rewarded my commentary by pledging never to coach me again in a "team situation." And he never did. And he was right in feeling the way he did. I should have been having a good time, which is what he wanted, and what the other kids wanted. Instead, I made a nuisance of myself. I just couldn't stand losing every week.

Years later in a playground league after the basketball team I was on got beat, the coach, a lawyer friend of Dad's, said to us, "We lost today because we didn't have enough intensity out there." And I piped up: "Coach, the reason we lost is because you don't know what you're doing. You don't substitute right. You don't know who to put in or when to put them in."

My dad was in the stands. He could see me gesturing and

pointing at the guy. When he asked what it was all about and I told him, he was livid. He said it was inexcusable (right again). That night he drove me over to the coach's house and made me apologize. He said if I didn't, I wouldn't play again the rest of the year. I apologized, sobbing all the way. I was twelve at the time.

In high school I loved my friends, but I didn't hesitate to let them know what I thought when it came to team and team effort. The intensity would show up in the workouts I'd organize. You could say I was just following Cooper's lead, but I was even more driven. Dad laughs about it now. He'd hear me on the phone on Saturday, coaxing guys to attend a Sunday workout, then on Monday getting on them when they didn't show.

He finally told me, "Look. For sixteen-year-olds, a lot can come up between Friday afternoon and Sunday night. A chance to go fishing. Surprise tickets to an event of some kind. A girl. Or just the chance to hang out." He told me to let up a little and gave me one of *his* daddy's rules: "It's better to be a good person than a good player."

I bought it, in principle, but I still didn't lighten up much. Not that I was a fanatic in any other area of my life. Just the opposite. I was *always* careful what I did away from the field, who it might affect. When you lose control and make a fool of yourself, it gets back. And in a drinking town like New Orleans, one false step can lead to another in a hurry. Wherever I went as a kid, I was concerned that somebody would know who I was and get the wrong impression. As Archie Manning's son, I was expected, I thought, to toe the line. People said, "Just go ahead and do what you want," but I never could. I didn't want anybody calling home and saying, "I saw Peyton and he . . . "

Except with Cooper, I didn't get into fights. But one night at a high school social, a coat-and-tie at somebody's house, a linebacker on the team came up and sucker-punched me from behind. He was a year ahead of me in school and was evidently upset because his girl had broken up with him and the word was out she wanted to go with me. That was the story, anyway. It could have been he was harboring a resentment and just looking for an excuse. It doesn't matter. He cracked me good and I went down.

I sat there for a second, stunned, but not really hurt. Then I got up and some of the guys got between us. I didn't push it. I knew it was the wrong place and the wrong time. You don't ruin a party for everybody by acting like a punk. And nothing more happened that night. But the next day I went to Coach Reginelli and told him I wanted to take so-and-so out on the field, privately, and "discuss" the matter. I went to the kid and said, "Okay, let's go." But now *he* had thought about it, and I got no response. Which was fine with me. The point was made. We dropped it.

Dad didn't like what happened; he preferred I not get into fights. A thoughtful citizen should be above that kind of thing, even if provoked. I believed that. In fact, I was darn close to being a pacifist in social confrontations, and still am. From the time I was out of short pants, I don't think I ever took a swing at anybody. The difference, though, is there are times when you have to stand up, and I think I'd made progress in learning that distinction.

But other times my stubbornness crept through in ways that weren't so noble sounding. Like that nonfight, things happened that I just couldn't—or wouldn't—let pass. They'd stick in my craw and just fester, even when it involved nothing more than hurt pride. I had a thing for a long time about Josh Booty, who's actually a friend of mine. But we're both from Louisiana, and competitive to a fault, and in our senior season in high school, football analysts rated us the two best high school quarterbacks in the nation. Josh was *USA Today*'s Player of the Year. I was the Gatorade Circle of Champions Player of the Year. But Booty was at Evangel High in Shreveport, where they threw every down and he hardly ever came out of a game, and he broke all the national records. I had some good statistics, but not like his.

What bothered me about Josh, though, was that when I'd

see him at LSU games I'd say, "How'd you do last night?" and he'd say, "Threw for four touchdowns, 534 yards, et cetera, et cetera." And then wouldn't ask *me* how *I* did. Not ever. A small slight, maybe, but it got under my skin. At the end of the season, the National Quarterback Club again recognized the professional, college, and high school quarterbacks of the year. When Booty won, I admit it, I was jealous.

Three years later the same organization alerted Dad that he was about to be named to the Quarterback Hall of Fame. He said when they told him, they said I was going to be their College Quarterback of the Year, even though I had only finished my junior season at Tennessee. He said they wanted me to come to Charlotte to accept the honor.

I said, "Tell 'em to call Josh Booty."

And I didn't go to Charlotte. I had "other commitments," which was true, but only to a point. Which all sounds silly, I know, and when Dad tells the story he shakes his head. But that's the way I was. And *am*, too much of the time. (I'm working on it.) I know I must be improving because I take no satisfaction in saying that Josh went to professional baseball out of high school, and after knocking around the minors for several years, he wound up back in Louisiana competing, at age twenty-three or twenty-four, for the starting quarterback's job at LSU. If it isn't too crazy, he could wind up competing against Eli.

The infamous Peyton Manning stubborn streak has cost me more than once. And sometimes dearly. The biggest loss to date: the last two years of varsity basketball at Newman. Which is another episode I'm not particularly proud of.

Billy Fitzgerald is a legend at Newman. Successful. Dedicated. One of a kind. And a fixture there. He's been coaching Newman basketball for twenty-seven years, and when you see his teams, it shows. The Newman family—students, alumni, parents, friends—call him "Billy-Fitz" and his style of play "Billy-Ball," and it's very good stuff. I mean, *five state championships*! Cooper said openly one time that if Billy Fitzgerald had been the Newman football coach, the football team would also have five state championships by now. Unfortunately, Cooper said it *too* openly and his remarks got back to the football coaches, who didn't like it at all. And I don't blame them. But Billy Fitzgerald can *coach*.

According to Dad, the root of my problem with Billy-Fitz was that he's just like me: hardheaded and strong-willed and stubborn, and he hates to lose as much as I do. Which is not news because he has never been very coy about letting people know. One year when Cooper first played for him, Newman lost in the finals of an early-season tournament, and at the awards ceremony when he was given the trophy, Coach Fitz's face showed he wasn't thrilled. The Newman team immediately got on the bus and went back to the school gym, where Billy always gave his postgame talks.

This one was short, but a lulu. He walked into the dressing room with the trophy, holding it like it had a skin disease, whirled, and *slammed* it against the wall. It broke into several bent, ugly pieces. He said, "*That's* what I think about runner-up trophies!"

As you would expect, Cooper couldn't let such an opportunity slip by. When Fitz was out of sight, he gathered up the pieces of the trophy. A couple days later the school had an awards assembly to recognize its latest achievements in sports. Cooper took the remains to Coach Fitz beforehand and plopped them on his desk. "Here, Coach. For you to show the kids." Fitz couldn't help but laugh.

Cooper was one of the few who could do that, make Coach Fitz laugh. And being Cooper, he was never afraid to try. One time when he and Fitzgerald's son, Edmund, who had gone on to Ole Miss on a basketball scholarship, were in Edmund's apartment in Oxford, Cooper put a call in to Billy. Disguising his voice, he said, "Coach Fitz, we got a little problem here. Your son Edmund really wasn't drinking much, but he was out buying a couple cases of beer illegally and he got stopped and we're going to charge him with a DUI and keep him in jail overnight."

Fitz paused for a second, then broke out laughing.

"Cooper, damn your lying hide, I know it's you! Even if it wasn't April first [which it was], I wouldn't believe you!"

Coach Fitz had a special place in his heart for Cooper. He was his whipping boy. Some coaches like to have one of those on every team, and Cooper was Fitzgerald's. He got on Cooper all the time—about mistakes, about goofing off, about anything he could think of to let the other players know what he expected. It didn't bother Cooper. He gloried in it, because he understood it. The criticism really wasn't personal at all, it was motivational. Coach Fitz knew Cooper could take it and would come back for more with his *own* remarks.

And they both knew something else, which also told you something about Billy-Fitz. No matter what he criticized Cooper for doing, he was never going to take him out of the lineup. Cooper was too valuable.

The crux of my problem with Fitz was that basketball at Newman is practically a year-round proposition. For a lot of parents that's "overemphasis," and what makes them mad is that kids get cut from the program—weeded out, discouraged out, cut—and Newman isn't supposed to be like that. I didn't mind when I was there, I thought that was the way competitive sports were supposed to be. But some parents were always talking about getting Coach Fitz fired "for the way he treats these kids."

Except Coach Fitz doesn't get fired. He keeps rolling along. On a teacher's salary, no less (and no more). And he works wonders with kids in a school that prides itself on being "privileged," which is no small feat in itself. The players who stick with him for four years develop a bond, both among themselves and with Fitz, that's absolutely beautiful. The kind of thing that can make high school sports so special. You watch his ex-players now when they come home from college during Christmas break. The first thing they do at a Newman game is go hug Fitz.

I didn't want to hug him when we had our blowup, though. I wanted to clobber him.

Coach Fitz starts basketball practice early in the fall, which limits the time Newman football players have to make the team. Cooper managed to, though, and was a starter his junior and senior seasons, so I had no doubt I could. I'd played on Fitz's JV team as a freshman and got into a couple of varsity games with Cooper when they won that first state championship. Then as a sophomore, when they won it again, I was what you might call the sixth man—big enough to play guard or forward, but generally the point guard. I wasn't a great basketball player, but I could run the offense without an ego. Meaning, it didn't matter to me if I scored a lot of points. Or *any* points for that matter. Coach Fitz liked that.

My junior football season, we went 11–2 and went to the quarterfinals of the state playoffs. Dad says my football blossomed that year. I threw 30 touchdown passes, and visions of playing at a major college were dancing in my head. So it could be that my heart wasn't into basketball as much as it had been. It also could be that I'd remembered—kept in my craw—what happened to Cooper with Billy-Fitz when *he* was being recruited. How Fitz gave him such a hard time. How when Cooper wanted to visit a college on a weekend, and it meant missing a Friday-night basketball game, Billy put the heat on, and Cooper would always wait and go on Saturday. That happened over and over.

From Coach Fitz's standpoint, I'm sure it made perfectly good sense. Cooper was a starter. He needed to be there. But I think in the process it took much of the joy out of the recruiting rites for Cooper, being so restricted in time. I thought the whole thing stunk.

Anyway, when I went out for basketball my junior year, I again had to report late because practice had begun while I was still playing in the state football playoffs. Making it worse, I had also skipped the last week of summer basketball to go to a football camp in Alabama. Before that last week, I'd been working with the first team. But apparently my cutting out didn't sit well with Fitz, because when I finally showed up for regular season workouts, I wasn't listed on the first team. After a few days of practice, I realized I was being punished. I wasn't getting nearly enough practice time, at least to suit me, and never worked with the first team at all.

The last straw was when Newman had its annual Invitation Tournament, matching some of New Orleans's best high school basketball teams. I didn't get off the bench the entire tournament. I was a noncombatant. Fitz's explanation was that they had put in a new offense that last week of summer training and I was behind in picking it up. I didn't buy it. I thought it was punitive, and I was boiling. I told Dad I had to have a talk with Coach Fitz. He said, "I think you should."

Dad never interfered in our relationships with coaches. He said it wasn't his place. He had made it a rule to keep his distance unless it was absolutely necessary. He remembered his own father telling his mother when she was tempted to lobby on Archie's behalf—for grades, sports, anything—at *his* high school in Drew that "if they want you over to that school, they'll call you and you can go. It's a short walk. Otherwise, stay home." So Dad never lobbied for his sons with coaches.

Except once. And it just happened to be with Coach Fitz. Dad called him when Cooper was a sophomore and, similarly, had just finished football and was practicing on the basketball team. Cooper had a lingering hip injury from football and Dad thought he needed time to heal. So he phoned Billy on a Sunday night. "Billy, I hate to bother you, but Cooper's had a hip pointer for about a month. I think it would help if he could rest for four or five days."

He says he doesn't remember what Coach Fitz said, but whatever it was made him feel like mud on a shoe. Like he had trespassed onto sacred ground. When he hung up, Dad told Mom, "I'll never call that man again."

The next time they talked by phone, it was over me. And Coach Fitz did the calling.

It was a Monday when I went in to see him. I'd had the

weekend to get charged up. Unfortunately, I was *over*charged. I went in too strong. I blamed Coach Fitz for "embarrassing" me in front of people. I said, "I was a starter last summer and you've got me practicing with freshmen!"

It was downhill (and more heated) from there. We got into each other's face pretty good and used words you'd never hear in Sunday school. It almost got physical. Dad said Fitz told one of his assistants later, "I'm not going to let this expletive deleted tell me what to do!" When I ran out of personal complaints, I said, "Besides, you screwed up all of Cooper's recruiting visits his senior year, and I'm not going to let you do it to me!" The clear implication was that I had more at stake with a football scholarship, so watch your step.

Dad was in his office when he got the call that afternoon. Coach Fitz said, "Archie, Peyton came to see me today, and I think we need to talk. The three of us. Can you be in my office tonight, say around eight?" Dad said sure.

But before we left for the meeting, Dad sat me down. "I have to ask you one thing, Peyton, and I need the truth. How badly do you want to play basketball this year? Are you sure you even *want* to play basketball this year?"

And I realized right then that maybe I didn't. I said, "No, I'm not sure."

He said, "Well, I know I've always told you never to quit something you've started, but this might be a time that you should."

I told him maybe the truth was I would rather have a big year in baseball. My future was falling into place, and there had to be some prioritizing. I knew I couldn't play both football and basketball in college, not the way the seasons run together, but I could play football and *baseball*. I said if I dropped basketball, I could devote more time to baseball.

There was, however, one acknowledged catch. Billy Fitzgerald was also the head baseball coach.

The meeting in Coach Fitz's office included his assistant, Ed Graf, which was good because it became more of a conference than a confrontation. Dad quickly got to the heart of the matter. He said, "Billy, I asked Peyton before we came in here if he really wants to play basketball, and I think you should ask him, too."

Fitz did.

And I said, "I don't think so." The die was cast.

Dad said, "I'm not blaming anybody for this, Billy. I think it'll be best all around if we just let it die. But I don't think it should affect Peyton's baseball chances in any way. I think this will actually help him with his baseball."

Coach Fitz agreed without objection. There were no harsh words.

Newman played the 1990 basketball season without me and won another state championship, its third in a row. I'd have enjoyed it, I know, but it was spilt milk. Instead, I got the early jump in baseball, and had by far my best season. As a reasonably good-hitting, six-foot-five-inch shortstop, I batted over .400 and had major league scouts sniffing around. Dad set them straight. He said it would be no sense drafting me because my heart belonged to football. In the off-season, I'd be running and working out, lifting weights, getting stronger (and, hopefully, faster)—for football.

The story about my "fight" with Coach Fitz got out, unfortunately, and was blown way out of proportion. Dad was *not* happy. Not just because I was more wrong than Fitz, which we agreed I was, but because people who didn't know what they were talking about were making more of it than was warranted, and have made more of it ever since.

The good thing was that it was settled. And in my senior year of football, nobody was a bigger booster of mine than Billy Fitzgerald—coming to games, complimenting me, cheering me on. The day I committed to Tennessee, I called, in the following order, the Tennessee coach, then my Newman football coach, Tony Reginelli—and then Coach Fitz. To thank him, too. For more than he might have realized.

One of the things I had to learn growing up was toughness, because it doesn't seem to be something you can depend on being born with. Dad says he sees it in me now and doesn't see the same toughness in *his* mirror. But his was always there, just understated. He says he knows he may have told me, "Peyton, you have to stand up for this or that," but the resolve that gets it done is something you probably have to appreciate first in others. Coach Fitz was a major source for mine, and I'm grateful.

As I said, we went 11–2 in football my junior year at Newman, and finished the regular season undefeated (10–0) when I was a senior. It was quite a year. Coach Reginelli let us really air it out, and I completed 168 of 265 passes for 2,703 yards and 39 touchdowns. The awards seemed to multiply like amoebas. Besides the Gatorade Circle of Champions award, I was named high school offensive player of the year by the Columbus, Ohio, Touchdown Club, got the Atlanta TD Club's Bobby Dodd Award, the New Orleans Quarterback Club Player of the Year award, and so many others it makes you wonder if they don't decide all these things with a single vote. Just as important, or more so, I made the Blue Chip Academic All-America squad. And for the second straight year, I was named Most Valuable Player in Louisiana for our classification.

But in the end, it wasn't all wrapped in glory. We got beat in the second round of the state playoffs by an all-black team from Zachary, Northeast High coached by Doug Williams, the quarterback who led the Washington Redskins to the 1988 Super Bowl championship. We played *at* Zachary, on "Doug Williams Field," which added to the experience, and it was the darndest offensive spectacle you've ever seen. I mean, Disneyland couldn't have produced more fireworks. I had one of my best high school games ever, completing 23 of 43 passes for 395 yards and three touchdowns. But every time we scored, they scored. And they scored more and won, 39–28.

After the game, a small army of Newman parents came onto the field to kiss us and the season good-bye. Mostly they were parents whose kids were seniors. There were a lot of tears. But not from me. I was upset we didn't win. I thought we should have, and still do, and I was mad we hadn't taken advantage of all our chances. But this time, losing really was easier because I could compare my place in life to Cooper's and be grateful this was more beginning than end.

I still had my football tomorrows.

Archie Manning could no longer avoid the obvious. Peyton's star was rising so fast, he had to scramble to stay current with all the implications. Whereas before he had been apprehensive about Peyton getting too absorbed in college football ambitions, Archie now felt obliged to provide whatever assistance or accessories he thought might be needed.

In the spring after Peyton's junior year, I got a number of letters from college coaches, asking if I'd please call them to "talk about Peyton." Which was just one of the many NCAA rules quirks you encounter when you're the father of the prize. I could phone a coach, but he couldn't phone me. Silly. But I knew most of the coaches who had written, so I called. And friend or not, they all said the same thing: "If Peyton were a senior, I'd take him right now."

I think Peyton was well aware at that point. He was already playing it cool, listening and watching instead of letting his head get turned. I was helping him in workouts with his Newman receivers at the time, and Peyton could see that I mostly worked with them, not him. He was sound in his techniques, he was very natural throwing the ball, and now he was taller and getting stronger—a lot stronger than I was at that age—and was totally motivated. I never had to get on him about anything.

Peyton dropped in on the Saints' training camp a few times when he was a junior. Jim Mora, now his coach at Indianapolis, was head coach of the Saints then, and he let Peyton jump in with his offense at practice a few times. I saw Mora later at a social function. He said, "The way he looks, the way he throws, I would have thought Peyton was a junior in college, not high school."

Peyton had already asked about going to football camps,

and before his junior year I had let him go to the Bowdens' in Birmingham. Peyton was now getting letters from college coaches, and after going to the Bowdens' camp, he got letters from Florida State, and we went on a series of "unofficial visits" to FSU, Florida, Texas, and Texas A&M. Just driving around, having a look. The way the rules work, if you arrive at a school on your own, they can talk to you, and Peyton was talking to whoever would talk, about everything he could think of. But he still was looking to improve his skills.

Football camps, if the teaching is sound, are good for the basics. That's what ours stresses at Hammond every year: three days of basic training for about four hundred aspiring quarterbacks and receivers. But there are others just like it, and though repetition is always good for mechanics, Peyton wanted something more advanced. About that time I ran into Bill Walsh, the former 49ers coach, in New York, and Walsh told me I should send Peyton to *his* camp at Stanford University in Palo Alto. He said, "I always pull out the top five or six quarterbacks and we work with them individually every day in the stadium. It's a terrific learning experience."

The opportunity was too good to pass up. That summer Peyton got a friend, Walker Jones, another prospect whose father had played at Ole Miss, to go with him . . . all the way to northern California to learn at the feet of an offensive master. They were there for five days. But the master, Coach Walsh, was there for only one. For pictures. And that was it. He never showed for any of the workouts. Peyton was *not* happy.

I told him something must have come up, that he should give Walsh the benefit of the doubt. (I sure could. Walsh once said I was the best quarterback in the NFL—and he said it the year the Saints went 1–15!) But Peyton gets ornery when he feels he has been misinformed. The night before the last day of camp, the coach who was running it called a meeting of the high school seniors-to-be to ask them what they thought of the operation.

Peyton's hand shot up. "Remember the first day when

you said practice starts at nine and you want the quarter-backs there at eight-forty-five to get their arms warmed up?"

The coach said, "Yeah."

"Well, it's pretty hard to get our arms warmed up when we don't get any footballs until nine-fifteen."

Walker Jones said the coach turned red.

The next morning at quarter to nine, an equipment man was out there throwing balls onto the field like confetti and shouting, "Hey, Manning, got enough balls now?"

The Stanford trip turned Peyton off the West Coast. He came back shaking his head. "Dad," he said, "those kids out there are *different*."

I said, "Yeah, and they think you're *different*."

The thing is, his football education had already pro-gressed to the point where he was way ahead of his peers. Drop-back passing is a staple in college and pro offenses today, of course, and Peyton had the techniques down before he was ten years old. I never completely mastered them. My advantage as a young quarterback was being a natural runner, like Fran Tarkenton, so my athleticism disguised some of my failings. But I was *not* a good drop-back passer, as Peyton later saw looking at films of past Ole Miss–Tennessee games. At clinics I teach the "Four Things Young Quarterbacks Do Wrong," and Peyton spotted the first one in those films: me looking behind as I dropped back to pass, as if there might be something lurking there to trip me up.

It's a cardinal rule, and I broke it all the time. If you even glance behind you as you drop back, you can lose sight of your receivers and the secondary long enough to get disori-ented, and then throw off your timing. The second big mis-take young quarterbacks (and too many older ones) make is taking a false step, a kind of stutter-step, coming off the ball. It slows you down. Third, they "pat" the ball before they throw it, as if to reassure themselves it really is a ball. That too can screw up timing, and it's a tough habit to break. One of the best pro quarterbacks in the game does that, and you can bet he'd like *not* to. Fourth, but just as important: Young quarterbacks set up poorly when getting in position to take the snap. They lean in too much (or out too much) with their shoulders, or they bend their knees too much, or they stand too upright. It's like golf, where a good swing begins with the proper address.

I point all this out because here was Peyton, a junior in high school, doing none of these things. Sure, we had discussed them at one time or another, and I'd shown him what I was talking about, but you only had to tell him or show him once. The Colts' coaches have found that out. Peyton studies football like the honors student he was, and he doesn't just log instruction in his notebook, he logs it in his thinking.

How much, then, does athleticism play in good quarterbacking? Somewhere between "enough" and "a lot" would be an unscientific answer, but you have to remember that coaches cater to the strengths of their quarterbacks and adjust accordingly. Moreover, every position in football requires a different set of skills. You wouldn't call Peyton Manning a better athlete than Deion Sanders, but Sanders couldn't play quarterback and you sure wouldn't want Peyton at cornerback. The differences range from sport to sport. Some people believe the best athletes in the world today are pro basketball players, and maybe they are. But if you watched Michael Jordan playing baseball, you had to think, "Well, he'd better keep his day job."

Some quarterbacks were and are outstanding athletes. Joe Montana and Joe Namath, for example. And John Elway. Others become starters without having great athletic skills because they've learned the game so thoroughly. You can't fake the cerebral part. Many times a better athlete isn't the starter because the starter is smarter. Howard Schnellenberger started Bernie Kosar over Vinny Testaverde at the University of Miami when they were both underclassmen, and Vinny was twice the athlete Bernie was. But Kosar was way ahead of the game mentally at that point, and with him the Hurricanes won the national championship. Now, years later, Vinny has come into his own as a pro quarterback—a late arrival, just as

Randall Cunningham has been, and people rave about their athletic ability. But as they'd be the first to tell you, it takes more than that.

It's gratifying, now, to be able to say that Peyton got to this point at a school (Newman) where football is most definitely *not* overemphasized, where the scholastic is valued over the athletic, and where there was no favored treatment. When you consider that only one other Newman player has ever gone on to see the fine print of a professional contract (a little wide receiver named Omar Douglas, who played when Cooper was there and went on to the University of Minnesota and then to the New York Giants for a couple years), you get a sharper image of the achievement.

But I'm proud of another thing, too. A "personal achievement." With all three boys participating in at least two varsity sports, Olivia and I attended more than 950 games over the years (and if that's not a record, this surely is: one January I saw seventeen basketball games in one week!), but in all those years, through all those games, I never once went to a coach to complain or make suggestions. Newman parents just don't do that, and though I might have been tempted a few times, I wouldn't have done it anyway. The unwritten rule is there and it's a good one. It keeps everything in perspective.

Funny. A Newman football coach invited me in one time to give the staff some tips about offense. I agreed, and spent a lot of time preparing, knowing it was high school and that I had to keep it simple, and knowing that it was Newman and I had to be low-key. As I got up I said, "I'm going to throw a lot at you, fellows, so just take what you want," and I began explaining and diagramming on the blackboard. I cut it short when I realized none of them were taking notes.

(Peyton had the same thing happen when they asked him for help years later. He showed them some plays he ran at Tennessee, concentrating on those he thought high schoolers could handle. The coaches expressed their gratitude—and never ran a single play he recommended.)

Arrogance? No. They're great people. It's just the blasé

way Newman approaches football. At Newman, coaches don't make kids report at 6 A.M. for summer workouts or lift weights three or four nights a week. And if the star halfback has to skip practice to go for extra help in math, he goes. Football comes second. The kids know there won't be many "have-tos" at Newman. If your family's going on vacation the first of August when practice starts, you go on vacation. No questions asked.

It works because it achieves what Newman wants to achieve. Newman prides itself that seventy-five or eighty kids go out for the team every year despite the fact that football does not attract a lot of interest from college recruiters. Moreover, every coach has to teach classroom academic subjects as well, and for them football is more a hobby than a living. Which is not to say they don't put in the time. You would see Coach Reginelli, and now coach Frank Gendusa, handling the equipment and lining the fields and driving the buses to the off-campus practices and you realize the difference: It's a labor of love. For *all* of them, players *and* coaches, it's a labor of love. I greatly admire Tony Reginelli and Frank Gendusa.

The only negative I see is that for those twenty or thirty kids who every year *do* put forth the extra effort—work out on their own, try hard to get better so the team will be better—it can be pretty frustrating. It was for my three, especially because they'd each liked to have helped Newman win its first state football championship. They argue that if Billy-Fitz can find a way in basketball, why can't they do it in football? But I have no regrets at all, and if I knew any or all of them could have won that championship by playing somewhere else, I still wouldn't have wanted them to leave Newman.

I'm probably more gratified—or at least more relieved—that Olivia and I got the three through the "tempting" years, and all those teenage social gyrations, without any real problems. New Orleans is a tough town for raising kids. It's the drinkingest place you ever saw, and you have to be so careful.

My buddies in Mississippi, even the ones you'd think of as all-league drinkers, can't believe it. The forms it takes are almost comical.

Where my kids played baseball growing up is one of the worst parks in town. The city was broke, the recreation department was broke, the park needed a transfusion. So the parents got involved, redid the facilities, and set new rules. And the program for solvency included a concessions stand where you could buy shrimp, jambalaya . . . and beer. Beer at Little League games! It's a daddies-coached league, and with beer handy the inevitable became commonplace. We had to put in a rule: Coaches on the bench or in the coaches' boxes couldn't coach with a beer in their hands.

Naturally, they all complained. They said, "Aw, hell, it's after work, it's hot, why not?" Only in New Orleans.

I'm sure our boys didn't lack for experimentation during those formative years. But uptown New Orleans is kind of an enclave, tied to other enclaves, and hanging out in the Quarter and on Bourbon Street was not a common thing for them. So the temptations weren't as awesome as they could have been. More important, they grew up in a loving, trusting environment that also stressed responsibility and the viability of their religious teachings, and they proved over and over again that *they* could be trusted. Of course, they had Olivia to ease the way—granting their requests to stay out "another hour," or to do this or that or go here or there instead of coming home at the specified time.

They knew my first inclination was to say no if a proposal sounded too, well, venturesome, but what they probably didn't realize was that when they opened communications with "Dad, can I speak to Mom?" I knew exactly what they were doing. And approved of it, too, because I knew that Olivia in her sweet, empathetic way wouldn't let them do anything dumb. She and I used to laugh about it, but it made for good balance. I think without that leveling influence they wouldn't have been nearly as easy to raise, Cooper's antics notwithstanding.

So did I secretly believe from the start that such an under-pinning and such support would lead to all three sons being good enough to play major college football? And that one of them would in a twinkling (so it seemed) be a star in the National Football League? The simple answer is: Not for a minute. It's been as much a surprise to me as anybody. And since I didn't have nearly the interest shown me when I was coming out of high school, I probably got as big a kick out of it as Peyton did when he started fielding scholarship offers.

A lot of coaches came to watch him during spring train-ing at Newman before his senior year, although it was against the rules for them to talk to him (or to me). A couple of times I picked up Eli from school and we went over to the field to watch the circus. We all still thought it was really just win-dow dressing, because Peyton would surely end up at Mississippi, but the alternatives were getting interesting. A coach from Michigan, Fred Jackson, was there, and he brought along Cam Cameron, who is now the head coach at Indiana. Jackson said he thought Peyton was the best high school player he'd ever seen.

In August, when they were allowed to call, our phone never stopped ringing. Peyton got close to thirty calls the first day. From the beginning, he enjoyed it. He'd have his friends over before practice and they'd kick around the pros and cons of each school, which ones offered the best academics, the best social lives, the prettiest girls, et cetera, et cetera.

My calls were mostly from Ole Miss people, reminding me to keep Peyton "true to the Red and Blue." Buddies I hadn't seen for years looked me up or called, and it was all they wanted to talk about. I had a stock answer: "Yes, I hope he goes to Ole Miss, but I've advised him to go where *he* wants to go." It didn't help. Mississippians just assumed Peyton was heading their way, and anything they heard to the contrary was written off as a smoke screen. It was a position taken even under our own roof. Olivia thought Peyton would go to Ole Miss right up to the very end.

I doubt anybody ever handled the recruiting process the

way Peyton did. To say he was thorough, and patient, would barely cover it. Normally, when a kid is considered a hot prospect and gets inundated by the scouts, the thrill wears off in a hurry. The calls get repetitive. The visits get repetitive. Before long he's making a decision just to get everybody off his back. He ups and announces, "I'm going to so-and-so"— and it's usually the school he wanted to go to in the first place. The dance ends right where it began.

Peyton, on the other hand, never tired of the process, because he made up his mind it was to his advantage to take it to the limit. He didn't throw his letters on a pile, he opened every one, and filed them in groupings on the Ping-Pong table upstairs. He scoured the press guides the schools sent and could recite the names of the offensive coordinators and who the quarterbacks were at each one.

When the calls started coming, he was ready for them. And since he kept up with other commitments, too, he could say to the caller, "Why would you want me if you just got the best high school quarterback in the Midwest?" Or "What would be my chances of playing in this scenario . . . ?" He even got a little reconnaissance network going with half a dozen other quarterback prospects around the country, calling back and forth to compare notes and tip one another off on a coach's line. Or his lies.

Peyton kept forty or fifty schools on the string for a long time, not because he was leading them on but because he wanted to be absolutely sure of his decision. He never seemed to run out of questions. It got to be October, and they were still calling, along with the recruiting services that flat-out drive you crazy trying to get "inside" information. I relieved him of some of the latter, and when they'd ask, "Which schools are in Peyton's top six?" I'd say, "He doesn't have a top six. He has a top forty."

As for under-the-table offers, the shiny red convertibles and the big cash outlays and the wardrobes of choice at the best haberdasher in town, historic inducements like that, there weren't any. I know those things still happen, especially when you get coaches who are desperate to keep their jobs and alumni who are so blind to the true meaning of competition— that when you cheat to win you haven't really won any- thing—that they do things, give things, promise things. But I know, too, that this is more likely to happen when the recruit comes from a poor background or has been "taking" all his life—given preferential treatment, given grades he didn't deserve, given spending money.

Peyton didn't fit the profile. Even if the scouts were inclined—and we had no reason to believe any of them were—Peyton wasn't the type they'd offer anything to. He'd have been insulted. In fact, those who stayed on Peyton's trail adhered to even the most nit-picking of NCAA rules, like the number of calls they were allowed per week. They were straight-up about everything.

We had a regular parade of in-home visits from head coaches. Phillip Fulmer from Tennessee was the first to come, opting to visit even before Christmas, and he brought his offensive coordinator, David Cutcliffe, with him—the first time we'd met Cutcliffe—and Randy Sanders, who recruited the area for the Vols. They came in coats and ties, and Olivia had to have food brought in for dinner—ironic, because that made Tennessee's the only coaches she didn't prepare a fancy meal for. Eli had something at church that night and our family policy was to have at least one parent at every function, so she just ordered in and left.

After that, Gary Moeller came from Michigan with Cam Cameron and Fred Jackson. One night we had two: Tulane at seven o'clock, Notre Dame at nine. Olivia put the food away after the Tulane coach was finished, then brought it back out for Notre Dame. (Imagine. Notre Dame getting leftovers.) Steve Spurrier came with an assistant the morning after his Florida team played in the Sugar Bowl. We had Florida State scheduled, and Lou Holtz was going to lead a second wave from Notre Dame, but Peyton by then had removed those schools from consideration and told them he didn't want to give any false encouragement.

The Ole Miss coaches came right after Peyton, Olivia and I had "unofficially" visited the campus in Oxford. That night Olivia and I got our first inkling that it might not happen. That Peyton might not choose our old school after all.

Billy Brewer, the Mississippi head coach, was a longtime friend of the family's. He was crazy about little Eli, and he and his new offensive coordinator came early so they could catch Eli's fifth-grade basketball game. At dinner, Peyton talked offense with Billy's coordinator, using Olivia's linen-napkins to write on, and you could tell it was awkward. It was as if Peyton had decided against Ole Miss without realizing it, and what he was hearing was not doing much to change his mind. He was going through the motions, and I think Billy sensed it, too.

Peyton went to Florida on his last allowable visit (he had also been to Michigan, Tennessee, Notre Dame, and Florida State), and I thought that might be where he'd wind up, given Steve Spurrier's pedigree: a Heisman-winning quarterback who had become a coaching genius when it came to the passing game. But again Peyton didn't commit. After all the visits, all the talk, all the mail, he announced he would make his decision a week before the official signing date. He said that way he would be giving the school of his choice time to sign others it might be courting (receivers, maybe?) who might be persuaded by his decision. He had covered all the angles.

Peyton got back from Gainesville on a Sunday in late January. His decision would be announced the following Tuesday. I suggested we check him into the Hilton Hotel downtown under an assumed name to distance him from all the confusion and give him the chance to go over the pros and cons of each school one last time. He liked the idea and asked me to stay with him. We checked into the Hilton on Sunday night. And early Monday evening he made his choice.

Peyton Manning says there was "no doubt" he would have gone to Ole Miss if his brother Cooper had still been on the team there. They had even talked about Cooper redshirt-

ing a year so they could have three seasons together, Peyton passing and Cooper catching. As it was, Peyton went into the recruiting process with a more open mind, and soon had it filled with alternatives. . . .

I loved the recruiting. All of it. I read all the letters, answered all the phone calls. I read the media guides cover to cover. I loved my visits to schools, I loved talking with the coaches who came to visit me. I loved to question them. It was an incredible learning experience.

August 11 was the first day coaches could phone. Mom and Dad had to be out of town, so I had about ten buddies over for hamburgers and to help field the calls. They grilled the hamburgers, I grilled the coaches. I'd ask the one who called what he coached, what town he was from, what he thought of this or that about the team or the passing game or the conference they played in. I'd probably have asked for his physical description and Social Security number if I'd thought about it.

The phone would ring and if one of my buddies answered, he'd act like he was screening the calls. "Yes, who's calling?" "Coach so-and-so." "Hold on please while I see if he's still here." At one point I heard one of them answer and say, "Sorry, Peyton's outside right now smoking a cigarette." I about choked. Turned out one of the other guys had sneaked upstairs to another phone to call me from there.

Steve Spurrier called on opening day, and Coach Fulmer. Don James called from Washington. James told me he contacted only four players that first day. I charted them all, but I knew I must be starry-eyed because they all sounded good. Some of the really sharp ones called from schools I had no intention of going to: Northwestern for one, and Kansas State. But they were so persuasive they still kept me on the phone. I told Virginia I wasn't interested from the start, however. I made it clear it was because of the way they'd treated Cooper.

When Coach Fulmer came to the house as the "first visit," he let Coach Cutcliffe do most of the talking. I think

Fulmer backed off after a few minutes because he could see Cutcliffe and I were hitting it off. I had a lot of questions: What was happening on the roster? Could I play without red-shirting? If the starter gets hurt, where would I rank as the backup? In a big lead situation, would I play as a freshman? I told them I'd like to play some that first year so I could compete for the starting job as a sophomore, "but I don't want to just come in for a couple plays and lose a year of eligibility. I'd rather redshirt than do that."

Cooper went with me to visit Notre Dame. We spent an hour with Lou Holtz in his office. Talk about a motivator. Holtz said, "You come here and you'll play in every game next season." Ron Powlus was his quarterback at the time. He'd been brought in as the "savior" of Notre Dame football, a highly respected All-America high schooler, but he'd gotten hurt his freshman year. Holtz said, "I don't know if Ron is going to come back strong or not, but if he beats you out, you'll still play at least a series every game." I admit I was tempted. I had gotten to know Powlus. We talked about the various schools I was interested in and he'd been giving me a lot of encouragement to go to Notre Dame. But when I told him what Holtz laid out as a battle plan, Powlus said, "You know, Tennessee might be a really good situation for you." He didn't like the sound of sharing playing time at all. He wanted to bump my butt right out of there. I can't really blame him.

I actually visited Tennessee the same weekend I visited Ole Miss. Dad went with me. And even now I can't say why I liked it so much. I'd never been there, never seen a game in Neyland Stadium. I knew it offered a good opportunity to play, but when I visited, there was an ice storm, it was bitter cold, and the stadium field was covered with ice. I told somebody later, "All I did was talk to people—students, coaches, fans, whoever. That's all, just talk." There was nothing else to do. I went to one party the whole time I was there.

But for some reason, Tennessee felt right. For some reason, I thought right then it would be a good fit. Evidently that's how these things play out. On gut feelings.

I'd gone to Oxford that Friday. By contrast, Ole Miss had rolled out the red carpet. In the locker room they had Dad's "No. 18" on a brand-new jersey hanging from a designated locker and said they'd bring it out of retirement for me. They gave me a tape to listen to—of *next* year's opening game with Auburn, with the announcer simulating a play-by-play in which I took the team on a two-minute drive to the winning touchdown. Me throwing the touchdown pass, of course. Dad's old coach, John Vaught, came around and chatted with me. Billy Brewer talked about it being the dawn of a "new era," but at the same time a return to the "good old days" with a Manning again at quarterback. It was all very touching.

They say after one of these visits, when you find yourself really smitten, you should go back two days later to see if it makes the same impact. Instead, on Sunday Dad and I flew to Knoxville, where the reception wasn't nearly as grand. And despite that, for reasons I had to think long and hard about, Ole Miss faded from my thinking. For good, as it turned out. At that point Tennessee became my number one.

The next weekend I visited Florida. My last recruiting trip. I said to myself, "Unless these people blow me away, I'm going to Tennessee." They tried. I went to a party at one house, and it was packed. Cars parked everywhere. And right out front was a sign: "Peyton's Place." Oh boy, here we go again. But when I went home, it was still Tennessee, though I wasn't quite ready to tell anybody.

Dad stayed with me at the Hilton, but early Monday evening he had to go out for a while. And while he was gone I decided to end the suspense. I called my mother with the verdict. She took it well, and so did my dad when he got back to the hotel. I met him at the door. "Dad, I've decided I want to go to Tennessee. I think that's the place for me. But I told Mom and I'll tell you. If you'd rather I go to Ole Miss, that's what I'll do."

He hugged me and smiled. He said, "Don't even think about it, son. You go where you want to go. It's your life, not ours. We're with you all the way." After that I called Cooper and my grandparents, and a couple of my buddies on the Newman team to tell them my decision, making them swear to secrecy until it was announced.

Why Tennessee and not Ole Miss? I guess mainly because my sights had been lifted a little higher from when I first thought of playing football in college. I wanted to be the best quarterback I could be, and Tennessee had the environment to make it happen. I love Ole Miss. I always have, from reading and hearing about my father playing there until now, when I'm looking forward to seeing Eli play there. Until my freshman year in high school, I didn't think there was another college.

But at that moment in time the Tennessee program was Up Here, and the Ole Miss program was at a low ebb and going lower. I didn't know it, it was only rumored, but the team was about to go on NCAA probation for two years: no bowl games, no television appearances, and Billy Brewer would be fired in the aftermath. It wasn't a good place for me to be. Not then.

I know deep down my mother wanted me to go to Ole Miss, but she never pushed it. Never made me feel "lobbied." Which wasn't true of Ole Miss fans. I got more mail from them than anybody. "We love you . . . We loved your dad . . . Be loyal." They talked about loyalty a lot, not thinking, I guess, that for me acting on that basis would have been to go to Tulane or LSU. I wasn't born in Mississippi. I was born in New Orleans.

And the fact is, I didn't want to be an instant celebrity. I knew some people would know me at Tennessee, but I wouldn't be going there to save the program or anything close to it. It didn't need saving. Tennessee had done, and would continue to do, quite well without me. So in the end, I thought to myself, "Okay, I can go to Ole Miss and make a lot of people happy. But would *I* be happy?" And I applied what Dad had said from the beginning. "Before anything else, go where *you'll* be happy." Case closed.

First thing Tuesday morning I made my calls. I'd told the

last four schools I was still interested in I'd call then, starting at 6 A.M. Coach Fulmer called my mom the night before and gave her the number where he could be reached in New Jersey. He was there recruiting another kid. He said, "Does Peyton mean six o'clock eastern time or six o'clock central time?"

Whatever time it was, I think I woke him up, because he sounded half-asleep. But when I told him my decision, he said, "Peyton, I'd do cartwheels in the street if they'd let me out there in my pajamas."

Next I called Keith Daniels, the assistant coach at Ole Miss who was the recruiter Brewer had assigned to me. I'd gotten to like Daniels a lot. When he recruited me, he gave me the "Top Ten Reasons You Should Go to Ole Miss," David Letterman–style. Number one was, "We have the best looking women in America."

Keith was obviously disappointed. I tried to cheer him up by telling him what a good job I thought he'd done, but I don't think he bought it. I then called Bob Sanders at Florida and Fred Jackson at Michigan, the last two "finalists." They were okay with it. I'd been antsy about telling them, but Dad had said from the start, "You gotta because it's only fair to let these coaches know so they can get their ducks in order."

I had made a whole slew of calls to recruiters before that and wrote fifteen letters to coaches from other teams, thanking them for their interest and their time. All of them were supportive. Several of them said they appreciated my writing because so many guys don't tell them anything and they waste a lot of time they could use recruiting somebody else. The coach from Southern Cal called, and I sort of stammered around until he laughed and said, "Peyton, you're going to be successful wherever you go, and I wish you well. I've enjoyed recruiting you."

After I finished my calls that Tuesday morning, I went off to school, and Dad arranged for an afternoon press conference at the Hilton so that the whole thing could be handled at a single sitting. One press conference instead of 150. Get it said, get it over. But the word was already out and spreading—I was going to Tennessee. So the place was jammed. Mississippi sent a battalion of newspaper and radio-TV crews, though the news, for them, wasn't good. But we got through it without too much trauma, thanked everybody we could think of, and went home.

Then all hell broke loose.

Dad started getting calls right away. Indignant calls, outraged calls, what's-going-on calls. *Brutal* calls. We both got blasted hard by Ole Miss people, and while it hurt me a lot, it hurt mainly because of what it did to my dad. He was devastated. The calls, the letters, the disrespect shown a man who had done so much for that school, not only on the football field but in all the years since, always being there for them, making appearances, raising money for this program or that— it was cruel. There's a room named after him in the new athletic building at Ole Miss, and he deserves it. He *didn't* deserve this.

But, of course, that's the flip side of college football. How the partisanship can go to such extremes. How so totally out of touch a lot of "fans" are with reasonable behavior. They weren't all that mad at me, they were mad at *him* for not *making* me go to Ole Miss. Knowing, as anybody with half a mind would, that if a father handles such a situation the right way, it'll be to let his kid make that decision for himself. As part of growing up. Dad should have been applauded for what he did, not condemned.

We divided the mail and messages between the "good" and the "bad." Some of them Mom and Dad wouldn't let me see. Some of them were written on business stationery; some were from doctors and dentists. Established people. They told me I'd made the "worst mistake" of my life. "We always loved your dad, but not after this." Some hoped for the worst. "I hope you get hurt." "I hope you break your leg."

I had a cushion between me and the bitterness: school. At Newman, then at Tennessee, because it continued for months afterward. Dad had to face it head-on, and often, because he and Mom still went back to Mississippi regularly.

He used to drive up at least once or twice a month, and when he'd stop to eat or get gas, he'd talk to people he'd gotten to know along the route. One day at one station, the good ol' boy who always pumped his gas said, "I don't think you should come back through here anymore." Dad just laughed and got in his car, but the man meant it. Dad said he tried to think, "It's good that people love their school so much," but it was just too ridiculous.

He got more than two hundred letters attacking my choice. The Jackson *Clarion-Ledger* supposedly received seven thousand negative calls on the subject. At Ole Miss, Cooper had his antennae up. And his guard. He was dying for somebody to say something, but nobody did. When a "Peyton Who?" T-shirt was introduced on campus, Cooper started wearing a Tennessee baseball cap. He wore it the rest of his time there. He was more fired up than anybody about me going to Tennessee. *"Yesss!"* he said when I told him. "I *like* it. I *like* Tennessee. *Great* receivers. *Big* stadium. This is terrific!"

He knew more about Tennessee than I did.

Most of the negative reaction was just out of ignorance, of course. And when all the votes were counted, I think Dad and I both got more good letters than bad. No real friendships were lost, not the ones that mattered. I know Dad would never have let Eli go to Ole Miss if he hadn't gotten over it—and wasn't also convinced that Mississippi had gotten over it. He and Mom have a condo in Oxford now that they'll be using when they go for Eli's games.

I went back to Oxford on a visit when I was a sophomore at Tennessee, to spend some time with Cooper. I was a little hesitant, but we'd just beaten Alabama, and I was on a high. Ole Miss was playing Alabama that week. Tennessee had an open date, so I spent the weekend.

And nothing bad happened. Not a single discouraging word was said. I was suddenly surrounded by best friends. I shook hands like a Louisiana politician, signed autographs galore, and had a wonderful time. I thought about matching up some of the houses in Oxford with the return addresses on the slanderous letters we got, just so I could drop by and say hello, but what the heck. It was finished.

Over the next few years, the bad feelings subsided. Dad, sadder but wiser, was back in high regard at his alma mater (if you could truly say he ever left). But every now and then we'd still get some fallout. He and I were on a plane going somewhere a couple years later and this guy who evidently knew him came down the aisle and reached over me to shake his hand. Just ignored me and stretched across, and said, "Hey, Archie, how about Eli? Is he going to Ole Miss?" As far as he was concerned, I wasn't there.

I guess some people will never get over it.

9

If it were a crime to scourge record books, Peyton Manning would be doing time today instead of starring in the National Football League. His four years at the University of Tennessee resulted in such a wholesale revisal of school and Southeastern Conference records that future sports historians weighing the figures will think there were three of him instead of one. Peyton broke thirty-three Tennessee quarterbacking records. In a conference where the quarterback pantheon includes such names as Namath, Tarkenton, Conerly, Parilli, Sullivan, and Spurrier, he broke SEC career records for most victories (39, in 45 games), most completions, most passing yards, most total offense, best completion percentage, lowest interception percentages, and most 300-yard games. He broke NCAA records for lowest career interception and single-season interception percentages (when he had only four of 380 passes intercepted in 1995, a minuscule 1.05 percent). And this does not count the times he is in the books for "seconds" and "thirds." While he was at it, Peyton completed his bachelor's requirements in three years, was a three-time Academic All-America, and graduated cum laude with a 3.61 grade point average. Tennessee clearly had never had, seen, or heard of anything quite like him. . . .

passed up the Louisiana High School All-Star game and enrolled in summer school at Tennessee in July 1994 so that I could get a jump on everything (and everybody). I was hoping to play some as a freshman; Coach Fulmer had said I might. I didn't want to redshirt, so if I played I wanted to be sharp enough to challenge for the backup spot to whoever the starter would be, and maybe compete for first string as a sophomore. I was confident enough to believe those things could happen. I did *not* expect to wind up the starter myself, and close out the final eight games of that season at number one. Dreams like that would have been categorized as "pipe."

But I made up my mind to go in with the best possible attitude and the best possible work ethic. If I wasn't in class, I was doing something to make myself a better football player. I was in the athletic complex every available minute, hanging around like a gym rat. I'd go to class at eight, then at ten be there to lift and work out, then on to the film room to watch Tennessee games and practices. Teammates took to calling me "Caveman" for all the time I spent alone in dark rooms studying film.

And when workouts started, I was so anxious to apply what I was learning that I was even more gung-ho. If the quarterbacks were scheduled to throw at five o'clock, I'd be dressed out at four, looking for somebody to throw to. I was determined to the point of being obsessed. I was resolute. I was single-minded. I was boring.

I look back on it now and realize that a lot of my friends, the ones I consider close, I didn't get to know hardly at all until my junior and senior years. As a freshman, I didn't meet a lot of people. I didn't go through fraternity rush. I didn't go to many parties, didn't pledge, never went out during the week and seldom on the weekends. Guys who called to go eat or hang out, I'd say, "Sorry, I have things to do." I wish now I hadn't been so fixated. I'd like to have gotten to know people better, sooner. But I was cramming. Chuck Noll, the former Steelers coach, is the source of my favorite football quote: "Pressure is something you feel only when you don't know what the hell you're doing." I wanted to know what the hell I was doing.

And the truth is that if I hadn't had that drive, that dedication, who is to say where I'd be now?

The bright spot socially was meeting Ashley Thompson,

the girl who would one day occupy *all* my "coeducational" attention. It was in August, at one of the few fraternity parties I went to. We were introduced and only talked a little while. I didn't make a big first impression (she said later my pastel shirt was a turnoff) but *I* was certainly impressed. She was beautiful, she was bright, she was charming. I had a curfew, however, so I told her I'd sneak out after bed check and we'd talk. But once I got to the dorm, I didn't think I should risk it and didn't go back. If I'd been a little more like Cooper, of course, I wouldn't have hesitated.

I didn't see Ashley again until we were into the season, but the memory kept me interested and mutual friends kept us in contact. Besides the obvious, she had something my dad had found in Mom: a football background. Ashley's grandfather, Van Thompson, had played at Tennessee in 1939 and '40 when the Vols had consecutive undefeated seasons under General Bob Neyland before losing in bowl games, and her brother, Will, lettered at the University of Virginia. The only negative I saw was that Ashley was also going to Virginia—a four-and-a-half-hour drive away, as I soon discovered.

I was listed no higher than fourth or fifth on the quarterback depth chart going into fall practice. The incumbent starter, Heath Shuler, had turned pro early, leaving number one to another senior, Jerry Colquitt. Junior Todd Helton, a baseball player now with the Colorado Rockies, was behind Colquitt; then a redshirt freshman, Mike Grein, who wound up quitting when the season started. My direct competition for number four was another incoming freshman, and he couldn't have been more impressive.

Branndon Stewart was recruited the same time I was. A superathlete out of Stephenville, Texas, he could run the ball as well as he could throw it, could power-lift 465 pounds, had won awards as a baseball player, and could high-jump six feet eight inches. He'd been the Southwest Player of the Year before Fulmer coaxed him to Tennessee. All he lacked was an "S" on his chest.

It was kind of ridiculous, but it tells you how competitive coaches are. Coach Fulmer had told Branndon Stewart he wasn't going to recruit any more quarterbacks. When Branndon told me about it, I laughed. I said, "Maybe that's why Fulmer's such a great recruiter," and told him that Fulmer had told *me* Ole Miss wasn't on the Tennessee schedule. That mattered because I didn't want to have to compete against my dad's old school and my "first love" among college teams. Fulmer had fibbed about that, too. Tennessee was booked to play Ole Miss both my junior and senior seasons.

Despite what people later thought, there was never any animosity between Branndon and me. We were always friendly, and the competition never got confrontational. But it was still him against me for the job, and just the sight of him made me want to head for the weight room. That night after we met I called Dad. "I need to bench-press 225 pounds! I need to get bigger! I need to get stronger!"

Dad said, "Don't worry about it. They're not going to demote you for not being a great weight lifter."

I thought to myself, "Yeah, but you haven't seen Branndon Stewart."

A couple nights later Branndon asked me if I wanted to go watch some game film with him. Of course I wanted to. That's *exactly* what I wanted to do, study film. So naturally I said, "Naw, I gotta study for a quiz tomorrow." He said, "Well, okay," and he didn't go. He went to his room, and I went to mine.

And when I saw his door close, I slipped out and went over and watched film by myself for two hours. Sneaky? Sure. But I felt if we were looking at the same things, and comparing notes, how would I get an edge? I mean, if I watched a certain play, say "62 slant," every time Tennessee used it during the previous season, I could watch that play fifteen or twenty times and come to some definite conclusions about how the play developed, how deep the quarterback's drop should be, what they played off of in the secondary, and so forth. If we were watching together, we might interpret what we saw differently and adjust to each other's thinking. I couldn't get the edge I wanted by trying to reach a consensus.

I watched film all summer and into the fall, usually alone. I don't know how often Branndon watched, if at all, but I doubt it was nearly as much. After that first invitation, he seemed to lose interest. I didn't object. It was a very competitive situation, and I wasn't above taking advantage of every opening.

I locked him out of a quarterback meeting one night. Or at least part of a meeting. We were scheduled to meet with coaches at eight o'clock, when a lot of the buildings on campus are closed and everything looks deserted. I was walking through one of the doors they had kept open for us and it "accidentally" closed behind me, locking automatically. I knew Branndon was running late and that he'd have to get through that door. I didn't bother to prop it back open, I'm now ashamed to say. He eventually got in, all right, as I knew he would, but the opportunity was there and I took it. A sudden response to a competitive urge.

But I think my willingness to put more time into preparation was what really gave me the advantage over Branndon in the fall. I was always trying to find a better way. Todd Helton used to call me "R2D2" for being so analytical. I think it bugged him. For such a good athlete, Todd didn't have a quarterback's mentality. He had a baseball player's mentality. You don't study in baseball the way you do in football. He thought he could get by on ability alone. But even when I knew he didn't have all the answers, I bombarded him with questions, him being a junior and my "superior." He just didn't relate. At one point, I asked him so many questions he said, "Just shut the hell up for a while, will you?"

In the first few practices that fall, I didn't throw particularly well. We had brand new balls, and the field was wet, and I had trouble gripping them. Passes kept coming off my fingers like they'd been tipped. Branndon had no such problem and did well. After one day, the media were already making predictions, and if I paid any heed I would have written off my chances of making the top three. I didn't let it bother me. I just kept plugging away on things I knew I had to do better. Then in the first scrimmage I went 10 for 12 passing, and everything started falling into place.

One advantage from the beginning was my relationship with David Cutcliffe. We developed something all quarterbacks and offensive coordinators need to have—total communication, available around the clock. It had started with that first recruiting visit, when he was so open and honest, and it carried into the season. We had candid conversations about teams, about individual players, about what I had to do to contribute, what I had to be careful of. I never felt embarrassed saying, "Hey, Coach Cut, I don't understand this," or, "Why do we have to do that?"

We became friends beyond the field. He'd invite me to his house for dinner, and I'd play with his kids. And as the years went by, we got closer and closer. I'd come into his office on a Monday and he'd close the door and give me the plans for the week, the new plays that were being installed, what to expect out of the ordinary. And many times before and after practice we'd just sit and talk.

Some of that is the natural order of things in football, of course. It was natural to be closer to the offensive coordinator than to Coach Fulmer. A more respectful distance is generally kept between players and the head coach, who by definition will always be a little above it all. A little more forbidding. Which is as much to his advantage as the players'. A clear understanding of "he's the boss," the last word. With Coach Cut, I had a mix of coach and friend, where last words weren't important.

We didn't just talk football. We talked about life, about girlfriends, about the pressures of schedules on football-playing underclassmen. It was like having a father away from home. He had a party at his house one night shortly after I'd been on campus and invited certain players and their "significant others"—girlfriends or wives. When I told him I'd try to bring Ashley Thompson, he ragged me pretty good. "You've only been here a couple weeks and already you've got a girl-friend?" Well, not quite.

Dad quickly saw the value in my relationship with Cutcliffe and didn't hesitate to give Coach Cut the credit. He said, "Sure, Peyton and I spent a lot of time on the field together when he was growing up, but mostly what I did was help him with his mechanics, and tell him he had to get a little quicker, a little stronger. After a certain point in high school, there was nothing wrong with him otherwise that I could see. But I was his ex-quarterback father. David Cutcliffe was his quarterback *coach*. He knew all the drills, all the insights. He got into Peyton's thinking, teaching him the dos and don'ts of plays or formations against this or that defense. I wouldn't have pretended to know what Tennessee had in mind."

Dad always kept a respectful distance on those things. I mean, he didn't even *want to* know our plays, or what the thinking was about them. When Coach Cutcliffe came to New Orleans that June to go over the offense with me (the NCAA having recently allowed coaches to visit signed players), he said he wanted Dad to be there. But about thirty minutes into the session, I looked over and Dad was sound asleep in his chair, with his mouth open. It was his way of saying, "I don't care about your plays, I don't want to know about them. You coach my son and I'll be there for the other things."

I admit it was harder when Dad first said, "You do what you think is best, and I'll support you." But it was his way of giving me my rite of passage. He was saying, "You're a man now. It's time to take charge." When it came to life, he had never hesitated to tell me to be smart about my choices, about the places I went, the times I went to them. He'd say, "Peyton, don't give people a chance to think bad things. If you're out late drinking beer, put it in a cup, don't make it obvious. . . . Hold your tongue when it's time to be quiet. . . . *Sign* that autograph. It only takes five seconds." Now he was letting go, or at least giving me a freer rein.

Don't get me wrong. We still talked football, and after games even now we analyze the good and the bad. He stays current. If he wanted to, he's certainly qualified to say to a coach, "What are you doing? You call this play on third down and you make my son look bad!" But he wouldn't, and never did. Not when I was in high school, not in college, not now in the pros. If he saw something he might ask me about it privately, but otherwise he bit his tongue. That's very impressive. As a result, all my coaches have been candid with him. They've gone to *him* with observations.

Cutcliffe told Dad he'd never had a player more eager and willing than me. I appreciated that because it was precisely what I tried to be. I had studied the Tennessee offense before I even got there, and knew enough when I arrived to "keep the coaches on their toes," as Dad put it. Cutcliffe said he had to get to work earlier "just to get ready for Peyton's questions." I liked that, too.

More recently, Dad put a handle on something I had never really articulated. He said, "What David Cutcliffe appreciated most, and what I already knew, was that from grade school to the pros, Peyton's desire wasn't to make himself the center of attention. It was to be the catalyst for helping his team win. He was never looking to throw the ball fifty or sixty times a game, because he knew teams that did that weren't going to be consistent winners. He understood the value of the whole game, running and passing, and how you win with that balance."

To be sure, I knew from that first season that to even *think* about throwing fifty or sixty passes a game for Tennessee was out of the question. More likely it would be fifteen or sixteen. Fine with me; whatever it takes. I also learned that being ready "just in case" was every bit as important as I thought it was. Fulmer had said I might get to play as a freshman. I did. And in the team's very first game, albeit briefly.

Branndon Stewart and I stayed fourth-fifth/fifth-fourth through two-a-days, and were still bringing up the rear when we went to California for the opener against UCLA. I called Grandfather Williams in Mississippi from the hotel before we left for the game. Always the optimist, he said, "Be ready, Peyton. You might get in there today!" I said, "I'm not playing, Paw-Paw. No way in the world. Watch for me on the sidelines."

For a raw recruit from Louisiana it was quite an introduction to major college football. UCLA. In the Rose Bowl. Before a national television audience. I remember everything about it. The beautiful weather, the bands playing, the pregame warm-ups, the crowd spreading like some out-of-control amoebas to cover the seats before the game. I remember waving at Bob Griese and Keith Jackson at the practice on Friday. They were longtime friends of Dad's, and were there to do the game for ABC. And I remember just before we went out on the field asking Jerry Colquitt if my pants looked all right, as if anybody on the planet was going to notice.

My assigned task was a no-brainer. Branndon and I were to stand along the sidelines in such a way as to shield one of the assistant coaches, Randy Sanders, from UCLA's view when Randy signaled in the plays to Jerry Colquitt. That's all we had to do, ostensibly.

Then on the seventh play of the game Colquitt got hit hard running an option and came up limping. The trainers had to help him to the sidelines, but I'd seen enough of those to think, "He's okay. He'll be right back in there."

Then I heard one of them say, "A-C-L." Anterior cruciate ligament.

Chilling words in sport, because the A-C-L is a part of the knee that when injured can be the kiss of death for a player's season, even his career. It turned out to be both for Jerry Colquitt, though we didn't know it then.

It still didn't hit me that I might play. I was thinking instead how unfair it was for Jerry, a fifth-year senior who had finally gotten his chance after three seasons of backing up Heath Shuler. This was going to be his year. And now he was out. Todd Helton started warming up.

To my surprise Coach Fulmer came over to Branndon and me. "Be ready," he said. "You're both going to play today."

My heart jumped, then started pounding so hard I could feel it through my jersey. I hadn't been that nervous for a long time. I felt like saying, "No, Coach! Not yet!" It wasn't that I hadn't prepared, it was that I hadn't prepared for *this*.

I went behind the bench and began running little sprints back and forth to warm up. I could feel the hair lifting on my arms. A veteran offensive lineman, Bubba Miller, who plays for the Eagles now, came over and said, "Don't worry, Peyton. We'll take care of you out there." Was I *that* obvious?

I must have been, because in the Tennessee section of the stands, down near the end zone, Mom tugged Dad's sleeve and said, "Peyton's going in!"

Dad said, "Naw. What makes you say that?"

"He's got his helmet on. He's warming up."

"Relax. It's not going to happen. He's had his helmet on all night."

But it did happen. Todd Helton quarterbacked the next two series and got nowhere. UCLA was ahead, 17–0, when Coach Cutcliffe phoned me from the press box. "All right, Peyton, you're up. Get us going."

I'd been advanced from fifth to fourth to third to in-the-game without a hearing.

I could feel the crowd noise swelling as I jogged onto the field. It wasn't, there was no reason for it to, but it seemed that way. I tried to focus on something Dad always told me: "Peyton, no matter who you're playing for, no matter where the game is, when you go in, you're the quarterback. Act like it." And I remembered what coaches preach in practice about calling plays: "Speak up! Speak the hell up!"

In the huddle, I said, "All right, guys, here we go!" (Was that me? That strange, squeaky voice?) I was clapping like a cheerleader to cover up my nervousness.

In the press box, Bob Griese said to the national television audience, "Yeah, you see him clapping, but believe me, he's nervous."

In the huddle I babbled on. "All right, guys, I know I'm just a freshman, but we're gonna take it down the field on this series and score, then . . . "

And Jason Layman, our left tackle and another veteran, said, "Just shut the f—— up and call the play!"

Well, okay. I could do that. I called the play, said, "Ready . . . break!" and followed the center up to the line of scrimmage.

It was anticlimactic after that. On first down we gained nine yards, but got stuffed on second. Third and one, we went to the line, and UCLA was in the middle of a substitution and taking its time getting set. One of our guys said, "Snap the ball, Peyton, they're not ready!" If I heard that now, I'd say, "We'll snap it when *I'm* ready. Just pay attention." But then I blurted, *"Hut,"* and a UCLA guy slammed through and dropped us for a loss. I trotted off the field.

In the stands, Lynn Swann brought his ABC sideline camera crew over to where my folks were sitting and asked Mom, "How does Peyton look to you, Mrs. Manning?"

"Young," Mom said.

That was it for me in the game. I was a little upset afterward that I didn't get a second chance, and Dad was surprised. But that was it.

Branndon Stewart also played some, but in the end it was still Todd Helton, who engineered a great fourth-quarter rally and almost pulled the game out. We lost, 25–23.

I didn't play at all the next week against Georgia, when the running game won it for us. Against Florida, though, when we got behind early and it was 24–0 at the half, I played long enough to throw five passes, and had one for a touchdown called back by a penalty. On *me*. I had scrambled around when the pocket broke down and crossed the line of scrimmage just before I threw the ball. Jimmy Harper was the referee, a highly respected SEC official who knew my father. After the pass went upfield he started waving his arms and shouting, "No good, no good!"

I said, "C'mon, Mr. Harper, give me a break," hoping

maybe he'd remember I was Archie's kid. But of course, he didn't. Give me a break, I mean. They called it back.

We lost, 31–0. It would be the first of four defeats by the Gators in my years at Tennessee. We were more competitive in the last three, but in the end Florida would account for half of the six losses we suffered when I was the starting quarterback for the Volunteers. I still get asked why we couldn't beat Florida during that period. The answer was as simple then as it is now: Florida was better.

The following week, lighting struck again—Todd Helton went down with a knee injury in the first quarter against Mississippi State in Starkville. He, too, was as good as finished for the season. Coach Fulmer immediately went to me. A much less nervous me. No misgivings, no jitters this time. On our third play, I threw my first touchdown pass as a Vol, a 76-yarder to Kendrick Jones. From a purely aesthetic standpoint, it was one of the best I made in college—the deep-out route everybody says you have to be able to throw if you want to make it in the pros. Kendrick caught it on the dead run right in front of Jackie Sherrill, the Mississippi State coach. The State cornerback said afterward, "I didn't think Manning's arm was that good."

Two series later Fulmer put Branndon Stewart in, and on third down Branndon threw an interception. I hate to say it, but that made a good situation even better for me. I finished the game with by far my best statistics of the season—14 for 23 for 256 yards and two touchdowns. But the downside spoiled everything: we lost, 24–21, when Mississippi State scored 10 points in the fourth quarter. We fumbled the ball away four times in the second half.

Dad missed the game, the only one he couldn't make in my four years at Tennessee. Mom was there, though. In keeping with their vow to always be "represented" when any of us played, Dad attended Eli's junior high game at Newman that day. With one eye on Eli and the other on a little handheld TV, he watched most of our game sitting in the stands at Newman. He said the reception left a lot to be desired. Was it snowing in Starkville? Not exactly. It was ninety degrees.

By the process of elimination, I was suddenly on the verge—so it seemed—of being the starting quarterback for Tennessee as a greenhorn freshman. But Coach Fulmer didn't let anybody jump to any conclusions. The following week Branndon Stewart and I took an equal number of snaps in practice and Fulmer kept saying, "You're both starters. I won't say who'll actually be in the game first until Friday."

That bothered me, because I thought I'd earned it against Mississippi State. Dad calmed me down when we talked Monday night. He said, "Peyton, Coach Fulmer is doing what he has to do to pull everything together. This is a major decision for him. The last thing he needs now is a big controversy over who he chooses as his quarterback. It's better for you *and* him if he waits until Friday."

So instead I concentrated on the opponent, Washington State, which came in as the top defensive team in the country by NCAA statistics and had a reputation for being a very physical team. Two of its linebackers were later drafted high by the NFL.

Coach Fulmer's routine during a practice week called for his starting quarterback to sit next to him in team meetings. It's an honored spot, front row, left. That week an offensive lineman sat there—until Friday, when Fulmer announced that I would be his starter against Washington State. The seat was mine from then to the end of my career at Tennessee.

This time Dad was the only member of the immediate family who could make it to the game. He got tickets for his sister Pam and her family and they joined him in Knoxville on Friday, and he and I hooked up. We had talked regularly by phone, but I hadn't seen him for a while and I missed him. We had some catching up to do. As good as it had gotten for me, it hadn't been good for him.

Archie Manning spent his son's first year at Tennessee in a kind of emotional no-man's-land between Peyton's gathering status and his own painful estrangement from Ole Miss. It was, for him, a year of exhilarating highs and dispiriting lows. He was glad Peyton was, at least geographically, a state or two removed from the lows. . . .

From his arrival in Knoxville, Peyton and I had talked almost every night. Usually I'd just let him ramble—about school, about what he was doing, about the competition. He was frustrated at times, and confused, like all freshmen are, but he never let any of it get him down, and each step was a step up. He got better in a hurry. I could say the same about my troubles with Mississippi, but I'd be lying.

For Peyton's sake, it was good that when he came home for breaks, home was New Orleans, not Oxford or Jackson or Drew. But he heard enough to be educated for a lifetime about what "fans" are capable of, and to develop a sense of proportion when it came to judging their actions. As for their occasional spasms of gross immaturity, I don't think you ever get used to that. What surprised me was how long some of them held the grudge. Even years later, people would come up to us and identify themselves as Ole Miss alumni and ask for my autograph and ignore Peyton. Just ignore him. I never did go back to some of the places I used to patronize in Mississippi because of the criticism I got traveling back and forth.

We should have seen it coming from that first announcement at Newman. The questions asked by the Mississippi media weren't "Why did he pick Tennessee," but "Why *didn't* he pick Ole Miss?" Every interpretation was negative. One television station from Jackson sent a reporter and crew to New Orleans, not to cover a boy making his college choice, but to stir things up. The reporter said, "Don't you think you let Ole Miss down, letting Peyton go to Tennessee?"

I said, "No. And listen, I'm current with Ole Miss. As far as I'm concerned, we have nothing to be sorry for or ashamed of." I had, in fact, just headed up a $10 million funding drive for the school, so I wasn't in the mood to have my loyalty questioned. I'd been an Ole Miss season ticket holder for decades—six seats that I kept buying all through Peyton's time at Tennessee even when I didn't use them.

A picture ran in newspapers the next day showing me looking sullen and gloomy, like I was beaten down by the process. The captions implied that poor ol' Archie was grieving over the turn of events. Hardly. I had introduced Peyton, then sat down with my arms folded and my eyes cast down to let him talk. From that angle, I might have looked dejected, but the truth is I had positive feelings about Peyton's choice. And from his calls once he got to Tennessee, I got an even better feel for the things that drew him there: the "top ten" program, the big-time facilities, the big-time stadium, the big-time everything. Sure, the Ole Miss side of me was disappointed, but the daddy side of me was proud. He had chosen wisely.

That one long first day stretched into a very long year. Our telephone number is listed, and I got call after call, month after month. One guy said he'd been encouraged by me to donate a lot of money to the $10 million drive and that I was now a "traitor to the cause and should be ashamed" of myself. But it was the first call that was the worst, because it involved my old coach, John Vaught. An insurance man who had been a friend of mine called the very morning of the announcement. Coach Vaught was on his board and through his company hosted an annual golf tournament on the Gulf Coast that I was always invited to.

The insurance man was abrupt. He said, "Archie, you need to call the coach."

I said, "What . . . ?"

"You need to call him right now!"

"I'll call him, but I'm not sure I like the way you're presenting this."

"Just call him!" And he hung up.

I called Coach Vaught. He said, "Archie, you have to talk Peyton out of this. He's making a big mistake."

I said, "Coach, he put a year and a half into this decision. He studied it from every angle. It's something he wants to do. It's not for me to stand in his way."

He said, "Yes it is. You've got to talk him out of it, that's all there is to it."

Now I was *really* upset.

I waited two or three weeks and finally wrote Vaught a letter, trying to put into better words what I'd said hastily on the phone. He waited two or three weeks to reply. A man who was close to him in the meantime told me I had to understand that Coach Vaught still harbored a long-running bias against Tennessee, dating back to his days competing against his nemesis General Neyland. We had inadvertently poured salt in an old wound.

Within the official Ole Miss family, everybody else showed their class. Then-chancellor Gerald Turner said he understood. The vice chancellor, who is now chancellor, Robert Khayat, did likewise. So even did Coach Billy Brewer. Peyton called him after his decision, and Brewer wished him well. I suppose he had enough problems of his own at that point. In time, the bad vibes I first got from Coach Vaught abated, too, and we were friends again.

But I never got invited back to the insurance man's golf tournament.

Over the next few months, there were four distinct levels of reaction.

One: the close friends and family who willingly accepted Peyton's decision and were glad for him. They appreciated the fact that we didn't live in Mississippi anymore. Two: those who felt strongly about Ole Miss and didn't like it but were willing to let go. Jim Poole's dad Buster's reaction when he heard was "Oh, shit!" but he came back around. Three: the hypocrites who said, "I fully understand" to our faces, then said what traitors we were behind our backs. There was one in Jackson who had played basketball at Ole Miss with Olivia's brother and with whom I had a small business partnership. He said it was fine, then trashed us to others. The others told us about it. I saw him once after that, at a function in Oxford, but I looked the other way.

And finally, four: the group who flat-out will never get over it. Some of them were in a bar watching a Tennessee–Arkansas game the next season when Peyton got hurt (not badly), and they *cheered*. One guy wrote letters every year to chide me about a game Peyton had lost (most likely to Florida) or a key interception he had thrown. The letters usually ended with "I hope he breaks his leg."

Those who came to me directly even from the beginning were taken aback to find me less than hostile. Defensive, maybe, but never hostile. I figured if they were loyal Ole Miss fans they deserved to be heard. And my motto since has been to kill 'em with kindness. It seems to have worked. The good has long since covered over the bad. Olivia and I now have a condo in Oxford to make weekends out of it when we go to see Eli play for Ole Miss. The season tickets I'd been buying all those years have come in handy.

What conclusions to draw from it all? About what you'd expect if you know anything about the passion college football generates, and has done with so many for so long. What needs to be understood about college fans—especially at those state school strongholds where the game is so big—is that for many of them the scoreboard on Saturday afternoon is the centerpiece of their lives. The affirmation of their "faith" in football. They get so wrapped up in the team that nothing is more important to them than winning. Whole lifetimes revolve around it. I love that allegiance to a large extent, but when it gets out of proportion to other priorities, it can turn ugly.

Anywhere.

I am grateful that, through it all, Peyton was tucked away in Knoxville, and doing fine. For much of that year I really worried more about Cooper. His health, his well-being, his being in Oxford, seemingly a convenient target for any residue of bitterness over his brother's "defection."

But I shouldn't have worried. Cooper was Cooper. As always, he was in control. Healthwise, his condition had stabilized, and he went about enjoying being an upperclassman—and a very conspicuous fan of Peyton's right there on the Ole Miss campus. He wore his Tennessee cap, and went to every Tennessee game he could get to. He wasn't about to let anybody put him on the defensive in Oxford. (I think he was hoping they'd try, but they didn't.) For Olivia and me it was odd in a way, because Cooper's role had been reversed. Now he was "Peyton's brother," not the other way around. It didn't bother him in the least. He loved flaunting it.

No, that's not quite right. He loved flaunting looking like Peyton.

As he tells it:

"I made it to a lot of Peyton's games, and the more I went the more fun I had because people kept mistaking me for him. We'd hit town on a Friday and go out to dinner that night, Dad and me and friends, and then I'd go on to maybe cut up a little and have some Scotch. And it would get to be one-thirty in the morning and some hillbilly would come up to me and say, 'Peyton! What the hell are you doing out so late? You got a game tomorrow!' And I'd say, 'Well, we're only playing Georgia.' And if Dad was still hanging with me, he'd be going, 'Oh, no, Cooper. That'll be in the papers tomorrow for sure.'

"I'd give 'em autographs, too, when they asked for them. Just sign right there, 'To Robert's son Jimmy, your pal, Peyton.' Arch says, 'Aww, Cooper.' But I say, 'Have some fun, guys. Ham it up.' One weekend Tennessee was playing Alabama and we were out walking the night before when a big Expedition pulls up beside us. One of the passengers is dressed to kill, white tie and everything, and he leans out the window and shouts, 'Hey, Peyton, what are you doing out here on a Friday night?'

"I said, 'Oh, I'm just getting drunk and chasing women.' And I waved and said, 'Go Vols!' I know what they were thinking in that car: 'Do you believe it? That's Peyton Manning, the guy I heard giving that F.C.A. [Fellowship of Christian Athletes] speech two weeks ago. Looks like he's tanked!'

"Dad loves to laugh at those things, but he isn't always comfortable with me doing 'em. It doesn't bother Peyton. He just laughs. I shook him up one time, though. During his sophomore season I got a sideline pass for Tennessee's game at Kentucky and was standing there with David Keith, the actor, when Peyton came off the field after an interception. The Vols were barely winning when it should have been a blowout, and I said something like, 'Hey, Peyton, get your ass in gear!' Peyton didn't even know I was there until that moment, and he sure wasn't happy to hear that. We fussed back and forth, like we used to when we were kids, and he threatened to call security and have me thrown out of the stadium.

"But, of course, he didn't, and it was the only time I riled him. During that freshman year, he was too busy improving himself to worry about my antics."

Cooper couldn't make it to the Washington State game with me, but I called him from Knoxville when I found out on Friday that Peyton was starting. He was elated. Imagine, Cooper said, a kid from Newman High, level 2A in Louisiana, being a number one in the Southeastern Conference as a freshman, and about to go against the top college defense in the country.

I've never been as nervous in my life as I was that Saturday. The only time I felt that way before or since was when Peyton started his first game with the Colts as a rookie. I have to hand it to him, though. Peyton did his part. It could have been a disaster for Tennessee. If Peyton had folded, and the team went to 1 and 4, no telling how bad it would have gotten. But he didn't fold. He played well. My reassurance beforehand was that I knew the Tennessee coaches, and that they would find a way to protect him. And they did. Partly by not giving him too much to do.

Peyton Manning's first start for Tennessee was memorable only for that: It was his first. As sure as quarterbacks are primary to team success, in this game he was kept as incidental to it as he would ever be. . . .

At that Friday morning meeting, Coach Cutcliffe told me we were deliberately going to keep it simple for Washington State. He said, "We've got a very conservative game plan. Run the ball, run the ball, run the ball, maybe throw a little pass, then run again. If the fans get bored and start booing, don't worry about it. It means we're getting the job done."

We did exactly that. We had a veteran offensive line and three NFL-bound runningbacks in James Stewart, Jay Graham, and Aaron Hayden, and we ran the ball. I threw all of 14 passes, almost never in must-pass situations, completing half for only 79 yards. Neither team moved the ball very well. But we won, 10–9, scoring on a 62-yard reverse and a fourth-quarter field goal. There were 95,556 in Neyland Stadium, and if anybody booed I didn't notice. We had averted what would have been a horrible start. After that the points were a lot easier to come by.

We won seven of the eight games I started as a freshman, and I never threw more than 23 passes in any one of them. I had my best game against South Carolina, when I was 18 for 23 for 189 yards and three touchdowns. But the following week we played Memphis State, and I had my worst. Maybe ever. I was certifiably awful: 5 for 12 for 32 yards, and an interception. At one point I had a receiver running wide open down the middle of the field for a sure 60-yard touchdown, and threw it into the ground at his feet.

This time I *did* hear the boos. Loud and clear. I deserved them, even though we won the game easily enough (24–13). Afterward the media and the talk shows openly debated the merits of Manning versus Stewart. I wasn't exactly unanimous as the people's choice. Branndon had produced the last 10 points in the game and had played a lot in the second half. I steered clear of the argument and tried not to listen, because so many times in such cases people say stupid things. But the experience told me what a humbling game football could be at this level, where so much attention is given it, and I kept that in mind even as we swept the last two against Kentucky and Vanderbilt, scoring 117 points to their zero. The strong finish got us an invitation to the Gator Bowl.

Branndon remained my backup throughout, playing less than a third of the time that year. He and I never talked about the decision or the aftermath. We talked about plays, and defenses, but never that. I liked Branndon. We'd laugh and tell stories, and never had a harsh word. But there was always that little barrier that exists between number one and number two. I used to think how much better it would have been if he were a tight end or a receiver so that we could have gotten really close.

The whole thing had to be a huge disappointment for him, but not just because he hadn't beaten me out. He was under a lot more pressure than I first realized. His mother had a reputation for being "involved," to put it politely, and word got around that the family was counting on him to make it big in the pros. Success at Tennessee was therefore mandatory, and it showed.

Dad saw some of it from the stands. At one game during that freshman year, he and Mom sat behind the Stewarts, and every time Branndon did anything, even if it was just a successful handoff, Mrs. Stewart would applaud like mad. In that game, I threw an interception, and instead of at least acting disappointed that it had happened to Tennessee, Mrs. Stewart jumped up and down like she'd won the lottery. Not exactly the image you'd want in a loyal fan.

It was a bad scene all around for Branndon. He couldn't just try to be the best quarterback he could be, which is all I was doing. He had to compete with his future in the balance. I got the impression he'd chosen Tennessee instead of a school in Texas to get away from just that kind of thing. It got even worse when the press hopped on it. Dad and I were asked for comments, but we refused to give any. At one point, even Branndon's high school coach got into the act. He was quoted as saying Branndon was going to be "a great pro player," implying Tennessee's coaches were missing the obvious.

I don't know how you could see that far ahead for an eighteen-year-old, but I thought then, and do now, that Branndon was plenty good enough to be a starter in college. But for the team's sake, it was better having the issue settled. The most *un*settling thing that can happen at quarterback is to have a 1-A and a 1-B. Pepper Rodgers, the former coach says it's like having a wife and a girlfriend. He says, "When you've got two quarterbacks, you've got none." You can get away with having interchangeable running backs, but the whole offense springs from the quarterback and when there are two, the players will take sides, the media will take sides, and everybody will suffer. One time while the issue was still in doubt I called Dad and said, "Can you find me Fred Jackson's phone number?" Jackson was the coach who recruited me for Michigan. I said, "Keep it handy. I might need it."

Branndon Stewart left Tennessee the following January, and I was sorry to see him go. He transferred to Texas A&M, where he sat out a season to get a third year of eligibility. I thought he'd do well there—he had a great arm, he could move, and he was back home in Texas. I was pulling for him. I remember bolting after a Tennessee practice one day to catch the television coverage of his first game against BYU.

But things didn't work out for him. I don't know if it was the system or what, but he got beaten out for first string his senior season, and though he did start in the Sugar Bowl against Ohio State, he wasn't drafted by the pros. Over the years, we kept in touch. When he was a senior, he called to ask if we could get him a room at the Jazz Fest, and we did. Evidently he had made peace with his fate. I hope so. He's a good person.

My first season as a Vol ended typically. We ran the ball 47 times and passed it 23 and beat Virginia Tech, 45–23, in the Gator Bowl. I was 12 for 19 for 189 yards, no interceptions and one touchdown—and "broke loose" for a 29-yard run (who says Manning is so slow?). After the game, Coach Fulmer gave me my first game ball. For the season, I completed sixty-two percent of my passes for 11 touchdowns and only 6 interceptions, and was named SEC Freshman of the Year. All of it was encouraging.

Two other notable things happened that season, both after the Alabama game, the only one we lost when I was the starter. In the postgame press conference, Coach Fulmer told the media that I had thrown to the wrong side on a crucial incomplete pass that killed our chances at the end. When they asked me about it, I bristled. I said, "I threw to the side I was coached to throw to!" Which was true.

Our little contretemps made the news, and Fulmer brought me into his office that Monday to clear the air. But it wasn't a "muzzling" by any means. I have never hesitated to speak my mind when I know (or have reason to believe) I'm right, especially when something has been said or done that's harmful to me or my family or my team. Dad would probably call it another manifestation of my stubbornness, or that "little mean streak" that faithfully emerges when I feel wronged. I react. Trouble is, I haven't always done it diplomatically. I'm working on it.

On a happier second note, Ashley Thompson came to the Alabama game and we got together. Her family were neighbors in Memphis with the Vols' punter, Tom Hutton, and we had communicated through him that we would meet after the game. She started coming to Knoxville often after that, and before long it was a habit. Both ways. She'd drive the four-and-a-half-hours from Virginia to see our games, then when we had an off week or when the season was over, I'd return the favor. I enjoyed the drives—a chance to see the countryside, clear my head, get away. In Charlottesville, there was nobody interested enough to get on my case about football.

Ashley had a lot going for her. She was making A's in the School of Commerce at Virginia, and when she finished in 1997, got sixteen job offers in New York City alone. For our benefit, she settled for a marketing position with Eagle Distributing in Knoxville. It made our times together a lot more convenient. In that respect, we had the kind of availability Mom and Dad had their last two years at Ole Miss. A full-time romance.

With all her qualities, I think what pleased me most about Ashley, though, was that she liked me for who I was, not what I was. We started dating before I'd gotten any real notoriety. At the time I was still pretty scrawny-looking, too, and my nose was too big for my body—a disproportion that weight training rectified, if you're looking for an endorsement—so she really had to like me for "my inner self." We hit it off, and I'll never forget one game day when the team was taking the traditional walk to the stadium through what has since been named "Peyton Manning Pass" (I'm proud to say). My folks were waving, and right there with them was Ashley in an oversized hat with my jersey number (16) on it. As fashion statements go, it was pretty comical, and I had to laugh. But that's what I liked about her. She was real.

The following spring, with Branndon Stewart gone, the starting job was mine from day one, and the coaches installed the rest of their offense. I tinkered with my passing technique that spring, trying to get rid of the ball a little quicker. I had watched film of some pro quarterbacks and realized I was dropping the ball down too low before delivery, almost as if I were about to throw a baseball. I worked on getting it up, and releasing faster, but I made it a point to alert Coach Cutcliffe, because sometimes when you mess around with your passing motion you develop a hitch and the next thing you know you can't throw at all. It happens more often than you think.

Coach Cut checked me over and said it made sense to him, and when I went home for a few weeks in the summer and showed Dad, he, too, saw the improvement.

I don't say that was a factor; the coaches opening up the offense was what did it. But I threw almost three times as many passes (380) in 1995 for almost three times as many yards (a school record of 2,954 that I broke as a junior), and until I'm the quarterback on a winning Super Bowl team, I won't be able to say I ever enjoyed a season more. We won 11 out of 12, beat Ohio State in the Citrus Bowl and wound up ranked second in the country behind Nebraska in the coaches' (*USA Today*/ESPN) poll and third in the AP's. I set a school record for completion percentage (64.2), and at one point went 132 straight passes without an interception. I later finished sixth in the Heisman vote, a huge kick for a sophomore. It was one of those years you brag to your grandchildren about and they look at you like they know you're lying.

Our only loss was to Florida (imagine that), and I don't think I've ever seen another game quite like it. I *know* I've never been in one. I passed for more than 300 yards and didn't throw an interception. I threw two touchdown passes to Marcus Nash in the first half when it looked like we were going to run away with it. Twice we led by 16 points, and went into intermission at Florida Field ahead by nine, 30–21. We looked absolutely unstoppable. But we weren't. We went into a total swoon in the second half. Florida outscored us 41–7 and won going away, 62–37.

It was a habit, losing to Florida, that dragged on for the next two years, though we made it closer (35–29 in Knoxville, then 33–20 back in Gainesville). Nevertheless, each year we finished in the top ten nationally, and won the SEC championship my last season before losing to Nebraska in the Orange Bowl. We had clearly reached the point where we could beat anybody (Alabama three in a row, for example) and when the Vols won it all—the 1998 National Championship—the year after I left, Coach Fulmer told Dad they "wouldn't have gotten here" were it not for me.

I appreciated that more than he could know, not only out of pride but also because it was a vindication of the work ethic I believe so strongly in—and have had the temerity to push on my teammates. By that sophomore season I was already just as big a pest in Knoxville as I had been at Newman High. I was always after my guys to go the extra mile, usually in the form of unsupervised summer and off-season workouts that most players loathe. Not Tennessee's.

They responded. So much so that I sometimes got carried away—too carried away to suit the Tennessee coaches. I put up signs: "Throwing at 5:30, Seven-on-Seven" (meaning the seven offensive players involved in pass plays versus the seven defensive players who would ordinarily defend against them). Or "One-on-One Drills, 5:30 Wednesday. Mandatory!"

When they saw what was happening, the coaches tore the signs down. They said, "You can't have 'mandatory' work-outs in the summer, Peyton. It's against NCAA rules." So I changed the wording, only half kidding: "Mandatory VOL-UNTARY Workouts." They said no to that, too.

I said, "What the hell am I supposed to do? We need the work. I can't go around knocking on doors trying to find guys to practice."

What I should have done was change the signs to read: "Keg party, 5:30 P.M. Bring your cleats." There wouldn't have been a single no-show.

Another time I locked horns with the athletic director, Doug Dickey, on much the same issue. I'd organized some perfectly legal off-season throwing with the quarterbacks and receivers in the school's $10 million indoor facility, but on this one rainy day the baseball team came in to practice, and the baseball coach insisted we keep to an area that limited us to about fifteen yards of turf space.

We started, and pretty soon we were using twenty-five yards, then thirty. More complaints, and now I really got riled. I'd gotten the receivers primed and ready, no small accomplishment in the off-season, and now I'm being told we can't work? The next thing I knew, Doug Dickey was there to arbitrate—mainly, it seemed, to point out that this was "the baseball season and you'll have to wait your turn."

I got huffy, and pushed my case a little too hard, telling him something he already knew: that the sport that paid the bills was football and football deserved a little more consider-ation in situations like this. I said, "The reason we've been throwing the ball so well in games the last couple years is because of the work we do in the off-season. If you're telling me we can't throw, you're cutting into our chances to win."

It was overkill, and Dickey got his dander up. But he was also sympathetic, to a point. He'd been a star quarterback in college himself (at Florida), and had been head coach at Tennessee for six years, winning two SEC championships. His Vol team beat Dad and Ole Miss, 31–0, in 1968—and Dad's beat his 1969 Vol team, 38–0. So even though the negotiations were not exactly cordial, he agreed to a compromise. He gave us an extra five yards.

As Dad says, to call me "a little stubborn" is to call Niagara Falls a little wet, and by the end of that sophomore season I had made up my mind about something else. I went into my junior year fully determined to make it my last at Tennessee—to declare for the NFL draft when the season was over. A lot of players are doing that nowadays, too many times sacrificing their education in the process, but it made sense for me because I had been just as resolute with my studies as with my football and was poised to get my degree a year ahead of schedule. I'd be out the same time Ashley graduated.

But as a team, we weren't as good as we thought we'd be in '96. Besides the Florida loss, we got upset by Memphis State, and after the Citrus Bowl game when we beat Northwestern to finish 10–2, I felt unfulfilled enough (for a number of reasons) to be having second thoughts about leaving early. Ordinarily you wouldn't have time for second thoughts. The pros always made underclassmen declare for the draft in January, only a couple weeks after the bowls. But through a special academic exemption for graduates, the NFL now was allowing you to declare in April. I gave myself more time to decide.

I completed graduation requirements in the spring, loading up on my communications major and dropping my business minor. But the answer to my turning pro seemed more elusive than ever. I was bouncing back and forth like a volleyball. I'd be hanging out with the players in Knoxville and thinking, "This is just too good. I'm staying." Then I'd go home to New Orleans, tap into some of the people Dad wanted me to discuss it with, and say to myself, "That's it, I'm going." Back and forth, back and forth.

Dad arranged for me to talk with a whole lineup of sports figures, some who had faced the same dilemma. I reached most of them by phone from his office: Roger Staubach, Fran Tarkenton, Hank Stram, Troy Aikman, Bernie Kosar, Drew Bledsoe, Michael Jordan, Rick Mirer, Phil Simms. And the more I talked, the more I realized I didn't want to go pro yet. I found myself twisting every argument that said "go" into a reason to stay.

Bledsoe, who had left Washington State as a junior, said he hadn't wanted to stick around because State had a bad team coming back. I thought, "But that won't be true in my case. We could have our best team at Tennessee." Bledsoe said he also knew he'd be the NFL's first pick in the draft, so it was a no-brainer. I said to myself, "Yes, but you don't know how much fun I'm having at Tennessee, and how much more I'd like to have." Troy Aikman advised me to go, but told of the pride he felt in making first-team All-America his senior season. I hadn't done that yet, and making All-America to me was a bigger deal than being a high draft choice. The former is based on what you've done, the latter on what you *might* do. Being the number one draft pick is an honor, but not a trophy.

Stram and Tarkenton both brought up the dreaded "injury factor." If I played another year in college and got hurt, how many millions would it cost me? I said to myself, "Yes, but Dad has been taking out generous insurance policies to cover some of that, and I wouldn't be doing it for the money anyway. And if I sacrifice that final year at Tennessee, how could money buy what I might miss?" The thought of having a pro career aborted by injury was never really a factor in my thinking. I had Cooper in mind when I told the questioning media, "Injuries are a fact of life in football that you learn to accept. But all of life is a gamble. Heck, the roof could fall on me while we're doing this interview."

Phil Simms encouraged me about my qualifications to go pro. "I've seen you," he said, "and you're ready." But I identified more with Mirer when he said he wouldn't give anything for the senior year he had at Notre Dame. He talked about friendships that meant so much to him (as mine were now beginning to mean to me). Jordan dwelled almost exclusively on the contract I'd be getting. He assumed I was going pro and he talked about ways of "protecting your money." He said he never regretted leaving North Carolina early, and if I left, "Don't look back."

And I thought, "Yes, and if I stay, I won't look back either."

One last factor gave me pause. The way the draft would go that year, the New York Jets had the first pick, and Bill Parcells was their new coach. Parcells said he had seen videos of "every pass" I'd thrown as a college player, and that he liked me. And I'd be lying if I said I wouldn't have wanted to play for him. In *New York City*, yet. But Parcells had been quoted saying the Jets were pathetic on defense, and defense was a top priority. I thought, "What if he drafts me, then trades me for defensive help? Or what if he passes me by and I go as the second pick?" The Saints had the second pick. After what Dad went through, I wasn't sure I wanted to take that one on.

At the end, my head was spinning. But that last semester on campus was the clincher. I said to myself, "Hey, I can have one more year of this and still go pro. And won't it be even better for me in the next draft, having been a *four*-year starter at Tennessee? And maybe an All-American to boot?"

I realize that most players with pro potential at that point would have gone for the gold. Especially those who came from nothing and were struggling to help their families. When they go pro early, you have to say, "God bless 'em." But I'd been blessed, too, with parents who could make it possible for me to stay and it not be a burden. And I have to say that when I look back on it now, no dollar amount could equal what that last year in Knoxville meant to me.

I made the decision official on March 6. It was a Tuesday. I'd told Dad the previous Saturday, and he advised me to "sleep on it over the weekend." Monday morning I called him. "I want to stay."

"Good. Mom and I will fly up. Get Bud Ford at the sports information office to call a press conference for tomorrow."

At midday, I was eating lunch in the cafeteria and Coach Fulmer came and sat down beside me. "I understand you've got a press conference tomorrow?"

I said, "Yessir."

He looked at me funny. "Well, I got a speaking engagement in Nashville tomorrow. Do you, uh . . . "

I said, "Coach, you go ahead, but I'm not going to commit until my parents come and we talk face-to-face. I want to be one hundred percent sure, and I don't want to have to eat my words."

I worked out that day, and got asked a lot of questions. Some people thought I was setting it up for a big show at the announcement, but I wasn't. In fact, by then everybody should have already figured it out. I mean, would I be calling a press conference in Knoxville, on the campus of my university, to say, "I'm leaving"? Give me a break.

That night when Mom and Dad got there we closed the issue. I called Cooper and Eli. And about 1 A.M., I called Coach Fulmer. Woke him up. I said, "I'm staying, Coach." He said, "I love you, man!"

Coach Parcells was on my short list to phone. He was nice as could be. He said what I was doing was "refreshing," and wished me luck.

A couple of New York writers implied in stories that I might have been a little wary of the NFL at that point. Or that I didn't want to face being a backup. I thought to myself, "You just haven't spent enough time on the campuses of the SEC to realize what we have down here." I freely and gladly admit it: I wanted to put the same exclamation point on my college days with the same joyful experiences my father had at Ole Miss. I just wish I'd started the process earlier.

That fourth year I got some of the bonding with my friends that Dad had always talked about. And like him, not just with football players. I double-dated with Ashley and other couples. I hung out with the guys. We went camping and hunting. We lived in apartments, went on spring break together, took trips to Cancun, to Las Vegas. I'd never done any of that, because I been doubling up on my studies. Anytime I could afford a little vacation break, I just went home to New Orleans. I did enroll in graduate school that last summer. With a very light schedule.

At the press conference, one guy asked me what I was "getting" to stay, as if there had to be more to it than met the eye.

I said, "A scholarship, room and board, and the right to call one play a game. I also get to drive Coach Fulmer's Lexus."

Nothing happened during that season to make me regret my decision. To the contrary. But I had a terrific case of first-game jitters that sure made me wonder.

We opened with Texas Tech, a team we figured to beat easily. On the first play I completed a 15-yard pass—and our center, a "bonded" friend of mine, Trey Teague, was flagged for a *personal foul*, of all things. The officials brought the ball back and docked us 15 yards. I said to Trey, "How could you *do* that on the first play of the season? There's nothing to be mad about yet." He gave me a shrug. Neither one of us could believe it.

We then went three-and-out, and on our second possession I threw a terrible pass from about our 10-yard line and Tech picked it off and went in to score.

I thought, "Why am I here? Why did I stay?"

But the listing ship quickly righted itself. I wound up with five touchdown passes in the game and we won easily, 52–17. Afterward, Dad reminded me of what Michael Jordan had said: Don't look back. He added his own admonishment: "You've made your choice, live with it. Enjoy it."

We beat UCLA in Los Angeles the next week, but shakily, having to hold on at the finish to pull it out. Leonard Little, a great defensive end and my co-captain, stripped the ball from a UCLA back and we recovered to stop a possible winning touchdown drive. The next week we went back to Gainesville for our annual loss to Florida, which we accomplished despite the fact that I threw three touchdown passes. But after that we ran the table: Ole Miss, with Mom and Dad in the stands trying to decide who to cheer for (they cheered for me, naturally) . . . Georgia . . . Alabama . . . South Carolina . . . Southern Miss . . . Arkansas . . . Kentucky (where I passed for a record 545 yards and five touchdowns) . . . Vanderbilt.

For the season, I threw more passes than ever—477, completing 287 for 3,819 yards, all school records—belying my own conviction that a team wins on balance. But we had such great receivers that Coach Cutcliffe couldn't resist. Marcus Nash led the SEC with more than a thousand yards in receptions. Jermaine Copeland and Peerless Price (that's really his name, and it's appropriate) were not far behind. We actually passed the ball a hundred times more than we ran it, and for 2,000 yards more than we gained on the ground. Of course, we didn't have the stable of great running backs we'd had before either. The bulk of our ground game was left to a freshman star-in-the-making, Jamal Lewis, a 220-pounder who could fly. If it hadn't been for Jamal, we'd have probably passed every down. (Just kidding, Coach Cut.)

We won our last eight in the regular season, then came from behind in the fourth quarter to beat Auburn by a point in the SEC championship game in Atlanta. We rallied from being down by 10 midway the third quarter in that one, and I threw 73 yards to Marcus for a touchdown in the fourth to put us ahead for good. It was one of four touchdown passes I had for the day, and they voted me the game's Most Valuable Player.

That night a whole crew of us made the rounds in downtown Atlanta, singing "Rocky Top" at every croaky key and at every stop. I got a lot of hugs from Tennessee fans we ran into, thanking me for having stayed. I said, "Listen, *I'm* the one who's thankful. I wish I could stay another four years."

The next morning I could barely get out of bed, but not

for, well, "spiritual" reasons. My knee had blown up like a watermelon. I had to think twice to remember what did it. The answer wasn't very sensational: I slammed my knee into the artificial turf when I got hit from behind trying to make a tackle on an Auburn player who was running with a fumble. At the time, I didn't think it was all that bad; I didn't even leave the game. But it turned out I'd busted a bursa sac, and I couldn't treat it or rest it because the next day I had to limp around New York at one of the awards ceremonies.

Right after that I had to go to Orlando for another, then Louisville for another, then back to New York. And by the time I made it home to Knoxville, the knee was infected and aggravated enough to where I had to be hospitalized for five days.

Ironically, it was my first real injury in four years at Tennessee. Not a career-ender by any means (that would have been *too* ironic), but serious enough at that point to make my playing status questionable for our Orange Bowl date with top-ranked Nebraska. I didn't get the okay until two days before, but I played—it was, after all, a chance for us to win the national championship. A slim chance, but a chance.

Unfortunately, I played more as a liability than an asset. My knee hadn't improved enough, and I had to wear a brace, and for most of the game I struggled. I wound up giving way at the end to my backup, Tee Martin. And we wound up getting routed, 41–17. I doubt it would have mattered what shape I was in, though. Nebraska was too strong, too good, too everything. The Cornhuskers weren't "balanced" either—they rushed for more than 400 yards and only passed to let us know they could.

It was a downer for an ending, and in deference to the injury, I passed up all the postbowl all-star games. But in almost every other way, I'd had the season I'd wished for. My cup ran over when the season superlatives were announced. I won the Maxwell Trophy, the Davey O'Brien Award, the Johnny Unitas Golden Arm Award, the National Football Foundation Draddy Award, the NASDAQ Scholar-Athlete Award, et cetera, et cetera. And I *did* make first-team All-

America, on all the teams that mattered, from the Associated Press's to the Football Writers Association's. But if they told me I'd have to trade the enjoyment I had that year for all the glittering hardware, I'd say take away the hardware. Reluctantly.

Conspicuous by its absence from the above list is the Heisman Trophy, which a lot of people seemed to think I'd win hands down. But I didn't. And I didn't cry over it, even if I should have (for no other reason than the hurt it caused in Tennessee). Because I think I learned enough, from close up, to understand it—without necessarily liking it much. It's something you accept as "the way things are."

Some thought the Heisman was the reason I stuck around that fourth year. Not true. I'd be lying if I said I wasn't disappointed finishing second to Charles Woodson, the Michigan defensive back, but at that point I didn't expect it, and when Woodson's name was called it was no surprise. I'd already gotten a strong feel for how it worked, mostly as confirmation of doubts I'd heard expressed by others. I'd been voted sixth as a sophomore, a thrill, but then eighth as a junior, and was by my senior year a tad skeptical. When I had my best passing day ever against Kentucky, I went *down* in the weekly poll of Heisman voters, and I remember thinking, "What's going on here?"

I know my dad was skeptical, too, but he kept saying I'd win. He and I were in Louisville for the Johnny Unitas Award the Friday night before the Heisman Trophy weekend, and we were in our room watching ESPN's *SportsCenter* when the hosts started talking about the Heisman. One of them said, "Peyton Manning is the odds-on favorite." Dad said, "See, Peyton? These guys know what's going on."

And I didn't mean to, but I got short with him. "Dad, I'm *not* going to win the frigging trophy. Read the papers. It's going to Woodson."

It was the first time I showed any frustration over it, but I really did understand where it was heading.

So when Mom and Dad and I got to the ceremony in New

York, it wasn't only my knee that bothered me. I was tired of the whole business (that being what it mostly is, I'm afraid). And while there, I have to say I didn't much care for the attitude of some of the people involved. I thought they were rude, and the event poorly organized. From almost the minute I arrived, I wanted to go home. When the announcement was made, I remember being glad it was over—but at the same time sad for Tennessee fans. Another runner-up without a Heisman to call their own. Johnny Majors, Hank Lauricella, and Heath Shuler had just missed, and now I was the fourth.

But I think if you're honest about it, you have to take the Heisman with a grain of salt, because it *is* so political and because it is so subject to conditions. Nobody seems to know for sure what it represents. I mean, is it really for that one year of accomplishments, or does a player's entire career factor in? How much do character and leadership count, if at all? (They should, but the evidence suggests otherwise.) How much does it mean to be on a "better" team (i.e., one that wins a lot of games)? Or even from a "better" school? Paul Hornung won it back in the '50s on a Notre Dame team that lost eight out of ten. Would he have won if he played for Colorado State?

The politics of regional considerations are ridiculously obvious. If a wide receiver from UCLA wins the Heisman one year, you're not going to see a wide receiver from Southern Cal win it the next. It'll be a fullback from Alabama, or a running back from Nebraska. There's only one Heisman, unfortunately, and they parcel it around. I knew my chances were slim from the beginning because Danny Wuerfful, the Florida quarterback, had won it the year before. Did anybody seriously believe they'd select two SEC quarterbacks in a row? Compounding the problem nowadays is that there's so much lobbying from so many vested interests. ABC and ESPN pushed Woodson. You can't blame them; they had the Rose Bowl coming up and he'd be in it. But does that mean if you're not going to *any* bowl, with no potential affiliations, that your chances drop? Is all this just too mind-boggling or what?

Dad, who had finished third to Jim Plunkett in the 1970 Heisman vote, says if I'd won I'd feel differently about it twenty years from now. A memory to cherish down the road. Flawed as it is, the Heisman Trophy still represents great achievement. Dad also likes to say in that regard, that for the Heisman's sake it's important that the trophy, in turn, be represented well. That when they have a big reunion of past winners, you want to see the likes of Roger Staubach and Earl Campbell and Steve Owens, not only because of how great they once played but because of, well, the stature they give the statue. He was definitely turned off in New York when he saw three or four former Heisman winners drunk as skunks at the presentation.

But as it is, the politics are always going to get mixed in, even if the voters try their best to keep them out. Dad and I share a common belief that too often that's the nature of individual awards given in "team" sports, where mutual effort is the key ingredient and the award recipient is really little more than the front man. Especially in football, the ultimate team game. Yes, I'm very proud to have been honored so highly so often, but I agree with Dad that my teammates were as deserving as I, and that too much of team sport has evolved into pandering to the individual. And worse, to individual self-absorption.

Television has been a big influence in this. You see a guy make a sack on the screen, and the next thing he's dashing 10 yards downfield so he can get in a few disco moves to draw more attention to himself. And while he's there dancing away, you look at the scoreboard and his team's losing, 30–3. Which tells you that either the guy's so stupid that he doesn't know the score, or that he really doesn't care about his team at all. I just don't get the practice of celebrating something you're expected (or even paid) to do—make a tackle, make a sack, make a catch. It tears me up.

I feel the same when I see teammates of mine laughing

and cutting up after a loss. Not that they ought to commit suicide or wear sackcloth and ashes on the team plane home, but you'd think they'd have a little more remorse, or at least some respectful silence over a common effort that failed. Maybe even stop to reflect on their own contributions, good or bad. Sure, if you see a friend from the other team on the field afterward you want to exchange pleasantries. But when you get your butt beat, more often than not you should just say, "Nice game, congratulations," and make your exit as inconspicuously as possible.

I don't think fans who have paid all that money to support a pro or college team enjoy watching players celebrate after a defeat. If the name on the shirt means something to them, it should mean at least as much to the player. And that's true at any level, no matter how high the price of a ticket. In the pros, of course, it's *much* higher, and the loyalty problem is getting much worse. Now that I am one (a pro), I have to say my feelings haven't changed a bit. If anything, they've gotten stronger.

Tennesseeans made much more over me than I deserved after that final game. They retired my jersey. They had a life-size mannequin sculpted and included with an exhibit of my career in the Tennessee Hall of Fame at the athletic complex. I don't think it looks much like me, but maybe that's a good thing. I go by and glance in now and then, just to make sure I haven't been replaced. And as I said, they named the hundred-yard street and walkway the team takes from the athletic complex to the stadium on game days "Peyton Manning Pass," which I really did appreciate because nobody loved that walk more than I.

Most of life goes by in a blur, but I'll remember that last one—down the hill, down the little street, and into Neyland Stadium—in detail for the rest of my life. (Actually, it was more memorable than the game, an unimpressive 17–10 victory over Vanderbilt which we seemed to play in a blur, too.) Coach Fulmer led, as always, and as always I made it a point to be one step behind. The band was playing "Rocky Top" and the cheerleaders were cheering another impending victory, and you could feel the fans' excitement building. I remember looking to see if my parents and grandparents were there, and getting chills when I saw they were. Dad could relate—a different time and place, but the same feelings. It was the kind of thing that every time I did it, I wanted to go back and do it again.

Yes, I got emotional. Yes, I cried. I always kissed Mom as I passed her, and she was crying, too. I thought about what I would do when we went on the field through the "T" that the band forms as a pregame tradition. I knew I didn't want to go too fast and miss anything. I knew, too, I didn't want to dance around like a clown in front of 106,000 people. So all I did was tuck my helmet under my arm as I came through, wave to both sides of the stadium, and jog on out. Not very original, but I'll never forget the cheering. I thought it would go on forever.

I have a ton of vignettes stored away in memory of that season that I'll be passing on one day to *my* children and grandchildren.

I remember before the opening game, giving the team my inaugural "captain's speech." I remember mainly that I kept it short. We'd had captains who just jabbered away, forgetting how brief the attention spans are for most college kids. I said our goal was to "win every game." Somebody interpreted that later as suggesting I had stayed the extra year "to win a national championship." I said that was dumb, even if all you considered were the odds against it. But if I had said that and we *didn't*, wouldn't I be obligated to feel bad about my last days at Tennessee? I sure didn't want that.

I remember after our third straight victory over Alabama, when I'd been kept on the field for a TV interview. The Tennessee band director grabbed me and said, "Wanna lead the band?" I'd already missed the team celebration in the locker room, so I said, "Sure. Rocky Top?" And he got down and I climbed up the ladder and started waving my arms like John Philip Sousa. I thought I was doing a great job until I looked back and saw the director furtively working his baton.

I remember being in the huddle against Arkansas, trailing late in the fourth quarter on a very cold night in Little Rock, and thinking, "If I don't hit this next pass (it was third and 10) we won't get the ball back. It'll be over." We were heading toward the SEC showdown with Auburn and couldn't afford to lose. The coaches called a 12-yard curl pattern to try for a first down, but in the huddle I told Marcus Nash, "Their corners have been playing us tight all day. If he [the defensive back on Marcus's side] sits on you, I'm going up top," meaning deep. Sure enough, the cornerback lined up too close, Marcus zipped by him, and I threw a 60-yarder for the winning touchdown.

I also remember Steve Spurrier's comment after we lost to Florida again, but I'd as soon forget it. He said, "Now Peyton Manning has a chance to be a three-time Most Valuable Player . . . of the Citrus Bowl." I thought for a head coach to trash a player like that, especially after winning the game, didn't show much class. We shook hands afterward but he didn't look me in the eye. If I saw him today, though, I'd be nice. He had, after all, tried to recruit me four years before. Maybe he forgot. Besides, the way coaches bounce around in the NFL, I might wind up playing for him some day.

And, too, I remember the Ole Miss game in Knoxville, worrying about how listless we were in warm-ups, like we were still thinking Florida, and me saying, "Guys, let's take advantage of this time in college. If you're looking forward to the NFL, remember that the NFL is work, not fun"—I didn't know at the time that the NFL could be fun, too; I was going by all those years Dad twisted in the wind—"so the hell with last week's loss. We'll go from here to the conference championship." Which we did.

Dad and Mom were there, on pins and needles. It was, after all, Mississippi we were playing, with all that meant in past "ups" and recent "downs." As it turned out, we won both the Ole Miss games Coach Fulmer had "promised" weren't on our schedule when he recruited me. We won in

Knoxville that day and the year before in Memphis. John Grisham sat with Mom and Dad in Memphis, probably discussing what character he was going to name after Dad in his next novel, and everything came to a happy ending. Dad said they never heard a negative word either game, and haven't since. (Eli's matriculation probably had something to do with it.) Case closed. At last.

I don't know how you could possibly sum up those four years with a statistic, but I have one that works for me. I was told later by Ellie Wilson in the sports information office, who handled requests for such things, that I signed more than 250,000 autographs in my years at Tennessee. Dad was as proud of that as I was, because he knew it to be an expression of mutual appreciation. He also knew "big-time" athletes are inclined to be big-time jerks when it comes to that kind of thing. After he quit playing and was doing color for the Saints' broadcasts, I'd go down to the locker room with him after games—I was maybe eleven or twelve—and he'd *still* get besieged for autographs. And never once did he storm through saying, "No autographs today!" the way some athletes do.

I realize it's hypocritical when I say this, because I get paid, too, at autograph shows, but I don't think it's right to charge for acknowledging someone's allegiance and affection. If I was outside on the street after one of those shows, and someone came up and asked me to sign a football or a jersey or something, I'd do it. It's a way to give something back. I think that's why in the end, the recognition I appreciated most (besides "first team All-America") was the Sullivan Award, given to the top amateur athlete not just for what he does in sports but for what he does in school and in the community. Not every Heisman winner has been a model citizen. The Sullivan people honor you for at least trying to be one, as well as for being a good player. They vote on it for reasons I hold dear.

A lot of people will read that and say, "Aw, you're just saying that." No, I'm saying it because I mean it. Whether

I'm believed or not doesn't matter. If nothing else in life, I want to be true to the things I believe in, and quite simply, to what I'm all about. I know I'd better, because it seems whenever I take a false step or two I feel the consequences. Like with the "mooning" incident that made such a stir in Knoxville before my junior year. Cooper would have sailed through it unscathed. Not me.

The way it happened, Tennessee had hired a female trainer, and never mind that women in the men's locker room is one of the most misbegotten concessions to equal rights ever made. When Dad played, there was still at least a tacit acknowledgment that women and men are two different sexes, with all that implies, and a certain amount of decorum had to be maintained. Meaning when it came to training rooms and shower stalls, the opposite sex was not allowed. Common sense tells you why.

I admit that even in the context of "modern" life, what I did to offend this trainer was inappropriate. Not exactly a criminal offense, but out of line. I certainly didn't dislike her. I thought she had a vulgar mouth, but I always tried to be nice. A couple times I went out of my way to help her, once giving a talk to a group at her invitation, another time when I was at the University of Virginia visiting Ashley and she was there with some young athletes who needed to be escorted to a party. I agreed to do it for her.

Then one day I was in the training room and a track athlete I knew made some off-color remark that I felt deserved a colorful (i.e., Cooper-like) response. I turned my back in the athlete's direction and dropped the seat of my pants. Cooper would have applauded, whether the trainer saw it or not. He'd been mooning people since he was twelve years old— out the back of buses, out car windows, wherever he felt the urge. He's the mooning champion of the world.

But I did it thinking the trainer wasn't where she would see. (Cooper would have done it so she *could* see.) Even when she did, it seemed like something she'd have laughed at, considering the environment, or shrugged off as harmless. Crude, maybe, but harmless. But as luck would have it, this particular trainer had been accumulating a list of complaints against the university that she intended to take action on—alleged sexist acts that, when her lawyer finally put it together, resulted in a lawsuit charging thirty-five counts of sexual harassment. In the end, the university settled with her for a good bit of money. My "involvement" made headlines.

It's all past history now, of course, but it hurt me. Probably much more than it should have. I'd have to say that in such cases it's easier being Cooper.

So with the four years at Tennessee over and all the facts in, how would I advise other players who come to that juncture before their senior seasons with a chance to make a lot of money if they turn pro early? Not because I did it, but I think even the NFL would prefer there be a rule (one that would stand up legally) that players *have* to finish their four years—develop to the max as athletes, but get their degrees as well, because too many leave early now and go bust in the pros, shorting out both ways.

And you have to know colleges would prefer that everybody play through their eligibility, because it's so disruptive to the team when players are counted on and bolt. It's costly for the university, too, having spent all that money recruiting and educating them. You could also argue that when a kid leaves early, ninety-nine times out of a hundred he'll never get that degree that could matter so much to him if he doesn't make it in the pros. Which the vast majority don't.

The flip side is that there are kids in the system who simply can't afford to stay. And a lot more now who don't intend to. And when the money gets piled under their noses, they really have no choice. It's a different world from when Dad played. The colleges now serve as one big farm system for the pro leagues, and a lot of hotshot athletes use it just that way, never really appreciating college life, never concentrating on their education (except enough to stay eligible). The dollars make the difference.

So maybe it's time to end the pretense, on both sides. Maybe it's time for the pros to put some of the millions they throw around into a real minor league that will allow good athletes who have no hope or interest in a college education to prepare in a more realistic (and more honest) way. Maybe it's time for the colleges either to be a lot more selective with their recruits or to make the recruits sign contracts that will refund all the money that's lost when they go for the gold early.

Because the bottom line is, there is no single rule that could be written to solve the current dilemma. The big gamble goes on, with imperfect choices all around.

Meanwhile, I had gone through my own gamble and come out the other side, having had my cake and eaten it, too. I was no longer going to be playing the game I love so much for fun. I was going to be playing it for money. A lot of it. Welcome to the National Football League.

10

Of the hundreds of outstanding players then eligible, Peyton Manning was chosen first, by the Indianapolis Colts, in the 1998 National Football League draft. The Colts then made him the highest-paid rookie in the history of the league. Figuring everything, the contractual dollars for the six-year deal totaled 38 million; were he to reach all the additional incentives (making the top five in the league in touchdown passes, top five in yardage, et cetera, et cetera, which now seem to have been foregone conclusions) the grand total would come to $48 million. Or about $7.9 million a year. Or about $8,000 every time he brought his team up to the line of scrimmage. Or about $14,400 every time he threw a forward pass. When his father was picked second in the 1971 player draft, he, too, signed the "largest contract ever given a rookie"—for $410,000 over five years, or $82,000 a year. Peyton would be making ninety-six times that. When he talked about this breathtaking dichotomy, Archie Manning could not help but smile, not only at the surrealism ("Can anybody relate to such money?") but at how little impact it had on his son. He was proud to say that Peyton Manning made an unlikely multimillionaire.

From the beginning, Peyton deliberately stayed a step removed from the process. Tom Condon of IMG handled the negotiations with the Colts, and Frank Crosthwait, our lawyer friend, oversaw everything. I served as a kind of go-between. Peyton knew what was happening; he knew what the figures were. But they were not something he dwelled on, except in the comparative sense (being the hard-nose competitor that he is, he wanted to be paid no less than he was worth, whatever that might be). When the deal was closed, Tom was excited about it, and, obviously, so were Frank and I. But for Peyton it was almost as if it was happening to somebody else. He just wasn't going to let it be a life-changing influence.

The biggest purchase he made for a good while afterward was $200 for a a cowboy hat when we were vacationing in Wyoming. He topped that a little later when he bought cowboy boots for his entire offensive line, totaling about $6,000. Then he splurged and paid for Cooper and Ellen's honeymoon in Paris, for which the bills are probably still coming in. He was funny. At the rehearsal dinner, he said, "When I told them I'd pay for their honeymoon, I thought they were thinking along the lines of Destin or maybe Panama City." He said he noticed one change in going out with his old buddies from Tennessee and New Orleans. "Now nobody else reaches for the check." But he said it like he was glad to be the one who does.

I think what happened was that Peyton knew he'd never had a real job in his life and was now worth half the budget of some third-world countries, and down deep he didn't quite see the equity in it. That's why he has moved so forcefully into his Peyback Foundation to benefit children, and all the other charitable things he does. He wants to do something for Newman High, for his university, for his hometown. As a Christian, he wants to walk the walk. Up till now, he still hasn't bought the big mansion on the water, or the Maserati, or the diamond-studded nose ring, heaven forbid. He did decide to build a house in a nice section of Indianapolis, mainly as an affirmation of his bond with the city. That's important to him. But his is still a long way from an ostentatious lifestyle.

Appearances are only part of it, of course. Peyton cares how people perceive his actions. Especially fans, who might not resent all the money players make these days but have every reason to resent the way they flaunt it. Things they do that say, "Look at me, I've got it and you don't." I read the other day about one—an Ole Miss grad, I'm sorry to say—who at the Super Bowl rented a $1,000-a-day Lamborghini to tool around in. You say, well, it's his money. But what kind of message does that send? Football is a blue-collar sport. Blue-collar fans want to identify with their favorites on the field, who are at least partially paid by their ticket purchases. Can they identify with that? And when they no longer can, will they still be fans?

Peyton's money comes in stages, of course, and when he got the first $2 million (isn't it amazing how the numbers roll off your tongue, like it's Monopoly money?) he just put it in a bank and went on up to Indianapolis to practice football. It bothered him that his contract was such a public matter, down to the last subparagraph. He didn't want it to be an issue with the players. Like me trying to hide my Continental years before, he didn't want attention for the wrong reasons. He knows you can't really "earn" the kind of money he's getting, but he wanted his teammates to know he was going to try his darnedest, without being a prima donna.

He practiced as hard or harder than anybody to make sure there'd be no doubts. He low-keyed everything else. He said the first thing he wanted to establish was his team's respect. He shared a locker with a rookie free agent, the way rookies normally do, and told Craig Kelley, the PR man, that if an interview or commercial had to be done, he'd do it when his teammates weren't around and not have it rubbed in their faces. As a result, nothing negative happened. No undercurrents, no wisecracks. Before one of the preseason games, a teammate nicknamed him "Powerball," after the big-money lottery game, and he took it as a positive—like, "Hey, Manning, you're okay. You're a rookie, and you're loaded, but we accept you. Let's play ball."

The route that got him to that point carried through all the now-familiar NFL rituals. The primping and eyeballing that go on at the special workouts teams hold for individual prospects, then the big "combine" super-workout (the part Peyton calls "one huge meat market") held every February in Indianapolis before the NFL draft. Then the draft itself in mid-April, when fortunes are won on the whim of a selection made in the first or second round—or lost on the whim of a selection made a round or two later, the figures seemingly based only on *when* you're chosen, not why. And finally the ridiculous cat-and-mouse games management plays during contract bargaining to wear down a player's resolve. Peyton kept shaking his head because it's all so given over to impressions instead of performance.

Word was out well before the draft that either he or Ryan Leaf, the Washington State quarterback, would go number one. The Colts had "won" first pick by having the worst record in the league the year before, which is why they call it the "equalization draft": the worst team gets to pick first, the next worst second, and so on in an annual (if forlorn) effort to balance the competition. With the Colts' recent history of nonachievement, however, we were advised more than once that Peyton should make it clear he wouldn't sign if they drafted him. That he would "pull a John Elway." The Colts were also on the bottom when Elway was eligible for the 1983 draft, and he threatened to sit out a year and play pro baseball if they picked him first. Elway's agent used a vaguely familiar example of what can happen when a player gets mired on a losing team. He said, "I don't want John Elway to be the next Archie Manning."

Actually, as I understood it, a major factor was Elway's father, who didn't want John to play for Frank Kush, then the Colts' head coach. But things had changed since then. The Colts were still struggling, but Kush was long gone, and Jim Mora, a man I'd gotten to know and respect when he coached in New Orleans, was the new head coach. Jim Irsay had taken over for his father as club owner and hired Bill Polian as the new president and general manager. Polian had done great things with the Buffalo and Carolina franchises.

Besides, Peyton really didn't have a team he preferred

over the others. He wasn't a "fan" of any of them. He knew
Mora, too, and liked him. Obviously the Colts were feeling
the same about Peyton, or at least about Peyton and Leaf.
And Peyton really didn't want to go the Elway route. He
wanted to make a more positive entrance into the league. He
talked to Elway about it. John reminded him that the Colts
drafted him anyway, then traded him to Denver.

Tom Condon, meanwhile, had done his due diligence on
the Colts and determined they'd be a good place to land. He
had checked various trade possibilities that could spin off
the number one pick and judged them unlikely. Tom knew
the game; he was a former player himself—a guard for thirteen years with the Chiefs—and had been president of the
NFL Players Association. Peyton chose him after interview-
ing twenty-some other agents because he had a reputation
for fighting hard for his clients without alienating them (or
himself) from management. No easy task. It helped in that
light that he worked for Mark McCormack's group, IMG,
which had been the class act in pro athletes' representation
since McCormack himself had made multimillionaires out
of Arnold Palmer, Gary Player, and Jack Nicklaus years
before. IMG also had Peter Johnson, whom I'd worked with
and who was going to handle Peyton's marketing. It all fit.

So Peyton went into the "draft phase" satisfied that he
was well represented, and that if the Colts really did select
him first, he would be pleased to play in Indianapolis.

*The "combine" is an official tryout conclave where play-
ers earmarked for the NFL draft are invited to come for testing by the various team coaches, scouts, and doctors. Peyton
Manning was among "a select group of about four hundred"
that was assembled two months before the draft of 1998.
After he had gone through it, Peyton agreed with his father
that as a determinant for separating the sheep from the
goats, the process left a lot to be desired. In the end he was
probably appreciated more for what he said afterward than
for anything he did during.*

The combine makes you feel exactly the way I described it to Dad: meat on the hoof. It's all very organized and official looking, and I'm sure a well-trained eye sees things that others wouldn't, but as a test of football attributes, I have my doubts. About the closest thing you get to the game are the shorts they give you to wear that say "NFL" on them. Oh, and a T-shirt that says, in my case, "QB10." Which meant I was Quarterback Number Ten in the cattle run.

You are required to do things at the combine you just wouldn't do playing football: bench presses, 40-yard dashes, vertical leaps (which Cooper and I could *never* do; Eli can, he dunks the basketball), and they give you a physical and a body-fat test. There's a futuristic-looking computer now that some test centers use where they stand you in front of a screen, on a big circle of dots, and when a dot lights up you're supposed to move to it, indicating how well you react. The combine hasn't gotten to that one yet, but they give you an SAT-type written test, and you're obliged to make yourself available for thirty-minute interviews with the team representatives. I abstained from the physical stuff because my knee wasn't up to it yet. It's commonplace now for candidates to find reasons to beg off, but I probably wouldn't have. I thought I was ready for anything.

I did submit to the "beauty" contest—the body exam, height, weight, et cetera, which you do with your shirt off because they measure and probe and yank on your limbs. I was warned that some teams take the way you look seriously, which didn't thrill me. I'd been working out and eating right, and my weight was where I wanted it—230 pounds—but I still wasn't going to be mistaken for Mr. America. So for a finishing touch, I went to a tanning studio a couple days beforehand. As all gym rats know, a good tan enhances body definition. Then, right before I got tested, I sneaked behind a curtain and ripped off fifty push-ups. Real fast. To accentuate my arms and shoulder muscles. (I did *not* apply tanning oil.)

Evidently I made a better appearance than some of the

competition. Ryan Leaf showed up at the combine weighing 262 pounds, a sure sign of a less-than-dedicated off-season regimen. I won't pretend I was disappointed. Charles Woodson, the Heisman winner, left early, and Randy Moss didn't show up at all.

Again, though, I wonder about the whole process—the conclusions that might be jumped to. Say a guy has a great college career, makes all-conference or even All-America, comes to the combine and maybe runs a step slower, or doesn't jump as high. Do they mark him down? Do they draft him at all? Some guys *do* run faster when they're in a game. And some guys *don't* practice well but play terrifically on game day. With all the various skills involved from position to position, football players aren't easy to quantify. I guess that's why so many top picks now say no to the testing. Take us or leave us, but we ain't doing bench presses or chasing lighted dots.

I can understand how a thirty-minute interview might reveal something about a candidate, especially if he's a jerk. You wouldn't want him on your team if that were the case. But if you already know he's a good player, with a clean record, and you have his coach's recommendation, would you let a relatively brief conversation make a difference? Maybe undermine all the good stuff? I guess the answer would be that every impression helps, but to me it all seems like much ado about too little.

The Colts asked me after the combine if I'd submit to a private workout, in Knoxville, just me and them. Private workouts are allowed as long as they're held on the player's college campus. I hesitated but said okay, and we arranged to do it in the indoor complex at ten in the morning on April 1, a couple weeks before the draft. No media, no artificial attention. I got Marcus Nash to come catch for me so I could throw to good hands, and we got there about nine-fifteen to loosen up. Five minutes later, through the double doors, came seven members of the Colts' ruling family, including Bill Polian and Jim Mora, Offensive Coordinator Tom Moore and Quarterback Coach Bruce Arians. An entourage.

I told them I was ready, and one of them gave me two brand-new NFL footballs to throw.

I said, "No thanks. I've got my own."

"But we'd like you to use—"

"Nope, I've got my own." I didn't want to be throwing new NFL balls. They're hard to grip when they're fresh out of the box and take getting used to. Coaches know that, so the Colts didn't try to change my mind.

There was no official beginning or end. I just started throwing. And that's *all* I did. Drop back and throw. Drop back and throw. It was a good workout, at least for my arm. Jay Norvell, Tennessee's receivers coach, joined Marcus on the receiving end and I about wore him out running downfield. When they were quoted in the papers the next day, the Colts gave a positive but noncommittal answer. They said they "saw what we needed to see." To their credit, they didn't ask me to run or lift any weights, and I sure didn't volunteer.

The fact is, quarterbacks don't have to be great physical specimens. They have to be good athletes, but they don't have to run as fast as wide receivers or be as physical as fullbacks. Some of the great quarterbacks of all time wouldn't turn heads on a beach—Sonny Jurgensen, Bobby Layne, Dan Fouts, to name three. But what you found in them, for all the things they brought to the game, you wouldn't find in a linebacker or a defensive back or a split end. What a quarterback has to do goes way beyond the physical, and is far removed from what other players (and other players in other sports) have to do.

Somebody once said in comparing John Elway with Michael Jordan and Wayne Gretzky that Elway wouldn't match up as an athlete. My dad would argue otherwise, but from a slightly different angle. He thinks Elway might have been the best quarterback ever, not only because of his competitiveness and his intelligence and his strong arm, but because of his great courage and escapability—athleticism on call in a crisis situation. You'd see him in the pocket under heavy pressure, sometimes scrambling to buy a few more seconds but waiting, waiting, waiting until the last moment to get the ball off, *always* giving his receivers maximum time, not just because he instinctively knew what to do, but because he'd learned the hard way how close he could come to getting hammered while doing it. You can't possibly see that kind of athleticism in those agility drills or private pass-and-catch sessions.

What Elway did athletically, Gretzky and Jordan couldn't have done. Good quarterbacks don't get enough credit in that area. No, I take that back. They do. But you have to pay attention. Bear Bryant once said that Joe Namath was the best athlete he ever coached. He didn't say the best quarterback, he said the best *athlete*. Archie Manning, old Dad, was chosen Mississippi's "greatest athlete" in 1992. Not the best quarterback. Not the best football player. The best *athlete*.

As they say, it's academic. Besides everything else, all a quarterback has to know is every play in the playbook as thoroughly as the offensive coordinator. And his receivers as well or better than they know themselves. And an opponent's defensive backs and linebackers almost as well. And he has to be comfortable conducting business with a cyclone of human flesh swirling around him. And 80,000 people screaming in his ears. And with the sure knowledge that he'll get more credit than he deserves when his team wins, and more criticism than anybody else except the coach when it loses. Quarterbacking in a nutshell. More than a few times on the field when I'm tired I've said to myself, "Boy, I'd trade this job in a minute for some other position." But, of course, those thoughts pass.

In all modesty, I really thought I was the best quarterback available in the 1998 draft. And the best football player. I don't say that to brag, I say it because if a number one draft choice doesn't think that way, he shouldn't be number one. And I *wanted* to be chosen first. Not a money thing, a pride thing.

But at the beginning I admit not being so sure about playing for the Colts. The *Indianapolis Star* took a poll to see which quarterback the fans wanted, and Ryan Leaf was their favorite. Not by a wide margin, but their favorite nonetheless. I wasn't all that anxious to go to a town that might not want me. On the other hand, my competitive juices were flowing.

After the meeting in Knoxville, Mr. Irsay sent his private jet to fly me down to his place in Florida for a one-on-one. We talked a long time. I think he liked me; I *know* I liked him. He told me how the organization had been realigned, and where it was heading, and I thought, "Great, but is he telling the same things to Ryan Leaf?" So as I was leaving, I said, "You know, Mr. Irsay, I'll win for you." Just like that. A parting shot.

And I got in the van to the airport and took off.

Irsay said later he remembered those words.

Then, just days before the draft, the Colts brought me to Indianapolis and I met with Polian and Mora. They showed me the new facilities and gave me a rundown on their plans for dealing with the draft and possible free agency acquisitions. When the small talk was over, I said, "Mr. Polian, if you draft me on April 18, I'll be glad to come here. I really will. I'd like to be the quarterback of the Indianapolis Colts."

And I paused and added, "But if you *don't* draft me, I'm going to kick your ass for the next fifteen years."

Meaning precisely what I intended: that whatever team I'd be on would beat the Colts, and I'd be responsible.

I didn't say it disrespectfully, I said it matter-of-factly. I wanted them to know if they didn't draft me they'd be sorry.

I think it shook 'em up a little. Polian said, "Then I guess we ought to draft you."

And Mora grinned and said, "But if we don't, and you go to San Diego, you wouldn't be playing us *every* year."

I said, "Yes, but one way or another I'll keep you out of the Super Bowl."

I made my mind up beforehand that I wouldn't go to New York for the televised draft ceremony unless I knew I was one of the top-two picks, or at least knew what pick I'd be. I told

Dad I wouldn't play that game again. The Heisman ceremony had cured me. The Colts said they'd let me know the week before, on a Thursday.

But Thursday came and went. They said, "We're still deciding. We'll tell you next Wednesday, the week of the draft." Wednesday came, then Thursday, then they said it would be Friday, the day before. By then I was mad. Dad was in Nashville for a speech, but leaving Friday morning to meet me in New York, and Mom and Cooper were on their way from New Orleans. I told Dad to forget it, I wasn't going.

He said, "Look, Peyton, we're all going to be there, so come on and we'll still enjoy the weekend. If you find out before the draft that you're not the first or second pick, you can still go home Saturday morning. But if you *don't* come, and you're picked first, you'll look foolish and you'll make the Colts look bad."

He said he'd talked to Polian and Mora and part of the problem was they were involved in a dispute with the NFL on the disposition of their *second* choice, having to do with the league granting Oakland an extra pick at the end of the first round. It had been a major setback for the Colts, Dad said. Polian was threatening to sue the league.

So I flew to New York on Friday, and went on a media cruise with all the players who'd been invited in. Tom Condon was there, and I was fending off questions about what I knew of the Colts' leanings (nothing I would want repeated) when Tom got a call from Polian with the decision: "We're taking Peyton."

Tom handed me the phone as I thought, "How come they didn't know until now? How could they be so late deciding?" But Polian chirped, "You ready to lead the Indianapolis Colts to the Super Bowl?" and I forgot all about being mad.

I said, "Yessir, I'm ready."

I still think being drafted first is more an honor than an achievement. But it *is* an honor, a great one, because the people who make the decision are putting their money where their mouths are and wouldn't choose you if they didn't think you were the best. Dad found out later that Carolina offered eight players, including two number one draft picks, for the Colts' number one, with the intention of picking me. That's impressive. But it's even more impressive that the Colts turned the offer down.

In the aftermath, media people asked, "Do you really want to play in Indianapolis?" The short answer was "Yes." The unspoken answer was "San Diego had the second pick, and I'm not a California-type guy."

Dad had had a conversation beforehand with Bobby Beathard, the San Diego GM, and Beathard said if the Colts chose Ryan Leaf, the Chargers would definitely take me, so I guess you'd say I was covered, with reservations. My "official" position on going to Indianapolis was that it gave me the chance to do something that had never been done in that town. All of the Colts' real successes—the Unitas era, their championships—were accomplished during their days in Baltimore.

Somebody said, yeah, but what about the endorsements? Wouldn't I be better off in New York playing for the Jets? I said I didn't play football for endorsements, or whether or not a town had marketing potential. More important to me was *who* I was playing for, from the front office to the field. It was still my life, and I wanted it in the hands of the right people. Everything else came second. I said my impression was that "these guys can get it done. Mr. Polian can get it done. Coach Mora can get it done. Coach Moore can get it done. And Mr. Irsay is committed to letting them do it."

I didn't have that kind of confidence in some of the others I'd talked with.

My overall impressions of the draft? Pretty much the same as Dad's. It flies in the face of free enterprise, and puts a player in the position of being a kind of high-priced indentured servant, making millions but with little or no say as to whom he serves. Civil libertarians would be outraged if doctors were "drafted" by hospitals or lawyers by law firms, or if teachers were "traded" from one school system to another without their permission. You'd never hear the end of it.

But who's complaining with the money so huge? And even if they did, I'm not sure what could be done about it, presuming something should be. Congress has given the practice special exemptions even though it makes a joke of restraint-of-trade laws. The long-accepted reason is that without those restrictive covenants competition would polarize—the rich would get richer and the poor would go out of business. The Cowboys and three or four other NFL teams with winning traditions in exciting cities would get all the good football players.

Whether that's true or not is moot because it's been an accepted way of life for so long nobody really knows what would happen otherwise. I know the colleges don't have a draft and the rule *doesn't* apply in college football. The Notre Dames and Oklahomas and Alabamas don't win the national championship every year, and sometimes don't even come close. The talent gets parceled around and you look up and the surprise team on top is Clemson or BYU or Miami or Georgia Tech or Washington or Florida State. Lee Corso once said that "Notre Dame doesn't recruit, it gathers," meaning the much-beloved and well-fortified Irish pretty much get their pick of the litter every year. But they haven't won a national title since the '80s and haven't made the top ten in years.

As Dad would tell you (and he's given it a lot more thought than I have), the irony is that the draft only works as a competition leveler when all things are equal, and all things *aren't* equal. Clubs with superior management rise to the top; others with consistently bad management consistently bring up the rear. It's not hard to reckon. If you have better personnel directors, better coaches, and owners who can afford better players, you'll win.

And when you're better, you deserve to win. The American way.

Players, of course, now have more leverage through free agency, which allows them to entertain offers from other teams when their contracts are up. The result has been a fairly steady stream of player defections, and teams shelling out a lot of money to grab up the defectors. The consequence is all that frantic scrambling you read about when club payrolls get dangerously lopsided (from having bowed to excessive demands) under the salary cap. A lot of owners are now saying to hell with it; we'll build our teams through the draft and try to keep our best players paid enough so they won't bolt. Let's see if it works.

Free agency is also a factor in what Dad calls a critical wearing-away of player loyalties. Pro teams recruit free agents like the colleges recruit high-school prospects, going to great lengths to win them over. They spruce up their facilities, replace the carpet, wine and dine the athletes like they were royalty, and generally try to make them feel "at home," just the way the colleges do. Brett Favre made the grand tour a couple years ago. One of his stops was New Orleans. But instead of a limo, the Saints picked him up in a Chevrolet (the team owner has a dealership), and since the club hadn't moved into its new facilities yet, what Favre saw wasn't very impressive. Everybody moaned about the lack of "presentation," as if it mattered.

It doesn't, Dad says, because this *isn't* college. This is big-money pro sports. Nine out of ten free agents go where they can make the most money. One player, Jumpy Geathers, told the Saints when they courted him, "You guys don't have to send a limo for me. You don't have to take me to Antoine's for dinner, or put me up at the Royal Sonesta. I'm signing with whoever gives me the best deal." An honest man, Jumpy.

None of this sits well with the fans, of course. They don't call it free enterprise, they call it betrayal when a popular player opts to move to a bigger paycheck, especially when he turns down a nice-size contract renewal from the home team to do so. But let's not lose track of the realities. The draft itself strains loyalty, removing on its face the chances of a player "playing for his favorite team." And is there any real difference later on between that player jumping ship and the club trading him away? The knife cuts both ways. Management fires and trades players. Players skip from team to team. "Disloyalty" is a way of life in pro sports.

I think that bothers Dad more than anything. He thinks it might be time to at least think about implementing what advocates call a "territorial" draft, where clubs would have first rights on college players in their mutual geographic areas. If Roger Runningback grew up in Kansas City loving the Chiefs and played his college football at, say, Kansas State, the Chiefs would have first crack. The loyalties would come built in and the fans could relate. The same with Detroit fans getting to watch the star tailback out of Michigan State play for the Lions. Or Atlanta fans cheering the star receiver out of Georgia when he signs with the Falcons.

The obvious problem with it, Dad says, is that they'd have a hard time divvying up territorial rights in areas where you've got a cluster of pro teams, like Southern California. And some parts of the country—the Southeast and Midwest, predominantly—simply have more and better college players, so there'd have to be some kind of formula worked out to make it equitable. You could, of course, allow players to simply declare in advance who they wanted to play for, but that might just take you right back to the problem of the rich getting richer.

I know from my college recruitment exactly how much it matters to the athlete to play for the team of his choice: a lot. I *wanted* to play for Tennessee. Dad *wanted* to play at Ole Miss, and Eli is there for the same reason. But when Dad was drafted by the Saints, and I by the Colts, neither of us could argue that those were teams we were longing to play for. It can work out okay in the end, as it is with me in Indianapolis right now. The bonding is already happening. I'd love it if I wound up playing seventeen years for the Colts the way Dan Marino played seventeen for the Dolphins or John Elway sixteen for the Broncos. Marino and Elway can *only* be identified with those teams.

But whichever way you look at it, the system starts taking its toll on a pro athlete's allegiances going in, no matter how big the money is (maybe that should read "*because* of how big the money is"). Especially if the relationship is adversarial, which too many of them quickly become. In my case, though, even while the money was going to be *very* big, it really wasn't the main issue with me. My goals weren't monetary at all.

So I was hoping my contract negotiations would go smoothly. I didn't want them to be confrontational, and I knew I didn't want to be one of those "shameful holdouts." When I was a kid, and even when I was in college, I'd read about star players holding out for more money and I automatically disliked them. The news would tell how "so-and-so's been out for three weeks over his new contract," and I'd say to myself, "Just go play the game, why don't you? Play because you love it, not because it can make you richer."

It took me one summer, the summer of 1998, to understand. I wound up being a holdout myself. Not much of one by current standards—only four days of training camp, a total of eight practices as they fussed back and forth. And it still bothers me that I did it because I identify with the public's disgust. They see all that money and read about all the wrangling and they say, "What's the difference if you make twenty million or twenty-five? How could that matter in the long run? Hell, I could live the rest of my life on *one* million!"

But I learned—was *taught*, actually—by Tom Condon and Frank Crosthwait and my dad that you have to get market value because when all their income potential is maximized, teams and the league have it structured that way. A balancing act between management and labor that keeps both sides happy and on their toes. They said I'd waited a year for this, to go with all the years I'd played, and my contract had to be done right, even if it meant holding out. (My dad had to work with me pretty hard to get that one down because he knew I didn't like the idea.)

They said I shouldn't sit in on the talks. That it wouldn't be smart. They were right. I'd probably have heard the first offer and shouted, "Yes! I'll take it!" They said it could get ugly. That there'd be some media speculation and criticism when the negotiations dragged. They said I had to be careful what I said. I said I'd rather not say anything, because I didn't want the contract terms to be a public dispute. I just wanted them to be settled and over.

It started, as Dad predicted, with a stall. Bill Polian put off negotiating until training camp was looming, I think assuming there was no way an eager beaver like me would miss camp. Open up football practice and I'm on the doorstep. Management also knows (routinely) that if they drag their feet a little longer and don't get things settled until workouts start, they can say, "Well, we've started, and *he* isn't here. And *he* ought to be."

Which invariably makes the player look bad. Players I talked with said it was always one bluff or delay after another and they didn't like it, either. They said it gets tiresome. Which is the whole idea, I guess.

But the Colts' management was right. I did want to get it over with quickly. I mean, I'd have gone to camp the day after the draft if they had one open somewhere. I was pumped. I'd told Tom Condon, "Just get me there on time." But Dad said after Condon fielded the first Colts offer, "It's not right what they want to pay you, Peyton. You need to let this thing play out."

It took me a while. My only strategy was to stay in New Orleans and keep a low profile, not be out on a golf course in plain view or at some resort looking like I was having too good a time. Tom had weighed everything and had a figure in mind that he knew would be close—a number derived from what the Colts had paid other players in the past few years, and where the market was heading, and what the last quarterback had brought (there'd been a shortage of numberones in recent years). He gave us the figure after the first meeting with the Colts. I thought, "Boy, if I get half that it'll be great!" That's how little I knew.

A couple times when the process dragged I told Dad, "I'm

just going to pick up the phone and call them," and Dad said, "No, you don't want to do that. You have to remember this is not a one-year decision, it's a career decision." In other words, it made sense to just let Condon do what he was being paid to do. I finally told him, "Okay, Tom, if I have to miss some of camp, I'll do it."

The battlefields were in varied locations: Charlotte one weekend, Chicago another, Pittsburgh another. Two or three times the two sides met in Indianapolis. Sometimes their exchanges were bizarre. Once they met at the Canterbury Hotel, where Mike Tyson got arrested, and during the middle of a heated conversation, according to Condon, Bill Polian said, "You're trying to do to me what Tyson did to that girl!"

I was made privy to the content of most of the talks, but I'm not sure it was a good idea. Players are probably better off hearing nothing. Polian, who is a very impressive and intimidating guy, at one point said, "We can't pay Manning that much now because he won't be good enough to deserve it for three or four more years." Not what you'd call a ringing endorsement. I had to say to myself, "Peyton, if he really felt that way you wouldn't have been his first choice. Don't let it get to you. It's all part of the game."

How important was it that I kept a low profile during the holdout? The Saturday the Colts opened training camp, I went out to dinner with my folks at Mosca's restaurant in New Orleans, just to have a good meal and relax a little. I had a beer. One beer. And the next day a reporter from the *Times-Picayune* who had been in the restaurant wrote that Peyton Manning, infamous holdout, was "seen last night with his parents drinking beer at Mosca's." It was duly noted that I did the dirty deed while my teammates were sweating it out in the hot sun in Anderson, Indiana. Great image.

Actually, I had attended, unsigned, the Colts' minicamp in late April, and the May workouts, where you practice without pads (making minimal the threat of injury) as a first step toward familiarizing yourself with the offense. I'd also been poring over the Colts' playbook from the day they issued me one at the draft. But now I was squirming to get in and get on with it. The final sticking points weren't all that clear to me, but Tom Condon and Bill Polian were well matched, and had come to a point near where their limits extended. They settled on everything six days into training camp. I had been an official holdout for one extra-long weekend, from Friday through Wednesday. And during that period the Colts' "bottom line" came up a lot. Enough to suit us, anyway.

In the end I was pleased to say I would *not* be among the vast majority of number one draftees who put off signing until training camp is over, or close to it. Foot-dragging on contracts is epidemic now in the NFL, and it's dumb all around because it delays the necessary assimilation of the player into the "family" on the field. If you don't practice, you don't learn. Edgerrin James's negotiations were dragged out almost until the season started in 1999, and got everybody upset, including Edgerrin, who might very well be the best running back in the league. I know he was upset because he kept telling me how much he wanted to succeed as a rookie, and how frustrated he was not being in camp.

I could sympathize with him, and I only missed days, not weeks.

The difference between Friday and Wednesday, as I understood it from Tom Condon, was about $13 million. On Saturday they were at $35 million for five years; on Monday, they'd agreed to $48 million for six, including incentives and bonuses. "Real money" was $38 million, with the other $10 million in what they call "junk money" for a variety of incentives. Among those were "likely to be earned" incentives, such as my taking thirty percent of the team's snaps (I took one hundred percent) or passing for 1,600 yards (I reached that in six games, and threw for a total of 3,739).

Then there were the "*not* likely to be earned" incentives: finishing in the top five in the American Football Conference (AFC) passing statistics, the top five in touchdown passes, and making Rookie of the Year. As it turned out, I finished in the top five in some of those categories not only in the AFC but in the whole NFL, and set rookie records in completions, yards, touchdowns (26), and consecutive games with a touchdown pass (13). And I was quarterback on the All-Rookie Team.

So I achieved all but one of my incentives: a bonus I would get if the team made the playoffs (which we did the *next* year).

The money included a signing bonus of $11.6 million, to be paid over two years. My actual salaries were to start at the league minimum ($140,000) for my rookie year and accelerate from there. The whole package is divided into three-year segments. If the Colts still want me after three years, they have to come up with another $8.5 million bonus, and the salaries become increasingly significant, capping out at $8 or $9 million. If they don't, I walk away after three with about $16 million. Some walk.

Of course, if we continue to do well, and I'm still healthy, I'd more likely want to sign a new long-term deal before the fifth year, removing the "threat" of my becoming a free agent after the sixth. A way of mollifying both sides.

I offer these contract details not out of hubris—although the sports pages would make you think success is measured that way these days—but because they're already a matter of record. The truth is they make me uncomfortable, and I'm still flabbergasted by the whole thing. When I finally went over the figures with my CPA, John Palguta, I could hardly get my mind around it all. I said, "Boy, just what I'm going to have to pay in taxes is unbelievable!" He said, "Yeah, but imagine if you were playing back when big money earners were taxed at ninety percent." Yes, well . . .

Tom Condon called when the deal was made and said I should pack up and head to Indianapolis. He put Bill Polian on, and Bill couldn't have been nicer. I said, "Just get me on the first flight up there."

They did. I already had my bags packed and flew out that evening. I got into Indianapolis about eleven o'clock, and the gate area was packed with media. Condon and I went from there to St. Elmo's for a late-night celebratory steak. Tom said he'd already eaten there twice that day.

The signing the following morning went without a hitch. Polian seemed happy it was over. He actually volunteered to chauffeur me to camp the next day, up to Anderson on the west fork of the White River, and we talked for an hour about the team and the upcoming season.

I felt when I got in that I'd been careful enough and humble enough through the negotiations not to have ruffled any feathers among the coaches and players, and I'm glad to say that from the first day there was no friction anywhere. I credit Coach Mora for that, too. He'd stayed neutral through the arguments, which I was grateful for because some coaches would have been posturing about the good of the team and saying, "Manning better get his butt in here if he knows what's good for him."

I suspect Mora might have had something to do with speeding up the process at the end, not from anything he told me then but because of something he'd told me before. He pulled me into his office back at the minicamp in April and said the words I was hoping for:

"I want you to hear this from me. You are my starting quarterback, no matter what. We have that kind of faith in you. But I don't want you to think I'm doing you any favors. I'm actually doing you an injustice, because you're a rookie and it's going to be tough on you. But we feel for the future of this team that the way for you to get better as quickly as possible is to play. Experience will be your best teacher."

I thanked him for the "injustice" and told him how much I appreciated it. I appreciated it even more when he stuck with me the entire season, through a lot more bad times than good, and never took me out of a single game.

I arrived in Anderson in the morning and practiced that afternoon, dressed out proudly in jersey number 18, Dad's number from Ole Miss, and the next day we bused over to Champaign, Illinois, to work out with the St. Louis Rams. We practiced with them twice on Friday, once on Saturday morning, then scrimmaged against them Saturday afternoon. Boom, boom, boom, just like that. I never felt awkward, never felt out of place, never felt behind.

The preliminaries were over. And I thanked God and Tom Condon (*and* Bill Polian) that they were. All of it had been awkward, most of it annoying, the so-called negotiation phase. The "business" of the NFL. I'm not comfortable with any of it and totally empathize now when I hear people say, "I like college football better because you don't have to listen to all that money talk and read about all those contract disputes."

I agree with my dad. Pro sports should *never* have opened up the numbers to the public and the media. I know the Players Association did it—starting in the early '80s—so that agents would be able to bargain more effectively, but it winds up making both sides seem greedy and self-serving. Especially the players. "If I don't get so-and-so, I'm sitting this year out." "If you can't pay me what I want, trade me." "If they don't settle this thing soon, I'm going to have to sell one of my Jaguars."

I picture working men and women reading that stuff and I cringe. The sports pages even run the salary lists like they were standings, with the top-paid guy, say Kevin Brown in baseball, making $15.5 million a year, Shawn Green following him at $14 million, and so forth. Like that's the way they should be judged—not by how many pennants they've won but by how much loot they're accumulating. Dad said when he played he never told anybody what he was making—not his roommate, not his best friends, not anyone. He said, "I'm not even sure I told Olivia."

I think the reasons for *not* giving out the figures far outweigh the reason for giving them. Like Dad says, "If we aren't made privy to how much management makes, or how much the team orthopedic surgeon makes, or how much the media guys who feed on this stuff make, why should they know what we make?"

It's all very counterproductive. If I'm a starting defensive end, say, for the Bears, and they sign another end and have to admit they're paying him $500,000 a year more than me, think of the resentment that causes. Or, for that matter, the insecurity. It's bad karma all around, no good at all in a team atmosphere. With it comes the envy and the jealousies, not just among players, either, but among families. And you really can't blame them. I'd be jealous, too, and complaining, too, if I thought the open books made my husband or dad look bad, or made it clear he was being underpaid (though that's a very relative term given the circumstances).

Then, of course, you have the agents, swarming like locusts over pro sports and capitalizing on the windfalls. And not all of them straight-up IMG types, either. Most of those we interviewed were solid, genuine professionals in every way, but some were about as sleazy and unprofessional as they could be, and about as winsome as a meat grinder. Some of them didn't even talk in complete sentences. Couple that with a know-it-all attitude and the manners of a dockworker and you get the picture why their profession is so suspect.

Some agents we talked with had been on television as football experts, guys who never played a down in their lives, or even spent much time around the game until they latched on to a player or two, and they absolutely made you cringe with the stupid things they said. We were with one who had a string of first-round draft choices whom he had represented, and Dad said he kept thinking, "If he handled those other top players, what are we missing here?"

The bottom line, if you'll excuse the expression, is I just don't like to talk about money. And I don't like it when any-body else *wants* to talk about it. I was at a Wendy's in Indianapolis one day after that first season, a place I usually go for the peace and convenience of the drive-through, but this time I'd gone inside to order and I'd signed about ten autographs when a couple of cooks saw me and came over. "Hey, Peyton, what's up, man!" "Hi, guys, how ya doin'?"

And we were talking about signing autographs when one of the managers walked up and saw and heard just enough to be misinformed.

Without looking at me, he said, "Peyton Manning drives through here all the time during football season, and he *always* pays with hundred-dollar bills."

The two cooks didn't say anything, just let him plunge his foot deeper into his mouth. He said, "We even had him signing bags and napkins one day."

I wanted to say, "Hey, guy, I never gave you a hundred-dollar bill. I don't keep hundred-dollar bills in my wallet." But I didn't. I let it pass. And one of the cooks said, "This is Peyton Manning, right here." I gave his boss a nice smile and let that pass, too.

I remember when Joe DiMaggio died. They wrote what he had said years ago about making a lot of money, and why he still always played his hardest. Why he *especially* played his hardest. He said, "A kid may be at the park for the first time. Or maybe for the last time. And if he came to see me, he deserves my best." I didn't need that to be inspired; I was inspired already. But it hit home.

Here's the way I view being a "highly paid" quarterback. If I don't help Indianapolis win a championship one day, I'll feel I haven't lived up to my end of the bargain. No, I'm not saying I'd be dumb enough to give the money back. I'm saying I'll do everything in my power to *make* it happen.

A lot was written along those lines after I signed the contract, and I tried to express my gratitude. But somebody asked, with what sounded like a little too much sarcasm in his voice, "What do you plan to do with all that money?"

"Earn it," I said.

The football season of 1998 found Archie Manning dancing on the equator between opposite poles—the extremes of the game as experienced 1) by Peyton, for gobs of money and prestige in the center of the spotlight at Indianapolis, and 2) by Eli, for the sheer joy of it at little Newman High in New Orleans, where he not only wasn't paid, but Archie and Olivia had to pay the school (tuition, books, fees, et cetera). As parents, they never had a more frantic year. Jet flights to Indiana for luxury

*viewing of the pro game in the RCA Dome; car pools and tail-
gating at high school games in remote, dimly lit bandbox stadiums hard by the railroad tracks of Louisiana. . . .*

It was wild. What a year. If Olivia and I had had *six* sons, it
couldn't have been more exciting. What surprised (and
pleased) me most that season was how far Eli had come, both
as a quarterback and as a young man. He was starting for the
third straight year for Newman, and was about to run the
table of the "alls"—all-district, all-metro, all-state. And when
it appeared likely that he was also going to reconnect the
Manning name to Ole Miss as a prize recruit, I realized that
he'd practically done it incognito. Right before my eyes without me seeing it. Well, seeing it but not as clearly as I might
have.

Oh, I was there, all right; we all were. But I hadn't been
when he was younger, not like I'd been for Cooper and
Peyton. In his earliest formative years I was playing pro ball
in Houston, and then in Minnesota, and Eli grew up so unob-
trusively that when I was home I hardly knew he was around,
except when we did something physical together (like shoot
baskets or throw the football). The first word he said as a
baby was "ball" and he used to sleep with a basketball and a
football in his crib, but even as a kid he seemed almost distant compared with the other two.

His friends call him "Easy," a nickname he got from his
freshman coach at Newman who noticed he didn't say much
except "Yes, sir"—but didn't goof off, either, or shirk his
responsibilities. Nobody had to get on his case. He just quietly did what he was told (or what he had a mind) to do. The
coach started calling him that, "Easy," and soon everybody
did. When asked about his reticence, he said, "I talk when I
have to. Otherwise, I don't bother."

And Easy is what he's always been. Easy Eli. It used to
bother me that he and I didn't talk much, or that *he* didn't
talk to *me* much, except in monosyllables. Almost to the
point where he seemed unfriendly. He didn't volunteer infor-

mation, I had to drag it out of him. He had that rule: no kisses except Sunday night, and it was more like a concession than affection. It applied, I thought, directly to me and my status in his life. He was so quiet around me that when I returned to New Orleans full-time I was afraid I'd lost him for good.

But Olivia, of course, knew him better, and she said it was just something he learned to get away with. No offense intended. He had been told for years how shy he was and he thought, "Well, okay, that's easy." Being the life of the party can be a burden. Sometimes it's better watching (and laughing) from the edge.

Olivia says we simply accommodated him in his diffidence and it became a pattern. A way to go. When we tried to be attentive, he didn't need it, or at least not as much. He has so many friends now you'd think he had a factory someplace making them, but he's still that way, preferring to blend in instead of stick out (except when he can't help it, like on the football field). Most of the time you don't know he's there. People talk about empty nests, which we have now with all the boys gone or in college. But when Peyton went to Tennessee and Eli was still in high school, we felt ours was already empty. Somebody would call and say, "Is Eli home?" And I'd say, "Uh, yeah. He's upstairs." Pause. "I think."

Eli had had some learning problems early on, which probably contributed to his shyness. Reading was hard for him, and at one point in grammar school we pulled him out of Newman with the idea of holding him back a year. We found a school that specializes in language arts and wanted to have him repeat a grade, but the school administrators did an evaluation and found it wasn't necessary. They had a resource center where he could get extra tutoring, and he responded to the point where he soon could read at grade level.

And, of course, when given the option, he wanted to go right back to Newman, where his brothers had been so big in sports and where he had every intention of being the same—but mainly where, as he put it, "all my friends are." We accommodated him again. He was such a good kid, never get-

ting into fights or causing trouble, that you tended to over-
look the mischief in his eye (it not being as obvious as
Cooper's) and want to spoil him a little. Being shy is not the
same as being a shrinking violet. But if his self-confidence
had suffered, at Newman he got a lot of it back with his successes in sports. He lettered four times in football and basketball and twice in baseball.

Olivia was closest to him in the crisis times that all kids
go through. For one thing, she said, "Eli was the last, and
when I was pregnant I kept thinking how wonderful it would
be to have a girl, because a lot of times Archie would take off
with Cooper and Peyton and I'd be left alone. But when I saw
that big old fat bulldog face, I said, 'Oh, Lord, let this be a boy,
too.' And I wound up loving my place in *three* boys' lives
even more because I realized I wasn't being left out at all.
Boys go to Mom when there's anything emotional involved.
They're never going to let Dad see them cry."

Cooper says now that we were a lot easier with Easy
when it came to discipline. Ordinarily I'd take that with a
grain of salt, considering the source's record for taking us to
the limit. But he's right. Nothing catastrophic, but Eli got
away with things Cooper wouldn't have. He got away with
some beer drinking. He got away with a couple trips to
Bourbon Street that I didn't know about until Olivia told me
later. (Naturally, I blamed her.)

We'd always given the boys a pretty tight framework of
rules to go by. We believe you establish right from wrong
early, and try not to let your kids jerk you around in the gray
areas. Nothing complicated, and most of it just a matter of
good manners. Respect for authority, and elders. Respect for
property. That kind of thing. Kids in New Orleans don't say
"Yes, sir" and "No, sir," they say "Yeah" and "No." They're
given a much wider berth all around than I was used to.
Mardi Gras is more than just an event, it's a prevailing wind.
I mean, in this town some parents have no curfew at all for
their kids, and some allow them to do whatever they want,
whenever they want.

Within that context it was dicey at times but really wasn't all that hard raising the three because they understood the logic. And the consequences. And because Olivia was always there for them to negotiate with on the finer points. I was the heavy hand, the "absolutely not" to inappropriate requests. Eli likes to tell the story of inviting a dozen of his friends over one night in the summer, thinking Olivia and I were gone. But we weren't, we were just in bed. He had everybody in the pool when they saw me at the back window, looking out on the festivities. They scattered like field mice, heading for their various vehicles.

Eli had to walk right by me to go to his room. I didn't say anything. The next day he went to the Penn State football camp, then we went on vacation in Jackson Hole. With so much time having passed, he just knew I'd forgotten about it. But when we got back home from Wyoming, I said, "Eli, remember that swimming party you threw . . . ?" He made a face, like, "Oh, boy, the Secret Service never sleeps."

Olivia, on the other hand, knew when to relax the grip a little. When to give in without giving up. The softer edge. She could be an avid fan without knowing a winged T from a wing nut because she loved them so much, and when they were hurt, physically or otherwise, she hurt right along with them. The primary support system. She had her moments, though. One time when Eli's dirty, sweaty clothes were on a par with the rest of ours, and everybody was tracking stuff in and lolling around messing up the couches, she read us the riot act. When she was about done, she said, "And another thing. I'm *tired* of washing jockstraps!"

Difference in approach notwithstanding, Olivia and I had one hard rule we agreed should not to be broken at *any* time: We wanted to know where they were. If they moved from one place to another on their nights out, we wanted to know about it. No arguments, no compromises, because there's nothing worse for a parent than to have a kid "out there" without knowing where "there" is.

Sure enough, the night after his last football game at

Newman, Eli didn't come in at all, and when he called the next morning he was at a friend's house. Which, of course, Olivia suspected all along, having been so inclined herself as a well-placed teenager in Mississippi. Typically, she was less upset than I was. I was *very* upset.

I said, "Eli, why didn't you call?"

He said, "You'd have made me come home." He had it all figured out. He said, "I'll take the punishment. I just wanted to stay out."

I told him he could have, if he'd asked. But he knew better.

Cooper, who probably figured Eli out a lot quicker than I did, believes that a very big asset for the youngest brother has been Peyton, always and faithfully around as his "older influence." Especially so now in early adulthood.

Actually, Cooper says it more this way:

"Peyton isn't Eli's older brother so much as he's his second father. 'Did you lift today, Eli?' 'Did you work out?' 'You better study hard, now, Eli.' I'm older than both of them, but I've always treated Eli like a buddy. A pal. A fraternity brother, which is applicable now: 'You got enough beer for tonight, Eli?'

"Eli will do things at Ole Miss that Peyton wouldn't have, as Dad already found out with that frat-party incident. He'll be in a fraternity. He'll skip a class or two on a Friday to go off with his buddies. He'll do what I did with *my* buddies—take a weekend trip to California in a beat-up old LeBaron that we chipped in and bought. Go to a Giants game. Play Pebble Beach. Go to Las Vegas and stay up till five playing cards.

"Peyton was too busy. He had stuff to do. Practice. And worry. People watching his every move. Eli won't be that way. He's just not overly impressed about things. He doesn't care, one way or the other, about the stuff other people care about. Oh, he cares about his music and his clothes and his football, but he's not wrapped up in any of it.

"I mean, he doesn't have tunnel vision even about football. He can't tell you the names of the defensive backs for the Broncos, or even the Saints. He might be able to tell you the names of the quarterbacks, but that's it. I could tell you them all, but I can't do algebra, so how smart is that? He wears this dumb hat that makes his hair look long, which probably embarrasses Archie and Olivia a little. But Arch used to like long hair, too. His hair looked like it was tucked into his shirt it was so long. So he had no argument when Eli went for it.

"It's going to be great for me, with Eli at Ole Miss, because I'm already finding out I can get away with looking like him, just the way I did Peyton. I'm getting it all the time when I go to Oxford. When I was in Knoxville when he was being recruited by the Vols, somebody saw me and shouted, 'Hey, Eli, you coming to Tennessee?' I said, 'How much money you got for me if I do?' Dad said I'd get Ole Miss on probation before Eli played a down there.

"But here's the thing to remember about Eli. He's smart enough to see Peyton has set a terrific example. He might not accept every facet, but he'll latch on to the good stuff."

I guess what was most gratifying to see as that '98 season came on was how much ground Eli had made up athletically while he was getting his academic life in order. At quarterback, he'd turned out to be a quick study. He didn't play tackle football, in pads, until he was in the eighth grade, but he'd go to those all-sports camps (which he liked best, he said, because they were "good places to make friends") and come home throwing the football better, shooting the basketball better.

And he got better by the hour. With pride in it that didn't show. Quietly, without making a big deal out of it, he competed against his brothers. It pleased him when he could outrun Peyton (out of high school, Peyton ran a 4.9 forty, Eli a 4.8). He didn't say anything even after he did it, but he was proud to be the first Manning to dunk the basketball. But his perspective didn't change. I saw him beat Fisher High as a sophomore when he totaled 235 yards and 5 touchdowns on only 23 passes thrown (19 completed), and afterward I said something about "the next level," meaning college. He said, "Aw, I was just having fun."

The Newman offense is still not much more sophisticated than when Peyton played, but Eli was the starter for three straight years, and after his junior year, when he completed 142 of 235 passes for 2,547 yards and 26 touchdowns, the college scouts were picking up the scent. He got about twenty calls in May after that season, in keeping with the rule about how soon scouts could make contact. He came into his senior year clearly primed and qualified to play college ball. But he was still Eli. I'll never forget, one of the teams that expressed a lot of interest in him was the University of Texas. One Saturday when Texas was on national TV, I tuned in to the game, and he watched it with me.

For one quarter.

Then he went to his room and played video games.

Meanwhile, there was his emotional antithesis, Peyton, at the starting line of that first season in Indianapolis, so pumped up and ready he could hardly stand it. Healthy, now, too. And rich. *Very* rich. How would *that* affect him?

I hear the question all the time, and have for years, even before Peyton's good fortune. It's a legitimate concern these days. How does all that money affect you in a game like football? We're not talking about badminton here, we're talking about a sport where you dance on the hairy edge of serious, maybe permanent physical damage every time you suit up. With millions of dollars in a twenty-two-year-old's pocket, how does that impact his equilibrium? Is he going to give it his all if he knows he doesn't have to, at least for not very long? Given a decent financial planner, most big league players today could live comfortably ever after, and take some of their relatives along for the ride, with just what they get in signing bonuses.

So what will the player with a trunkful of money do when push comes to shove?

How will he perform when he knows he's already set for life? Is he going to submit to all the extra training that is now so necessary, and the extra time studying films, and the added emphasis put on this or that just because the coach says so?

What will he do when practice is long and hard and hot, and his tongue is ashes and his muscles scream for relief?

What will he do when the play calls for him to stick his head into a mass of writhing sinew and hard plastic, or to make that open-field tackle when it's him against the 280-pounder aiming right at his nose, or get the extra yard when there are two 280-pounders bearing down?

You could never convince me that any player who makes it to the NFL lacks courage. It's one of the factors that makes you a good football player in the first place, even if it's not equally distributed. But what if what's required of you is not a survival or win-lose proposition? Are you still going to be courageous? Can you still be counted on? Will you still perform "to the best of your ability"?

All the combines in the world are not going to be able to scope that out every time, just as they won't be able to tell you for sure whether this guy is going to make the key basket in the clutch or that guy is going to deliver with two on and two out in the ninth inning. We sit in the stands now, or in front of the television set, and we say, "Look at this kid, what a dud he turned out to be! In college he was a go-getter, now he's wearing enough gold around his neck to sink his seventy-foot yacht and he's not nearly the player he was. Look, there he goes, stepping out of bounds instead of taking a hit!"

It's so different now, when the pros are so much better at picking the talent than they used to be. But the intangibles are called that because that's what they are: intangible. The line between those who make it and those who don't is paper thin. Player A, taken in the first round, might be better than Player B, taken in the fourth—but often not by very much. And who can judge for sure how the talent and the courage will mesh when the checks are signed and the whistle blows?

The mistakes made in the selection process are legion, and the money wasted in the process is scandalous. You look up and the two star running backs in the Super Bowl are Terrell Davis and Jamal Anderson, who were practically ignored in the draft. One went in the sixth round, one went in the seventh. Bad measurements? Maybe not. Maybe just an intangible kicking in (or kicking out).

And here is why, with all of that said, I knew Peyton would make it in pro football (although I admit I didn't expect him to be *that* good so soon); why he was a worthy first-draft choice. Because he personifies exactly what they're looking for. The player who wants so badly to do well at anything he attempts, wants so badly for the achievements to mark him instead of the money, that he practically drives you crazy with it. Going in, he was the totally dedicated player.

When Peyton went to the combine with the four hundred other players and talked with the coaches, *he* interviewed *them*. That is to say, he asked more questions than they did. He brought a legal pad and had a list of things written down he wanted to discuss, and he plugged away at it. It was like a sign in the window: "I'm dedicating myself to being the best NFL quarterback I can be, so watch out."

He cared about the money, sure. Who wouldn't? But it didn't faze him. He cared about being a great player even more.

11

The very first pass Peyton Manning threw in a National Football League uniform went for a touchdown—48 yards to Marvin Harrison against Seattle in the team's 1998 preseason opener. An omen? Yes. He'd throw a lot more that first season—26 in all—while leading the American Football Conference in several passing categories and setting a half-dozen NFL rookie records. But no. Not the start of something big for the Indianapolis Colts that year. They would wallow in the sty they'd made for themselves for one more season (with another 3-victory, 13-defeat finish) while Peyton and head coach Jim Mora got their sea legs before making the turnabout that stunned the league in 1999. . . .

Shawn Springs of the Seahawks came up to me when we were warming up for the game at the Kingdome. I don't like to talk to opposing players before a game, but I'd competed against Shawn when he was at Ohio State, and his dad, Ron, starred for the Cowboys. Shawn had already been in the league a year. He's a good guy, and a good cornerback.

The ESPN camera was on us, and Shawn was being very animated, congratulating me on the draft, et cetera, and I said, "Thanks, Shawn, I appreciate it, and good luck." And as he was trotting away, he turned and yelled, "Better not throw to my side tonight or you'll end up on *SportsCenter*!"

I didn't say anything. When the game started, my helmet headphones went out on the second play. I was using them for the first time (they're not allowed in college) and I'd been told if they malfunctioned to make my own choices from what I knew of the game plan. I called a draw, and Marshall Faulk ran for 12 yards. No problem.

Then I threw my first pass, a slant to Marvin Harrison on Shawn Springs's side. Shawn froze on my three-step drop, Harrison broke and ran right by him. The play went all the way. Bam, 6 points.

Ordinarily I don't say anything to a defensive back after a touchdown; I don't talk to defensive players at all unless I have to. I've always felt that the guys who get the most verbal abuse (and sometimes the late hits) are the same guys who mouth off or dance around to show up the other guy. Besides, it's not supposed to be a big deal when I throw a touchdown pass. It's supposed to be my job.

But I couldn't help it. As I ran downfield, I said, "Hey, Springs! Springs!"

And I gave him one of those "How about that?" gestures. I couldn't resist.

The season went downhill from there, if you can imagine your first pass being the high point. We lost that game and two of the four in the preseason, which really wasn't bad as records go, but preseason games are really little more than scrimmages. If you're alert to what's happening, they can be good indicators, but the indications weren't so hot when I saw the film. I didn't realize how out of sync I was. Very seldom do I make a throw where the ball comes off my hand and I immediately think, "Interception!" Most of the time I feel like I've made a good decision, and when something bad happens, it happens. But everything I did that night was too fast. My footwork, my passing, even my demeanor.

Nothing else could be blamed. The Seahawks weren't that intimidating. The crowd wasn't that big. Pro crowds are never going to bother me because I played in a stadium at Tennessee that has a greater seating capacity than any stadium in the NFL and in a league where huge, vocal audiences are the norm. You might as a quarterback sometimes have to deal more specifically with crowd noise (it can be very distracting calling plays), but it wasn't any easier in college.

My dad had always said, "It doesn't matter who you're playing against, you play the way you know how," and I hadn't done that. On the phone that week he had said, "You belong out there, so just play your game." In other words, be smart. Be tough. Don't give them anything. Compete. I'm sure, though, that he was as nervous as I was.

I felt much more comfortable in the second game, at home against Cincinnati. Everything slowed down. From about 100 miles an hour to maybe 75 (I was aiming for about 30). I was more relaxed, calmer. We won, then lost in San Diego and finished the preseason with a three-point win at home over the Lions. In that game, on the first play, I threw an 80-yard touchdown pass to Harrison (of course). Marvin caught it about 45 yards downfield and ran in. When it was over I thought, "Well, two and two ain't bad," making a mountain out of a molehill. "Maybe we've got a shot here." Little did I know.

With the preliminaries out of the way, I felt we at least had a fire started. I wasn't overwhelmed by anything. I felt current with the offense. I liked the guys, I liked the coaches. I liked the offensive coordinator, Tom Moore, from the start. Moore had coached Terry Bradshaw with the Steelers in the '70s and had been with the Saints the year before coming to the Colts. He knew my dad. After I'd been at camp a couple of weeks, reestablishing my work ethic, he told Dad I was going to get the "Tony Dungy award for watching film until your eyeballs drop out." Tony had evidently been as obsessed as a player, and now as a coach (at Tampa Bay), as I was.

Dad said Moore told him I was already "as smart as most of the quarterbacks in the league," but I felt I was still in remedial training. There was just so much to learn. At one point, they were going to give Kelly Holcomb, my backup, some reps in practice, and I said to Moore, "Gee, Coach, I really need all these reps." He and Mora let me have my way. Holcomb was left to throw passes as fodder for the defense.

Which is one of the problems with pro teams. They allow only 53-man rosters, as compared with 95 (plus red shirts and walk-ons) that colleges can suit up, and you can't do as much with your practice time when you have players doubling up everywhere. When Dad played for the Saints, they were so desperate for bodies that he did practice service as a wide receiver.

Bill Musgrave, a veteran quarterback out of Oregon, was my first roommate as a Colt and my on-field soul mate. He'd spent three years with the 49ers, then Denver, and was destined to be a coach. But he wasn't a first-liner, and though Polian brought him in mainly to serve as my mentor (he was perfect for it, a smart guy with a great sense of humor), they were worried that if anything happened to me they might have to use him, so they let him go to make room for Holcomb. Bill wound up that year as quarterback coach of the Eagles and is now with Carolina. But that tells you how limiting the numbers are. In college, they'd have just made room.

What probably made it a little easier for me fitting in was that Coach Mora was in his first full season with the Colts and the system and the coaches were new to everybody. A crash course all around. If everything had been set in stone and the coaches established, I probably wouldn't have been able to insinuate myself so readily into the system. I was flattered that they felt I could handle it all in a short time, but like Mora said, in that regard he was doing me no favors.

But I got the impression immediately that I had the confidence of the coaches. Bill Polian had done the advance work. He knew the Colts needed a quarterback badly, and quarterbacks had been big-money busts in the '90s in the NFL. Only one, Drew Bledsoe of the Patriots, had performed up to rank. So he watched film of every pass I threw in college (that's 1,505 passes) and paid Bill Walsh $5,000 just to analyze videotape. Walsh had been very flattering. He told *Sports Illustrated:* "The great ones have spontaneity, intuitiveness, inventiveness. They're intelligent. They know they need to know everything. Peyton Manning . . . is further along than any college quarterback I've seen in years. Maybe ever." *That* pleased me.

Mora called Dad a couple times, too, after we started, just to chat and say, "Peyton's doing a good job." Dad and Polian talked once or twice, but Dad wasn't soliciting any of it, and certainly wasn't nosing in. He told me, "For everybody but you, I'm not around. I'm not involved." He said, "The last thing the Colts need is advice from the peanut gallery." But he and I were on the phone almost every night, and though we didn't talk X's and O's, per se, we talked about everything else.

How was I doing with the players? Well, I treated the offensive line to dinner at St. Elmo's on Thursday night before our first game, a ritual that pro quarterbacks are wise to follow. I included Marshall Faulk in the mix and asked him if he wanted to go "halvsies." He said the jury was still out on how much blocking he was going to get so, "No, I'll give 'em a couple more weeks." Maybe he was thinking about my new contract.

I always make a point of getting to know the offensive linemen. They're football's equivalent of the beloved American blue-collar worker and usually the closest unit on a team because so much of their duties are interacted with subtleties that involve team play—blocking schemes, double-teams, pull-out blocks, picking up blitzes, and so forth. Probably the most complicated jobs on the field. They *have* to be together.

I got to know the Colts' linemen quickly because there weren't many single guys on the team and the opportunities to pal around were limited. I had taken up residence at the Indianapolis Athletic Club, where I could have some privacy along with the conveniences—good food, a place to park my car, a barbershop. I didn't have a roommate, which didn't bother me. I had my telephone.

But privacy isn't really a "thing" with me, and loneliness is an equal-opportunity employer. It can get to you whether you're a lighthouse tender or the biggest-name sports figure in America. It turned out the offensive line ate together regularly on Thursday nights, so I started tagging along. I got to know their families and got invited to their houses or apartments for dinner. Later, to be able to reciprocate, I moved into an apartment at Lions Gate, on Eighty-sixth Street, in a nice section of town. Some of the Pacers and other Colts lived there.

Mom and Dad made that last preseason game, on a Thursday night. The first time they'd seen me in the flesh as a pro. They were excited about it. Dad had given up his regular-season color-commentary job for the Saints games, partly so he could watch Eli and me at his convenience, but he was still doing their preseason games, so he had to hop around some.

He and Mom were back ten days later for our opener against Miami, this time with Eli and Mom's folks. A full rooting section. There was a lot going on. The game was sold out well in advance and the city held a parade downtown for the team ("Do the Blue," they called it). And I have to say when looking at film of the mighty Dolphins, I was encouraged. I mean, they didn't present a complicated defense at all. Vanilla, actually. The defensive schemes weren't fashioned to confuse you, just to attack you. They lined up with all that talent and said, "Okay, here we are, try to beat us."

And we started like we were capable of it. The Dolphins blitzed on the first play and I dumped off to Marshall Faulk and he went 20 yards. I hit him again for another first down, then threw to Harrison for still another. The coaches were feeding me surefire completions on every play. Then at second and eight on the Miami 20, with Faulk on the sideline taking a breather, we ran a draw play to the fullback and got 6 yards—and fumbled the ball away.

Those things happen, of course. To everyone. But I thought later how huge that would have been: a long, successful drive on the first series. A touchdown, maybe; a field goal for sure, and who knows what that would have done in the play-out.

Miami drove right back and kicked a field goal for 3–0 and never trailed. I hit a couple of long passes and the crowd stayed with us, and loudly, but we were behind, 17–3, at the half, and on our first play of the third quarter, I audibled from a running play to a pass against a defensive set that just didn't look right, and sure enough, the Dolphins' Terrell Buckley cut in front of Marvin, picked it off, and ran it back to our 5-yard line. A good play for Buckley, but the first interception of my pro career for me. Miami went in from there to a lead we couldn't make up.

I had three interceptions for the day. At least two too many. On one, I had a receiver open down the middle on a play based on what the defense was showing us, and I missed him. The third was a tipped ball, which happens and you can't let it get to you. All in all, we passed for more than 300 yards. But we also scored only one touchdown. I threw a touchdown pass to Harrison on the very last play of the game to make it look respectable at 24–15.

I thought afterward we could have won. Could have beaten what was generally considered to be the best team in the division. And I thought, too, that we could move the ball on anybody. I even thought the unthinkable, the one thing Dad and I agree shouldn't be said out loud by a pro: that I hadn't seen anything I hadn't seen before. The game at that level was not Greek to me. Of course, the speed of it was. And all that talent on the field at one time, at *every* position.

But something happened after the game that I'm still sorry about, still reliving in my mind, involving as it did my dad. The television cameras picked him up in the stands during play, and as he said later, he was too busy dying for me to notice. Part of it was reliving his own experiences, recollecting how tough it can be out there when everything is coming so hard. He said his quarterbacking instincts rose up and jangled his nerves in a way they never had when he played. It made him almost sick. He said he wasn't looking at me as a mature, twenty-two-year-old quarterback, he was looking at me as if I was still his little boy.

And, of course, he was looking at me through the eyes of a man who had known fifteen years of professional frustration himself.

The trouble was, *two* television cameras caught every move he made. Captured every sour look, every syllable of negative body language. And in the postgame interviews, they showed me his reactions on a monitor in the dressing room. I could hear the announcers' comments—"Boy, Archie's not happy about that throw"—and I took it as my dad being embarrassed. Disappointed. Mad. Ashamed even.

When we went to dinner with the family afterward, I didn't say anything. But on Monday I saw the full video, and after practice when we got together again, I said, "I didn't like the way you were shown on TV. It looked like you were upset with me."

He said, "I didn't know the camera was on me."

I said, "You *should* have known. They'll always try to find you at my games. That's *your* fault."

I was hurt, and now with my hasty reaction I hurt him. And when he tried to explain his actions, we both got testy. I look back at it now and I think, "Boy, Peyton, you were stupid." Here's my father, the man I have so much respect for—if there's ever been anybody who had the complete, one-hundred-percent support of his mom and dad, it's been me. It was moronic, taking it out on him. But I guess it's true about human nature. You take it out on the people who love you the most. Human nature is wrong on that one.

The worst part from both our standpoints was that we let it go on for more days than it should have. And during that time I've never been so uncomfortable. It was so *different* from what I was used to. Weeks went by before we both finally came to grips with it and talked it out. Dad realized he had to watch how he showed his feelings at games (because seeing it really did hurt me), and I realized how sensitive he was when watching his boys. I'd never really seen it before. I was on the field, he was in the stands, so how could I? And you can't always mask those feelings. Thank God, we cleared the air, with no real damage to our relationship. I like to think it even strengthened it.

The thing is, the environment had radically changed. When I was in high school, I was exposed to his thinking all the time. Even occasionally at practice he'd suddenly be there and we could talk afterward about what I was doing. In college, the distance made a natural division. He wasn't there to come home to, or even to see at practice. But I still called, we still talked, and I still knew he'd be at every game.

Now it's the pros and I'm no longer a boy. I'm earning my way, on a team that is finding *its* way. And the distance between us can be measured in miles *and* opportunity. He's no longer at every game. We don't talk as often. And I'm getting used to what has to happen with all father-son relationships: The son fends for himself as he gets closer to being a father, too. The father understands. There's more independence to accept. That's the way it's supposed to work, probably the way God intended.

But I miss Dad more now, too. That, I hope, will *never* change. And I was probably more conscious of missing him when we lost so many times that first season. That's why I still take to the telephone so much. But when I call home now, though it's still father-to-son, there's a lot more man-to-man. And I like sharing that old closeness in the newer format. He seems to like it, too. When we're hunting or playing golf together, having fun, I think, "We don't have to change. Where does it say we have to give up being so close? What rule applies?" The only thing that makes it different is that I'm a man, too.

Sometimes he still comes out with things that make me say, "Dad, you don't have to tell me that." And he says, "I know, and I won't." It's just his nature to try to help me with everything. Good for him. And good for me.

I don't throw helmets or chairs after a loss. I don't rant and rave and abuse the media with profanity. I'm more a let's-get-the-hell-out-of-here-and-go-back-to-work guy. But what's frustrating in the pros is that when you lose on Sunday, you really don't go back to work until Wednesday. On Monday you watch videos of the game, look at some of the next opponent, and lift weights or work out. On Tuesday you're off. It makes for a long time between wanting to "get even" and actually starting the process.

So, naturally, I overworked the telephone that first year. Friends like Trey Teague called me regularly, and Cooper and the folks, and I made it a point to talk with Eli. Coach Cutcliffe was on the list, too, and he was great to bounce ideas off.

We were worse the second week at New England. A bad game all around. I threw three more interceptions, one returned for a touchdown, and hesitated on my decisions. I kept saying to myself, "Don't force it, don't force it, just throw it away if the receiver's not there," but I don't always do what I tell myself to do. I didn't have good timing. I was off-balance a lot, throwing off my back foot. I said to myself, "If you're going to throw an interception, Peyton, at least throw it with some authority. Follow through! Follow through!" All three were floaters.

New England is a neat place to play. The atmosphere created around the stadium is like that of a college game, with cars driving into a kind of pastoral setting and tailgate parties everywhere. It was a good crowd, too, for a Sunday-night game, nationally televised. But we never got anything going, never got into any kind of rhythm. From every standpoint, it was my worst game of the year—less than 200 yards passing, three interceptions, two sacks, a fumble, et cetera, et cetera, and we lost by 23 points.

On one of my interceptions, Dad was watching back in New Orleans on a little TV in the kitchen, where he'd moved to get a cold drink. There he sees me chased out of the pocket, going to my right, and he's repeating to himself (on my behalf) the cardinal rule for a right-handed quarterback rolling right: "Don't try to pass back over the middle, and certainly not to the left. It's an awkward, impossible angle to throw from." But I'm with the Colts in the "red" zone, inside the Patriots' 20, trying to salvage the play. And I'm looking, looking, looking . . .

And at that moment Dad senses that I'm going to throw back over the middle!

And he shouts from his spot there in the kitchen for me to hear in Foxboro, "No, Peyton! NO, Peyton! NO, PEYTON!"

But, of course, only my mom in the family room heard him. I threw back over the middle. *Thunk.* Interception.

Quarterbacks need that, unfortunately. They need to see for themselves what can go wrong when they defy the odds. And, in the broader sense, to get the most they can out of a defeat. When we talked on the phone shortly after the game, Dad said, "When you watch the tapes of the game, you'll see what's always true: You're never as good as you think you are after a big victory and never as bad as you thought after a loss." I called him a couple of days later to tell him I'd watched the tapes. I said, "You know, Dad, that part about it never being as bad as you think? Guess what. It was worse."

I was in the locker room after the game taking a leak, thinking that was exactly where I deserved to be, the toilet. Our secondary coach, George Catavolos, was in the next stall. The defense had actually played well, and I said, "Geez, George, I'm sorry. Your guys played their hearts out. You deserved better."

He shook his head. "Don't you apologize for anything, Peyton. You don't have to. We're all in this together."

I was glad he said it, but I didn't believe him. And I admit that at that point I was looking over my shoulder a little, expecting to find some finger-pointing. As he would all year, Coach Mora left me in for every offensive play, and we did score on a two-minute drive at the end. But it was small compensation, and *no* consolation, and I figured some whispering behind my back was due. I might have been whispering myself if I was looking at it from my teammates' perspective.

But I didn't hear a thing. At any time. Not a single negative word.

Coach Mora and I happened to be walking off the field together when the game ended, and when I saw the film clip of us later, I had to think, "This is *not* the way I want to start my pro career. Walking away from disasters with my coach. This is *not* fun." But Mora looked at me and kind of laughed. He said, "You all right?"

I said, "No."

He smiled. "Hey, you gotta hang in there. Believe me, it's going to get better."

I thought at that moment, with the dead body still warm on the slab, he could just as easily have said, "Dammit, Manning, this isn't working!" He could have pulled me out of the game. Even benched me. But he didn't. He was calm and reassuring. He didn't even act surprised at what was happening. Honestly, I was awed.

Mora is an ex-marine officer, and he looks the part with those hard eyes and that steel-gray hair. He's smart and insightful, and when he wants to, he can outcharm Auntie Mame. I think if you suggested at all that he wasn't approachable, he'd say, "What are you talking about? My office is always open." But he's got that sense of rank about him, and when he comes around, a noticeable silence settles on the scene. A lot of players try to fill it with awkward non sequiturs. "Great weather today, eh, Coach?" He doesn't like that. He doesn't like wasted talk.

But I learned to appreciate him quickly and to act accordingly. If we're meeting on something and he stops talking, so do I. If I have a point to make, I make it. But I don't tell him out of nowhere what I had for dinner last night at St. Elmo's. Some players think that's his intimidation mode, but I think it's just him. And his door *is* always open. And he *does* invite you in. Which is when you realize how intimidating he really is. He fixes you with that look, and when you say something, he waits for about ten seconds before he responds. Makes you think, "Did he hear me? What dumb thing did I say?" I think he likes to see you fidget. It's like a test to see if you hold the stare or look down at the carpet.

Ordinarily, Mora doesn't make a practice of yelling at his players; he's actually pretty quiet at practice. But he ripped me pretty good one day, and I was glad of it. When I need it, I need it. No, I don't like getting yelled at, but I don't want my teammates to think I've got immunity, either. At Tennessee my last year or two, a lot of guys got the impression I was being treated with kid gloves by the coaches, and my fellow seniors ragged me about it.

But in Colts' practice one day, I got careless and threw an interception, and Mora burned the air with his evaluation: "No, No, NO, *NO!* Don't *do* that! Don't frigging *do* that! You do it out here and you'll sure as hell do it in the frigging game!" Except he didn't say *frigging*.

The players in the shower afterward repeated his criticism, verbatim, over and over. They got a big kick out of doing it, too.

My respect for Mora grew in giant steps. We had our moments. A couple of shouting matches. But we've grown together, too, just as I've grown to appreciate Bill Polian more and more. It bothered me early on that they both seemed to feel the need to keep telling me to keep the faith. It was like damage control, and I didn't like the vibrations. It was new to me, no question. I was used to losing only as a rarity. I hated the fact that we were *talking* about getting better instead of *getting* better.

But at the end of the season, I told Mora what it meant to me. "Coach, I really appreciate your hanging with me this year." He said, "You can't learn from the sidelines, Peyton. And what you did was hard. It's easier to be yanked and go pout on the sidelines when you're throwing interceptions. The tougher thing is to go back into the game, ignore the boos, and suck it up. Try to do something about it."

And I *did* do better in those fourth quarters after getting my knocks early in games. I hung in there. I think Mora wanted me to see the importance of that. Staying focused, keeping cool. Baseball managers do that with pitchers sometimes—let them stay in a game when they're being pounded.

"Okay, you dug yourself into a hole. Let's see what you can do to get yourself out."

I think that first big step toward coach-quarterback reciprocity was taken that night in New England. But I still had a lot of humble pie to eat before it got any better. The next Tuesday night I heard a little girl, a twelve-year-old call-in, talking to a country-western host on the radio. I don't know what the question was, but she said, "The Colts stank with Peyton Manning!" Not much on the grammar, but strong on the sentiment.

Dad had reminded me more than once, and he reminded me again after the New England game, that pro football "isn't a sprint, it's a 20-game marathon." You don't go limp when you lose a game, you go on. The question we were both struggling with was "How bad are we?," meaning the Colts. And "How good could we hope to be?"

Going into the season, everybody knew we were hurting on defense. The draft and trades made were mainly on behalf of the offense, to get that going. Polian had picked up whoever and whenever he could to plug defensive leaks, but it was an ongoing project that needed the draft and the off-season. The defense wound up allowing more yards than the Colts had given up in seventeen years.

I had a chance to talk with Mora about it late in the season, and he was receptive enough to let me say that he ought to consider hiring "a couple of bad asses" on defense.

He said, "What do you mean?"

I said, "Everybody you sign at this level is going to be a good player [as if he didn't know that]. What we need on defense is somebody who's vocal, who's got some fire, who'll jerk a teammate around if he catches him goofing off or yukking it up the Saturday night before a game. A guy who hates to lose, and isn't afraid to let his teammates know it when they're not being the same way."

All football teams need tough guys. You'd love to have eleven on offense, eleven on defense, but they'd probably wind up killing one another, and the truth is, like anything else, a team is made up of differing personalities. Our players didn't lack toughness so much as we just didn't have the vocal leadership.

The week after the Patriots loss, we demonstrated how much ground we really had to cover. We got slaughtered by the Jets in New York, 44–6. Vinny Testaverde threw four touchdown passes and the Jets rang up 503 yards. The fans and the talk-show hosts were singing duets. "Same old Colts." That week Dad sent me a highlighted passage from a Father's Prayer. It said, "Lead me, I pray, not in the path of ease and comfort, but in the stress and spur of difficulties and challenge." His mother had given it to him as a young man. I taped it to the bathroom mirror as a reminder. (It reminded me that things were going to get worse.)

We didn't win until our fifth game, and there was some irony in that because we beat the Chargers with Ryan Leaf at quarterback. Much was made about the match-up beforehand: Draft Pick number one vs. Draft Pick number two Which, of course, is a misconception. Quarterbacks don't go one-on-one. It's not like a batter against a pitcher or two fighters in a ring. You compete more against the opposing team's defensive coordinator (and, of course, his defensive players) than you do against the other quarterback. The added irony was the game itself. Neither Ryan nor I played very well. We won by playing less poorly, 17–12, but like I said afterward, "Twenty-eight other teams didn't even care that we played."

The victory was more cause for relief than rejoicing. But Mora was excited: his first win as the Colts' coach, and mine as the Colts' quarterback. And the one thing I've learned about pro football: *Any* victory is a big one, because nothing comes easy in the NFL. I mean nothing. Very little gets handed to you.

The positive after that was that we were in most of the games we played for the rest of the year. We beat the Jets by a point in the Dome when they were the hottest team in the league, and did it impressively: an 80-yard drive at the end capped off by a 14-yard pass I threw to Marcus Pollard with less than a minute to play. Later we beat the Bengals in a scorefest, 39–26. Our third and final victory, all at home.

By and large we spent most of the year blowing leads. Which I suppose was good *and* bad—the fact that we led was good, the fact that we led and lost was bad (better to have led and lost than never to have led at all). The worst was against Buffalo in mid-October. Four times in the first half we drove deep into Buffalo territory, moving the ball well, and each time had to settle for field goals. Instead of being up 28 to 7 at the half, we were ahead by only five, 12 to 7, and lost, 31–24. A matter of not being able to close the book on teams. Not being able to add the "finishing touch."

I got hurt in that game. Bruce Smith hit me late, and I suppose I should have thought of it as an honor, getting my knee battered by a sure Hall-of-Famer. But I wasn't happy about it because it was late, and though he assured me afterward it wasn't a cheap shot, he wound up getting fined $7,500 for it. I told him it was okay, and it was. I never even left the game. Maybe that's why they fined him $7,500. When Bruce puts you down, you're supposed to stay down.

My best game was against the Ravens in Baltimore. I had 27 completions for 357 yards and 3 touchdowns, and was especially pleased with (as the films showed) my mechanical improvements: good balance, good footwork, good releases. Taking the maximum time to throw. Alas, though we outgained them by more than 200 yards, we also gave up 17 points in the fourth quarter (again) and blew a 31–21 lead. The Baltimore fans enjoyed the last laugh: 38 to 31. Actually, they were screaming more than laughing at the end. One guy yelled at me going off the field, "Give us our trophies back!" I wanted to say, "Hey, man, I was eight years old when the Colts moved out of here."

But the worst collapse of all was in San Francisco earlier when we played the 49ers to a standstill and blew leads of 21–0 (in the first half) and 31–17 (in the fourth quarter). It was a dismal fourth. The 49ers scored 17 unanswered points to win, 34–31, despite the fact that it was the first game I didn't throw an interception. I stormed through the locker room after the game, showered quickly, did the interviews perfunctorily, and got out of there.

And as I was outside waiting on the bus, I saw Jerry Rice of the 49ers come out, wave to his fans, and get into a very fancy car. And as he drove slowly through them, the fans parted as if he was Moses going through the Red Sea. They were open-mouthed and wide-eyed, straining to get a glimpse of their hero.

And as I watched, the car passed three or four Colt players, also wide-eyed, also waving, and they bent to peek through the tinted windows at Jerry. And I'm thinking, "C'mon, guys, you just played against him. Are you now going to ask for his autograph? We lost, for crying out loud. Act like it matters."

I admit it. With each passing week, I got, as Cooper put it, "ornerier and ornerier." Cooper complained about it to Dad. The few times he'd seen me in Indianapolis, he said, "Peyton's so moody, so strung out. I'm worried about him." He'd been there with me one weekend with some of my pals from Knoxville, and when we went out after the game, I was just not any fun. Cooper tried to rouse me, but I couldn't pull it off. We'd planned to go to one of those country-western karaoke places, and we went as planned even though we lost. But one look at my face, Cooper said, precluded any thought of my enjoying it. There wasn't a happy note in me.

When it came to not handling my feelings, though, my worst moment was when we got beat by the Falcons in Atlanta in December. There was more orange in the stands than any other color because Tennessee fans in for the SEC championship game the day before had stayed over. The Vols had won and were on their way to an undefeated season and the national championship.

But after leading the Falcons 21–7 at the half and losing by 7 without scoring another point, I wasn't so communicative afterward. In the press conference, a woman reporter asked me about the Vols' SEC title (like one of the non sequiturs Jim Mora hates). I said, "Obviously, I'm very proud of them." And I was, and I was especially proud of Tee Martin, who'd been my backup the year before and was making the most of his emergence. It was a great year for Tee, Coach Fulmer, and Tennessee.

But the reporter wouldn't let it go. Finally I said (with just a little edge in my voice), "I'm really not thinking about that right now."

And in the papers the next day I was described as having "snapped" when discussing Tennessee's successes without me. I wish I'd had a second chance with the reporter who wrote it. I'd have said, "Look, we're not exactly having a banner year ourselves, and I've just spent six days busting my tail getting ready for this game. For three hours just now I was doing whatever I could to win, and we blew it. And I'm frustrated. Nothing else is important to me right now. I'm not thinking about my family or my college team or my girlfriend or anything. I'm thinking about what the Falcons just did to the Colts."

Dad didn't go to many games after our little "encounter." I let the Colts know he wasn't happy about being "eyeballed" by the TV cameras, and Bill Polian and Jim Irsay invited him to come back and sit in their boxes, but that really wouldn't have improved the situation much. He said he'd sit where he had been sitting when he came, but until late in the season he made the family-room floor his favorite spot for my games and confined most of his on-site football watching to Eli's senior-year season at Newman. He said the last thing I needed was for him to cause any commotion or for him and Mom to smother me.

But he also knew that when I was a kid he'd watch forty or fifty of our baseball games a summer, and if he didn't show up until the fourth or fifth inning, I'd say afterward, "What kept you?" So they came for a few more games, and we talked on the phone. Not as frequently but just as avidly. If I got distracted and maybe let four or five days go in between, Mom did what any unsinkable mother would do. She called me.

When the season, mercifully, was over, I asked Dad to come to Indianapolis and drive home with me. I said he could pretend to help me load up my Suburban, and we could talk for miles. We drove straight through, Indianapolis to New Orleans, thirteen hours in the car—except for food stops. Dad and I love road trips, and he has a list of favorite restaurants he always springs on me. One of them is a barbecue hangout in Tuscaloosa, Alabama, called "Dreamland." On that trip, trouble was he remembered it as being in Birmingham, and when we couldn't find it there and finally moved on to Tuscaloosa, I was starved.

When the waiter came, he suggested we "split a rack" of ribs, since Dreamland's rack is like a side of beef. I said, "Partner, I ain't splittin' nothing," and wound up eating *two* racks by myself. When we finished, I was so coated in barbecue sauce that Dad threatened to run me through a nearby car wash.

The drive home was one long series of great conversations. A chance to air everything out. Summing up the year, Dad said the thing I should remember is that in pro football, one year is all you get to "grow up." That after your rookie season, you're officially a "veteran." It's not like being a freshman in college, then a sophomore, then a junior. The line of demarcation is *one year*. And that you have to make up your mind to wear that hat. Especially if you're the starter.

I told him I felt some accomplishment about the season beyond having endured it. I'd been the only Colts quarterback in history to take every snap in a season (982 snaps). I was proud that I'd played so much and of the records I set. We both relived the significance of setting the one for most consecutive games with a touchdown pass (13) because the previous record holder had been Dad's first college hero, Charley Conerly (of Ole Miss, of course).

I told him how supportive Mora, Polian, and Irsay had been all year and how Polian had made promises after the season of "getting some defensive players in." He'd said that after almost every game. At one point, when I was particularly upset, he'd come in and said, "Hang with me, Peyton. I'm going to get you some help."

I'd said, "Bill, where the hell am I going? I'm not going anywhere." Dad laughed.

Tom Moore had been blunt about it when I left. He'd said, "Go home and forget about football for a while. Don't work out. Don't even think about it." Bruce Arians had said that I should just go to the beach for two months. (Dad had made other arrangements. I went hunting for two weeks and came back totally relaxed.)

By the time we got to New Orleans, I was feeling better. And I had to laugh telling Dad the story later. I'd gotten to meet so many of my heroes during the year. I mean, imagine sitting at a banquet table with Johnny Unitas and chatting with Troy Aikman and Steve Young, or doing a commercial for Gatorade with Michael Jordan. But what was best about it was exchanging recipes about football. And Troy Aikman told me that after a season he wouldn't pick up a ball again until May. He said that way he saved his arm. All he did in January and February was cardiovascular workouts, and in March, lift weights. But *no* football throwing until May.

As a result, I did something similar after my first year with the Colts. I didn't pick up a ball again until . . . March. (Or was it February?)

Archie and Olivia Manning's dedicated efforts to get their three sons safely into manhood, with character intact and prospects in bloom, were now just short of being completed. Cooper was married and working, hosting provocative sports-talk shows in New Orleans (when he wasn't providing comic relief at the Manning Passing Academy, Archie's quarterback camp in Hammond). Peyton, rich and famous, had hung his star in Indianapolis. And now young Eli was about to relight the way to his father's thirty-year-old place as quarterback of the Ole Miss Rebels. . . .

Olivia had a dream that Eli was in Oxford on a recruiting trip, being squired around by Ole Miss's new coach, David Cutcliffe (yes, the same David Cutcliffe who had been Peyton's honored offensive coordinator at Tennessee). In the dream, Eli was so impressed with all that he saw that he had signed with Ole Miss on the spot and was calling to say he'd just as soon spend the week. The ringing of the telephone was the alarm clock going off next to Olivia's ear at 5 A.M. "Darn," she said. "What a nice image."

The part about Cutcliffe was true. He'd taken over for the departed Tommy Tuberville. The part about Eli was about to be. But if you had asked either one of us if we really could have predicted it, we'd have told you that Eli didn't talk until he was almost three. That the most you could get out of him before then was "unh" and "unh-unh." And that when he finally spoke it was in a complete sentence: "Whose cat is that?"

Some anthropologists believe that style is set early, and from that reference point, I'd have to say Eli's certainly was. There he'd go, inconspicuously making his way, keeping almost everything to himself, and then, boom, out with it, like he knew all along but wasn't concerned whether you knew it or not. All he expected, rhetorically, was for you to be able to tell him whose cat it was.

Olivia says that I sold Eli a little bit short growing up and that I should remember I was a little like that as a teenager— shy, remote. I'd agree with her except that Eli was so deft at keeping his light under a bushel that I'd have to plead guilty only by reason of ignorance. With his return to Newman from his "catch-up period" at St. George's school, Eli had gone about establishing himself as the most inconspicuous superstar in Newman's history. He made all-state as a sophomore in football, and Peyton hadn't done that. Neither had Cooper. Actually, Eli made it three years in a row and, obviously, Peyton and Cooper hadn't done that, either.

If he'd had a publicist, maybe he would have made it four in a row. In his freshman year, Eli was the second-string quarterback on the Newman varsity and started for the JV team. He was doing fine, but I thought he stood out mainly for being tall and skinny. The starting quarterback was a senior, and about midseason, on a Wednesday night, we were having supper in what had become a very quiet house—Peyton was at Tennessee, Cooper was at Ole Miss, and Olivia and I were taking turns pulling conversation out of Eli.

And in the middle of the meal he says, "Looks like I'm going to be starting Friday night."

"What? Friday night? On the varsity!?"

"Yeah. So-and-so [he named the senior starter] is out and I'm starting."

We were dumbstruck by the revelation. Especially when he told us he had known about it for days.

When he was a sophomore and the full-time starter, Eli had a really talented group of receivers, all seniors. But I was concerned that he might not be able to get the ball to them. He was so skinny I doubted his arm strength. I shouldn't have. He got it to them so well, he totaled 22 touchdown passes and the team went 8 and 2 and made it to the first round of the state playoffs. Eli gathered up his first all-state recognition. Peyton as a sophomore hadn't even made all-district.

Olivia's theory is that Eli has always had a hidden agenda and only unveils it serendipitously—a pleasant surprise here, a stunner there. He sneaked up on Peyton in basketball and one day when Peyton was in town, Eli not only beat him one-on-one in our yard but dunked a couple on him, too. Peyton was flabbergasted. He said, "I always thought of him as being just this neat kid, as nice as could be, saying 'Yes, sir' and 'No, sir' to everybody and never causing me any problems the way I did Cooper."

Cooper has another theory. That Eli just refuses to show emotion. (Or maybe refuses to *have* emotion.) It drove Cooper crazy how stoic Eli was in his basketball and football games. Win or lose, touchdown or interception, he displayed no overt emotion. When Cooper finished at Ole Miss and started watching Newman's games the following year, he'd squirm in his seat whenever Eli made a play and didn't react.

Cooper'd say, "Eli, I'm going to quit coming to watch you if you don't show some life when you pass for a touchdown! If you can't feel it, at least fake it!"

But Eli never did. No histrionics, no end-zone discotheque. Just not his thing. He doesn't have a temper, so he doesn't blow up in the heat of battle. He's not a braggadocio, so bragging is out. He seems to get calmer with each new challenge and each new season. Which is very deceptive because he loves to compete. He'll chew you up playing one-on-one in anything. But he just refuses to lose his cool and never exhibits anything but total control. As they say, he don't talk, he do.

I happen to think that's an important quality in a young man today, being able to control himself. I mean, you don't know who's out there and what they might do. You come to a red light and glance over at the car in the inside lane, and the next thing you know the guy behind the other wheel has been "offended" and has a gun in his hand. It takes more courage today not to react. Kids don't settle things with boxing gloves like we did. They settle them with unspeakable violence.

The thing was, Eli really had no desire to be "the center" of any game's attention. He had no ego to make him want to be. In basketball, it didn't matter to him whether he scored or not. And because he didn't make mistakes, he hardly ever got taken out of a game. He liked to play, that's all. It didn't even matter who he played against.

And I mean *it did not matter*. During his senior year, he was playing in a basketball tournament over in Gulfport, Mississippi, and he called us the night before. I asked him the name of the team he'd be playing. He said he didn't recall. Newman lost in overtime, and afterward we talked. He still didn't remember the team's name. It just didn't matter to him.

In his junior year, with new, younger receivers, he worked harder and threw better, and with an improved running game the football team went 9 and 1, won 2 in the state playoffs, and got beat in the quarterfinals. Vince Gibson, my old coaching friend, saw him that season and marveled at how pretty his passes were. Not the hardest, not the softest, but laid out there beautifully. Gibson said, "Eli can play. He'll make it at a major college."

He was up over 190 pounds as a senior and solid. There's something almost magical about turning eighteen; a rite of passage that seems invariably to include greater savvy and poise and a more finished quality to the skills. That September you could tell that Eli had "arrived" and was thinking clearly. He gave up baseball to concentrate on football and basketball, saying there was just so much time. He'd worked on his speed early in the mornings (quietly), and at the Penn State camp that summer had run a 4.8 forty, which is certainly respectable. My best time was 4.65. Cooper was about the same. Peyton was 4.9.

As a senior, Eli was doing things in games that made it more and more evident that he was a prospect. He had reached a new level. He was making the sideline pass, the one that separates the good quarterback from the mediocre. He connected on post patterns in crisis situations, with defenders in his face. He didn't have quite as good an offensive line, so he was under the gun a lot. He made throws sometimes when he was badly rushed and off balance, performing some very impressive athletics to escape. Scouts are impressed when you make good throws under duress.

Newman went undefeated in the regular season but lost again in the quarterfinals of the state playoffs. This time, besides all-state, Eli made the high school All-America team and was named *USA Today* Player of the Year in Louisiana. He threw for 30 touchdowns and averaged 17 yards a completion, and before the season was over (actually, before it started) the college scouts were swarming. Eli's indifference was monumental. Yes, he certainly wanted to play college football, but did I think he could get the decision done by December so that he wouldn't be distracted from his basketball?

You knew from the start that he wasn't going to go for having a hundred schools on his list the way Peyton had or have to field twenty-five calls a night. He said he'd just as soon not fill out papers sent by schools he wasn't really interested in. Cooper "advised" him on how to con the schools he *was* interested in. Cooper said, "In the place where they ask you to list your three favorite teams, put their name, then the two who are their biggest rivals. Like if it's Florida, put Florida State and Georgia. They'll want you just so they can beat the opposition."

Eli told a lot of schools right up front that he wasn't interested. He sailed through the calls from September 1 on. Every night that first week the phone would ring for Eli and he'd take it up in his room. A while later he'd come down and say, "Well, I cut Baylor, I cut Ohio State, and I cut Texas Tech." And I'd say, "Eli, can't you at least wait until the second week?"

I presumed it was mostly assistant coaches he was brushing off, but one night he said, "I cut Vanderbilt." And I asked him, "Which coach called you?"

"Coach Woodenhoffer."

"Woody Woodenhoffer?"

"Yessir."

"Eli, he's the head coach! He's been a friend of mine since he coached the Steelers in the '70s."

Eli shrugged. "I didn't see myself playing at Vanderbilt."

I had to call Woody to apologize. He laughed and said he understood.

Eli cut twenty that first week and before very long had eliminated almost fifty. It seemed like in no time he had whittled the prospects down to his top three: Texas, which offered a great coaching staff; Virginia, a terrific school all around, and . . . Mississippi (any reasons necessary?). He could officially visit five schools, but only accepted invitations from those three. He went (at our expense) *unofficially* to a few others, including LSU and Tennessee.

Texas made a very big impression, especially on Olivia.

She and I went with Eli on that trip and got the red-carpet treatment. The Texas facilities are unbelievable, and about two hours before the game we were invited to see, we walked out of the new complex into the stadium and over the public address system they started playing the Three Dog Night song, "Eli's Coming." Olivia said, "I commit! I commit right now!"

A pretty hostess showed Eli around, and after the game (won by Texas) we all went over to Mac Brown's house for dinner. Mac had been at Tulane at one time before he became Texas's head coach and Olivia knew his wife, Sally. It was all very impressive. When we flew home the next day, I asked Eli what he thought and he said, "I had a good time." The equivalent of a ringing endorsement.

But once David Cutcliffe took the Ole Miss job, I think deep down Olivia and I not only suspected but hoped what the outcome would be. I had managed to steer clear of the "replacement process" that brought in Cutcliffe, so besides being pleased with the choice (I shared Peyton's high regard for David), I had no fear that there would be any link to Eli. The fact is I had been called by a number of coaches interested in the job or trying to get my recommendation. A couple Ole Miss guys even tried to talk me into applying, which I had no trouble refusing. To all I had the same response: "I'm not going to offer any influence either way, because it won't be fair with Eli being a prospect to go there."

Funny. After church one Sunday, Olivia said, "Why don't you just go back to Ole Miss and coach the team." Like it was that easy. This was before Cutcliffe had been hired, and people were calling every five minutes for my opinion.

I said, "No, that's not for me." Olivia had always said I'd wind up coaching. I'd always said I wouldn't. If my career had ended early, by injury, say, at twenty-five, I might have looked at it, but I was thirty-six when I quit playing, and that's too late to get into coaching. It was certainly too late to get into at my age now. Besides, I'd had too many coaching friends over the years who had been fired or jerked around in one way or another tell me, "Whatever you do, *don't* get into coaching."

When Eli and I went to Oxford for an unofficial visit, it was clear enough that there was chemistry. He sat on the sidelines during a game with the other prospects and went out afterward with his cousin, Amzie Williams, who was playing for Ole Miss. We didn't really talk about it definitively afterward. We didn't discuss my preferences, and I didn't intend to give them. In his quiet way, Eli can make you feel pretty awkward about prying. I think he figures, "I don't throw a lot at you, don't throw a lot at me," so after about four questions, you get a look that says, "That's enough."

I intended only to be his friend and to be a sounding board during the recruiting. So I returned from Oxford only with suspicions. Cutcliffe made it clear that Eli would be the first quarterback on his list and the first he'd try to sign. Yes, I was secretly excited that Eli might be leaning that way. So was Olivia. To say the least.

The one thing I did know was that Eli was very much in demand all around.

Through his senior year, Eli's stock rose dramatically. He consistently ranked in the top ten among quarterback prospects in the country. But while I might have been wanting to see his talent in red and blue, I have to say at that point I had a little bit of a sinking feeling. The way the buildup was going, I was afraid there was no way he could be as good as people were expecting. And if he went to Ole Miss, the expectations would go over the top. Eli Manning . . . Peyton's brother. Eli Manning . . . Archie's son. An immediate smash hit looking for a marquee, or isn't that what genes are all about?

Eli took an official trip back to Oxford around exam time. Ole Miss sent the school plane to bring him up on a Sunday night, then David Cutcliffe turned right around and came down to New Orleans to visit our house the next night. And by this time Olivia was going nuts. She didn't want to pressure Eli by asking, so she said to me, "Why don't *you* ask him? You're his father!" I said nope.

On the following Wednesday, I went duck hunting with Bert Jones, the old LSU and Colts quarterback. On Thursday night, when we were sealed into our lodge, Eli called. He'd come home after basketball practice and asked Olivia, "Where's Dad?" (He always seems to forget when I tell him where I'm going.)

"Why?" Olivia asked.

"I need to ask him about putting together the press conference for this announcement."

"Okay, we can reach him at camp."

Long pause.

"Do you mind telling me where you're going?"

"Oh. Ole Miss, of course."

Like we both should have known all along. Later, I found out he'd already told Cooper and Peyton. Parents, unless assisted by osmosis, are always the last to know.

I got back in time to change out of my hunting gear and give my face a lick or two with the razor before the press conference at Newman. The patio was packed, the Newman team and students hanging from the railing upstairs. All the TV and radio stations were there. I hadn't had a chance to talk with Eli except on the phone, mainly to remind him to call the coaches who were waiting on his decision. But I'd have wanted to give him some dos and don'ts—like not talking about "playing right away" and being careful not to discredit the other schools. But I didn't have time. He'd have to fly solo.

When I got there, I hugged him and he said, "Am I supposed to make a statement or something?"

I said, "Just give 'em a couple sentences on why you picked Ole Miss and then let 'em ask questions."

And he sat down and delivered as nice a little acceptance speech as you'll ever hear. Instead of a couple minutes, it was probably ten. He told about his choice and how he came to it, he thanked the right people, he offered the right predictions. And before they asked, he said, "This really didn't have anything to do with my father playing at Ole Miss. That was over thirty years ago."

Everybody laughed.

You got the impression without him saying it that basketball was always secondary to Eli. He was never a gym rat. He seldom played pickup games. You'd never see him go to the gym and shoot for an hour by himself. He'll play in the backyard with his brothers or his buddies, but that's just for fun. And he played basketball at Newman for just that reason: the fun of it. He had no interest in breaking scoring records or getting a bunch of college offers. Which makes it all the more amazing how good he was.

He was six-four plus (towering over me; I think I might be getting shorter) when he played his last game for Newman—in a tiny gym up in a little-bitty town called Pine, Louisiana, two and a half hours from New Orleans. It was the playoffs, the first round. Typical Eli, he saved his best for when they needed him most. He scored 26 points, about half the team's output and much more than his average. Maybe the best basketball game he ever had. But Newman lost, in overtime.

Billy Fitzgerald, the basketball coach that Peyton had had the run-in with, came over to Olivia and me afterward. He said, "It's a sad day for me, folks. I'm done coaching the Mannings."

It made Olivia tear up. Not Eli. He didn't mope around, he went right on being Eli. The next day he and Cooper went out and played golf.

When he graduated and went on to Ole Miss, I didn't hide my feelings that I hoped the Rebels would red-shirt him. I thought if they did he could "grow into" his potential (and expectations). Cutcliffe said that's what he intended. But you never know what's going to happen with football players, given their vulnerability. Look at Peyton, starting as a freshman at Tennessee when the first two quarterbacks went down.

So all that next season, with Eli dressing out for every Ole Miss game, I kept waiting, and dreading, for the other shoe to drop. I kept waiting to hear, probably a day before the game, "Dad, I'm starting Saturday."

Gratefully, the call never came. He was red-shirted and

came to his "official" freshman year as the clear-cut backup to the Ole Miss starter, Romaro Miller. Right where everybody hoped he would be, and where Cutcliffe said he should be. I, of course, quietly agreed.

When he came home at Christmas break, we went out for lunch, and he was so outgoing, so expressive, telling stories and reliving his first season at Ole Miss, that it was as if he were another person. I don't think we'd talked that much in any ten previous conversations. Olivia had Cooper and Ellen over that night and Eli invited his girlfriend, Marin, and we watched the Pro Bowl "announcement show," in which Peyton was revealed to be a unanimous choice for the game.

Then after Cooper and Ellen left and Eli and Marin went out for something, Olivia and I were there alone, and I put a tape of the Pro Bowl show in and we watched the replay showing Peyton's selection, with a little piece on Eli.

And Olivia broke into the biggest cry I'd ever seen. I said, "My gosh, what's wrong?" But I realized without her telling me what it was. Peyton was up there by himself, and it was two days before Christmas.

In eighty seasons of play, the National Football League had never known a change of direction equal to that taken by the 1999 Indianapolis Colts. From 3–13 in 1998, the Colts flipped to 13–3 in '99 and won the AFC Eastern Division championship, their first in twelve years. It was also the first time since 1977 that the Colts had won in double figures. Their three offensive standouts, runningback Edgerrin James, a rookie, wide receiver Marvin Harrison, and quarterback Peyton Manning, were all unanimous choices for the Pro Bowl. Each one for the first time. Assessing where that put the Colts in the larger picture down the road, Coach Jim Mora said ominously, "We're just getting started." Peyton Manning agreed.

I made a list of all the things I wanted to do, all the things I wanted us to do, before the 1999 season. An athlete has to have goals—for a day, for a lifetime—and I like to put mine in writing so that afterward I can check the design against the finished product. I won't tell you whatall I covered and what the figures were; they're not something you'd take public anyhow (although I will say I cut my interceptions almost in half and still didn't get them down to where I wanted them).

And I sure didn't see us winning 13 games. A 10-game swing isn't something that happens very often in the National Football League (every few decades? every half century?) and to even suggest it as a game plan is wishful thinking. More dream than scheme.

But I will tell you that from minicamp to training camp to opening game, I knew we had something going. I knew we were on the verge of being special. I knew it from the day the guys I asked to come out for off-season workouts actually came. I knew it from the attitude of those who didn't have to be there but were. And wanted to be.

And when those guys happened to be as talented as Marvin Harrison and Marcus Pollard and Ken Dilger and E. G. Green, and then Edgerrin James, when he came in after a delay over his contract, and Terrence Wilkins . . . well, please direct me to the nearest victory dance.

Call it something corny, like "dedication," but there are no secrets about what makes a good passing game, what gives you the edge in timing and knowledge that's so vital to it. I've said it before (and will keep on saying it): It's the work you're willing to do in the *off*-season. It's having guys do in the blazing sun (without compensation) the things they're going to do better and win with in the regular season. I've always believed that, and have had it proved to me over and over.

Football is so much of a concert of individual talents and limitations, of working together in very complicated sequences. Lines and X's and O's on a piece of paper only give you the road map. The enlightenment comes when you realize that everybody is different, and those differences have to be accounted for. Where Marvin Harrison will be on this play might be a step farther than your second-stringer, and if you're being pressured and have to throw the ball when he's 15 yards into the route instead of 18, he's *got* to be on the same page because if he's not—as he should have found out in practice—then you don't have teamwork. You lay that cornerstone in the off-season.

I started learning this at Newman High and had it confirmed at the University of Tennessee. The result is all positive: It gives you the edge. When can you tell? Easy in this case. We didn't have nearly as many off-season workouts in 1998; I didn't get signed and into camp until regular practices had begun. We had them in '99. And great players with great attitudes. I can't tell you how refreshing it is to have an Edgerrin James in the backfield, so eager to work, so eager to get the ball, that when you finally feed it to him, he *grabs* it out of your hands.

Oh, sure. I improved, too. I set up better, the ball came out of my hand better. I knew where to go with it and made quicker decisions on when. I had a saying for myself, "Don't throw 'hopes,' throw 'knows.'" No disrespect meant to the purists, but I was back doing it the way I did in college. And don't ask me why it took a year to regain that comfort zone. Rookie jitters, I guess.

But in 1998 we didn't have the same understanding of the offense, either, and the synchronization that comes out of it. This time my receivers were on the same page from the opening game against Buffalo. They were in sync. They adjusted readily when they had to. I didn't have to hold the ball as long. Marvin Harrison understands that, and so do the others now. Of course, it's also true that Tom Moore didn't want to overload us with complex stuff in '98. We were still babies in his offense. Now we were adding new plays every week and making better use of all that talent.

I talked to the team before the Buffalo game. I was thinking maybe I should; it was just the offense, and we're a young bunch as pro teams go. I had not made a pregame talk in 1998 like I had done fairly often at Tennessee. I didn't feel comfortable with it. And even now I won't do it every week, only when I feel I have something to contribute. As Dad would say, "You shouldn't even stand up otherwise." There's nothing worse than a speech that falls on deaf ears.

But I did it in response to what I felt was coming on as a kind of favorable wind. I'd had a conversation with Coach Mora about the importance of getting off to a superfast start and how that had to be inculcated into our thinking, and he liked the idea. He said, "Hell, yes! Let's do it!" He and the other coaches were at the meeting and stayed on as I got up.

I said, "No matter what happens tomorrow, let's be positive about this season. Play with a lot of energy. Don't point fingers at one another or at the defense. They're paying us to score every time we touch the ball so don't be saying, 'We wouldn't have done so-and-so if the defense had done a better job.' That's for losers. Let's not do that.

"We're not going 3 and 13 this year. We're better. We've worked hard. Let's stay together, be positive, get a fast start. Have a killer instinct. We didn't have that last year. We had leads in the fourth quarter and didn't hold them. We made mistakes, got complacent. Not this time. Let's put teams away in the fourth quarter, not let them overtake us. Let's close the door on 'em."

It was an exciting game, though Buffalo might not have thought so because we won, 31–14. I had good statistics—21 of 33 for 284 yards and 2 touchdowns. Two interceptions were on a tipped ball and a Hail Mary, so I felt I'd made good decisions on my throws. I could see from the beginning how much the extra work had helped. The receivers were adjusting, had a better sense of where they were, and I didn't hold the ball as long. That makes such a difference. In 1998 I was waiting, seeing, throwing too often after guys were coming out of their breaks.

Altogether it was a solid start. The game was a sellout. Mom and Dad and Ashley were there, and we went to St. Elmo's afterward. Mom and Dad stayed over to help me fix up my new apartment that week but went home before we went on to New England for game two, which we blew. We had 'em 28–7, and I threw 3 touchdown passes to Marvin, but we fumbled ourselves silly in the second half and lost, 31–28. Shades of the recent past.

There was really no hint in the next two games of what was to come. We beat the Chargers in San Diego, where I threw for 404 yards to break Johnny Unitas's Colts record for most yards in a game. It was a big win because it was our first on the road since I'd been there. And I scored the last touchdown on a 12-yard runaround end. As I said for the papers, "Speed kills."

Then we turned around and lost to the Dolphins at home before a sellout crowd, 34–31. Dan Marino drove 'em almost the length of the field with under a minute to go and threw a touchdown pass with thirty seconds left to beat us. Marino had apparently fumbled the ball away on the drive but the officials called it an incomplete pass. Very questionable. I kept saying to myself, "It's just so darn hard to win in this NFL." We were now 2 and 2 (but should have been 4 and 0), and going . . . where?

That's easy to say. Now. An 11-game winning streak. The Colts hadn't had one like it in twenty-three years, and then only one other before that. And never had one better than that.

It might seem a little awkward in the retelling, but right when we were launching into it—the second game of the streak, when we upset the Cowboys in the RCA Dome, 34–24—I had a huge blowup with Jim Mora the day before. It's worth a replay because it involves the fundamental difference I'd had to adjust to between the way pro players interact with their coaches and what I was used to for all those years in the "amateurs." It took awhile. I wouldn't be surprised if it didn't have something to do with the way I'd played the first year—schizophrenic.

The familiarity pro players have with coaches can take you aback coming into the league. I don't think I ever called one by his first name in college and certainly not the head coach. The formality, I think, helps create a buffer of respect, like you'd have for teachers and doctors and preachers. But right away with the Colts (as with any pro team) it was "Tom" and "Bruce" and "Jim," although for me it was still mostly "Coach" that first year. I like to think I wouldn't have been so forceful otherwise, although I'm a confirmed hard-head, because I really do have a high regard for "Coach" Mora.

In this case, however, I was also ticked.

I'd had a small run-in with Mora earlier when I jumped on one of my runningbacks for busting plays during summer practices. Mora, in turn, jumped on me. "We'll do the coaching, Peyton. And you don't have to swear at other players."

I said, "Fine. But you swear at 'em."

We exchanged a couple more words and dropped it.

Flash-forward to the Dallas game. Lots of excitement, big buildup, and when John Madden and Pat Summerall came in to do the telecast, the team's routine got screwed around so that I was scheduled to meet with them at eight-thirty on Saturday morning instead of on Friday afternoon. Bad move because you should never alter a routine to satisfy the media. I accommodated them, but I told Craig Kelley, our PR man, that I had a team meeting at nine that I had to make on time.

Sure enough, I got hung up answering their questions, and Craig didn't alert me to the time I needed (he had a watch, I didn't). All of a sudden it was nine o'clock, and I leaped up and sprinted to the meeting room—too late. The door was closed. I decided not to go in, thinking the last thing I should do is walk into a meeting late and have Mora rip my ass in front of the whole team. Which he would have.

Long story short, we wound up having words so hot, some people thought we almost came to blows (not true), and he fined me $1,500. Craig Kelley was very upset and offered to pay it for me, but I said no, it was still my responsibility. But I told Mora, "Dammit, Coach, if we're gonna play in big games around here, I think we should go about it without changing everything."

We finally calmed down. We had to. We had a game the next day.

When I got notice of the fine, I tried to get them to let me put the money into my charity foundation. I said, "I'd rather have it there than help pay for the new BMW Irsay just gave Mora for his hundredth victory as an NFL coach," making a joke out of it.

Later I was watching film when Mora came in to shoot the bull. He'd asked me a number of times to sign this or that for some auction he was chairing, and this time he said, "Hey, Peyton, how about signing this football for us?"

I told him I was working on a memo that would soon be on his desk. That any ball I signed from then on would cost him $1,500.

Dad and a contingent of his Ole Miss buddies came to the Cowboys game. They saw what Dad said later were the sure indicators of a good team getting better. We were decidedly better than Dallas that day—34–24, and 419 total yards to 232. We doubled their passing yards (313 to Aikman's 159). And to make it even sweeter—as sure an indicator as it gets—we were the ones coming on at the end. We scored the last 13 points, all in the fourth quarter when the Cowboys went zero and out.

It was our third straight, and we followed that into November with victories over the Chiefs at home (in a game "with playoff implications") and the Giants in New York, where we played just good enough to win. We didn't execute well, but I threw two touchdown passes to Marvin, one for 57 yards, and we put together a scoring drive that covered 99 yards and then survived a late Giants rally.

This time Cooper led a support group to New York City and didn't waste a lot of time there sleeping. The night before the game he rented a limo to take the guys to eat and it was waiting for them in front of the hotel when Mora and some of his coaches came out. Mora asked who the limo was for and when the driver said "Manning," he assumed it was mine and talked the driver into taking his group to dinner first (the restaurant was "only up the street"), then going back for the others. When Cooper found out, he made a big, exaggerated threat to bill Mora $1,500. Mora asked me about it and I said, "Coach, I don't do limos."

We were now 7 and 2 and showing so much improvement all around that I kept thinking how much better we were going to be. Our defensive team was clearly improved, a credit to our new defensive coordinator, Vic Fangio. Chad Bratzke, Ellis Johnson, Cornelius Bennett, Mike Peterson, Chad Cota, and Jason Belser made more big plays than I thought possible. The offensive line that had gotten so good in '98 was even better. You can't always see the individual heroics on the field, but in watching game films afterward I realized what a great blocker for running plays Kenny Dilger had become. I'd see him dominate an opposing linebacker and think, "Wow!"

And I'd see Tarik Glenn, one of the most talented tackles in the NFL, just manhandle defensive ends. For all their anonymity, offensive linemen have distinctive styles. Steve McKinney is a bodyguard type you'd like having on your side wherever you are (and whatever you're doing) because he's so tough. Larry Moore and Waverly Jackson don't say much, but they're strong, stay focused, and work hard. Adam Meadows is very athletic, with great footwork. He had become a close friend, and I could see him boil whenever I got sacked or hit hard after a throw.

Behind their blocks, Edgerrin James was making a head-long dash to the league rushing title and Rookie of the Year honors, and kicker Mike Vanderjagt was on his way to converting 34 of 38 field goal attempts. The line had a "no-sack rule" they laid on themselves for me, and worked so hard at keeping me vertical I got sacked only 15 times in the 16 games. It's rare when a team totals fewer sacks than games. As a result, I had more time to let pass patterns develop, and grew increasingly at ease with my receivers.

Harrison is unbelievably talented. I had learned in time how sensitive he can be, though, and not to get on him except to say "Hey, Marvin, you can do better." He'd respond in kind: "I know, man, I know." Mistakes bother him enough; you don't have to rub it in. But everybody's different, and you have to deal with the differences. As a communications major in college, I already knew not to give a fifth-grade speech to twelfth-graders, but now I was finding out that a soft, well-chosen word suits better—for some. Jerome Pathon, on the other hand, reacts more to "Jerome, that's unacceptable!"

But what they began to understand is that this wasn't about criticism, it was about improvement. Getting the utmost from them. It's a thin line. If you chew a guy out and for the next three series he pouts, you've failed. The only time I don't give it a second thought is when I think a guy isn't giving his all. Then I don't hesitate. But these guys were giving theirs all the time, and my knowledge of it came from getting to know them off the field as well as on it.

Thus I could talk to them more specifically about goals, about individual responsibilities. "Hey, Joe, we gotta block this play better." "Hey, Larry, we're counting on you this year, man. You working hard in the weight room?" If you're not compatible with your teammates, you can't say those things. Instead you say, "How ya doing, Paul? Been back home lately?" A sure sign you've got communication problems.

Now, however, we were going so well I had to keep reminding myself to take advantage of all the strengths that had emerged. I said, "Use your weapons, Peyton, use your weapons." It became a calming thing, because the more we played, the greater respect I had for the whole arsenal. I could lean on Edgerrin for the first two downs, knowing he'd get positive yards. I could count on Marvin and Dilger and Terrence Wilkins and Marcus Pollard and E.G. Green to make catches if I got the ball to them. Sure, I still had to throw well, but I told myself, "You don't have to do it all." And I went into games thinking how tough it was going to be for the opposing teams' defenses. I'd say to myself, "All right, defense, we've got a lot to put on you today. You can't just stop me. You've got to stop us all."

We had our first really easy game against the Eagles the next week; we jumped on them for a quick 17 points, led by 30–3 at the half, and when it got to be 44–3 late in the third quarter, Coach Mora "relieved me." First time I'd been out of a game since I came in as a rookie, and it was my twenty-sixth game. I'd played every down till then—1,590 downs. I don't know if anybody ever did that before, but I was glad to take a breather because it meant we were way ahead. But if I had my way, I'd *never* come out of a game.

As it turned out, there wouldn't be another easy game the rest of the season. One thing you have to factor in about the NFL is that the "book" changes on a team from week to week, just as surely as everybody studies the films and adds to the findings, trying to get an edge. For the last six games, every defense we faced double-covered Marvin Harrison and virtually eliminated him as a deep threat. Some of it was obvious enough so I could take advantage elsewhere, but the tactic became universal. As a result Marvin didn't catch a touchdown pass in any of those games, which was like a drought for him. We had to find other ways to get him the ball.

A big win for us in the stretch was at Miami. It was hairy at the end, before a big, hostile crowd. We had to pull it out (by 37–34) with a 52-yard Vanderjagt field goal as time expired, and it was two passes to Marvin in the last thirty seconds that set it up. Both times Marvin came inside and made the Dolphins pay. It pleased me afterward that Miami players made a big thing of my following through on my fakes, making it look pass when it was run or run when it was pass. Too many quarterbacks don't do that, and don't realize how important it is. How many defensive players can you fool when you execute a good fake? It only takes one to give you an advantage. If it's the right one, it can be a *big* advantage. On a touchdown pass against the Cowboys earlier, Deion Sanders made a wrong step off a fake, and Marvin Harrison blew right past him to catch a touchdown pass.

We won three more after that, the Patriots by five, the Redskins by three, and the Browns by one on a bitter cold day in Cleveland. In each one we felt we could have played a lot better. A disturbing trend seemed to have taken hold: making long drives and not scoring touchdowns. Our expectations had advanced to the point where we were no longer satisfied to be ordinary. The New England game was especially ugly, marked by some sophomoric-looking execution, but by winning we clinched a playoff bid. Edgerrin and I celebrated by buying our offensive linemen tailor-made suits. For the six starters we added digital camcorders.

Against the Redskins we completely shut down in the second half (after passing for 230 yards in the first). But by winning we clinched the division championship and a home field playoff advantage, so we went around the stadium afterward blithely high-fiving the fans in the Dome. They're great fans, and had become an important part of our success. Nobody wanted to go home. Dad was in the dressing room afterward and the evening news showed him giving me a big hug. They also showed him taking the price tag off my Division Championship T-shirt—typical Archie, making sure I looked okay.

Two days later, on Tuesday, the NFL announced that Marvin, Edgerrin and I had made the Pro Bowl. Actually, Coach Mora announced it after practice so that the whole team could hear. Howard Mudd, our line coach, pulled me aside and said, "Peyton, you'll never forget this day. You'll make the Pro Bowl again, and you won't forget that, either, but this one will be special." He was right. Because the Pro Bowl reflects directly the opinion of your peers. They're included in the voting. But I did feel we should have placed at least three more guys on the team: Chad Bratzke, Tarik Glenn, and Mike Vanderjagt.

We had to go to Cleveland, then Buffalo, to finish the season. It was brutally cold in both places. And very disconcerting. The Browns had us 28–19 into the fourth quarter when we scored 10 points to win. We weren't so lucky at Buffalo. We went up two days early to be in place in case there were any Y2K problems, and we celebrated the New Millennium in the hotel the next night. Mora ordered champagne for everybody and we toasted ourselves on the season. We should have known something bad was happening when we had to wait so long for the food that a pasta bar caught fire and turned on the sprinkler system. About thirty guys sprinted for the door.

On Sunday we got toasted by Buffalo, 31–6—the same team we'd beaten just as badly in the opener. Dad called it "an ambush." It was no contest. We couldn't make a big play. It's quirky, and there's really no explaining it, but it happens sometimes when you've been on a high, and we'd been on a long one.

We lost Cornelius Bennett, injured at Buffalo, for the playoffs. I can't say what it meant in the end, because you never really know how much those things influence a team, but he was certainly a key factor on the defense. The fact is we'd been pretty much injury-free all year so we couldn't complain. What we could complain about was that we'd now been less than sharp four weeks in a row.

I still thought we were ready for the playoffs. We were opening at home against the Tennessee Titans, a wild-card team that beat Buffalo to make it to our round, and I had good feelings about what to expect. I thought if we made the adjustments that had to be made, we would cut loose. It was a feeling generally shared, and the fans had caught the fever. For Indianapolis it was the first-ever home playoff game, a big deal, and tickets were tough to come by. I'd had to scrounge to buy twenty. Mom and Dad and Eli were up, and Cooper and Ellen, and, of course, Ashley, and a bunch of friends.

The celebration turned into a wake. We lost, 19 to 16. The defense played well, but the offense kept coming up short in the red zone. Three good drives got only nine points. We didn't score a touchdown until the last couple of minutes. Surprising was the noise the Titan fans made—something we hadn't figured on. Our front office was livid about it afterward, complaining that too many tickets wound up in the Titans fans' hands. But you can't exactly complain about fans yelling and screaming. We just hadn't made enough plays under the conditions. Communication at the line of scrimmage broke down.

I lay in bed way past midnight after the game, stewing over it, replaying it, trying to figure where we went wrong. But the logical conclusion was that this was still a big plus over '98. This was 13–3, and hope. This was a disappointment, but as Coach Mora said, a beginning, not the end. The reality made me want to go back on the field the next day and play the game over.

When the brain cells that were still working summed up, I thought, "Well, shoot! We're spoiled here. We had a great season." And the mood was already catching. Marvin Harrison and Edgerrin James both had taken me aside and talked about the need to "get together" in the off-season. Marvin wanted to take February and March off and start in April, which was fine with me. Edgerrin didn't want to wait. He said he'd like to get together as "soon as we've tied up all the loose ends" and start working on his pass routes with me.

Any review, subsequently, would have shown that it just wasn't our day. Great crowd, great excitement, and I think we were ready, but things happened that, even if you said they could have "gone either way," I would argue back that that's what makes football so wonderful. The big positive was the defense played so well. Take away one long Eddie George run and the Titans were pretty much shut down. Offensively, we'd always found a way during the season to get our act together after falling behind. This time it didn't happen. We kept having to settle for field goals before one unlikely touchdown right at the end—scored by me. Running the ball 15 yards.

I had no doubt later that the carryover would be positive. Somebody at one of my talks to kids asked me how my faith weighed in at such times. Like my dad, I make it a point when I speak to groups to talk about priorities, and when it's schoolkids, I rank those priorities as: faith, family, and education, then football. For me generally it had always been the big four: faith, family, friends, and football. And I tell all of them that as important as football is to me, it can never be higher than fourth.

My faith has been number one since I was thirteen years old and heard from the pulpit on a Sunday morning in New Orleans a simple question: "If you died today, are you one hundred percent sure you'd go to heaven?" Cooper was there, and Eli, but it didn't hit them at the time the way it did me. It was a big church, and I felt very small, but my heart was pounding. The minister invited those who would like that assurance through Jesus Christ to raise their hands, and I did. Then he invited us to come forward, to take a stand, and my heart really started pounding. And from where we sat, it looked like a mile to the front.

But I got up and did it. And I committed my life to Christ, and that faith has been most important to me ever since. Some players get more vocal about it—the Reggie Whites, for example—and some point to Heaven after scoring a touchdown and praise God after games. I have no problem with that. But I don't do it, and don't think it makes me any less a Christian. I just want my actions to speak louder, and I don't want to be more of a target for criticism than I already am. Somebody sees you drinking a beer, which I do, and they think, "Hmmmm, Peyton says he's this, that, or the other, and there he is drinking alcohol. What's that all about?"

Christians drink beer. So do non-Christians. Christians also make mistakes, just as non-Christians do. My faith doesn't make me perfect, it just makes me forgiven, and provides me the assurance I looked for half my life ago. I think God answered our prayers with Cooper, and that was a test of our faith. But I also think I've been blessed—having so little go wrong in my life, and being given so much. I pray every night, sometimes long prayers about a lot of things and a lot of people, but I don't talk about it or brag about it because that's between God and me, and I'm no better than anybody else in God's sight.

But I consider myself fortunate to be able to go to Him for guidance, and I hope (and pray) I don't do too many things that displease Him before I get to Heaven myself. I believe, too, that life is much better and freer when you're committed to God in that way. I find being with others whose faith is the same has made me stronger. J. C. Watts and Steve Largent, for example. They're both in Congress now. We had voluntary pregame chapel at Tennessee, and I attend chapel every Sunday with players on the team in Indianapolis. I have spoken to church youth groups, and at Christian high schools. And then simply as a Christian, and not as good a one as I'd like to be.

How do I justify football in the context of "love your enemy?" I say to kids, well, football is most definitely a "collision sport," and I can't deny it jars your teeth and at the extreme can break your bones. But I've never seen it as a "violent game," there are rules to prevent that, and I know I don't have to hate anybody on the other side to play as hard as I can within the rules. I think you'd have to get inside my head to appreciate it, but I do love football. And, yes, I'd play it for nothing if that was the only way, even now when I'm no longer a child. I find no contradiction in football and my faith.

Ah, but do I "pray for victory?" No, except as a generic thing. I pray to keep both teams injury free, and, personally, that I use whatever talent I have to the best of my ability. But I don't think God really cares about who wins football games, except as winning might influence the character of some person or group. Besides. If the Colts were playing the Cowboys and I prayed for the Colts and Troy Aikman prayed for the Cowboys, wouldn't that make it a standoff?

I do feel this way about it. Dad says it can take twenty years to make a reputation, and five minutes to ruin it. I want my reputation to be able to make it through whatever five-minute crises I run into. And I'm a lot more comfortable knowing where my help is.

New Orleans had been Archie and Olivia's home for almost 30 years when the millennial clock turned 2000. To all intents and purposes, Archie was entrenched. He had marketing and public relations contracts with seven companies, had kept a hand in Saints' television coverage, and was in such demand as a motivational speaker that he had to turn down three offers for every one he took. But when son Eli enrolled at Ole Miss, Archie and Olivia purchased a condo in Oxford, and marveled again (without surprise) how close they still were to their Mississippi roots. . . .

You never know, of course. One day we could very well go back to being full-time Mississippians. But New Orleans is home now, and I guess you'd say we're vested. Oxford, however, is just as appealing, with the town square and the football weekends and all that easy living that's so much smarter than casual observers realize. Oxford is thriving now, too, and though few of my old football buddies live there, it seems to have become a retirement haven for Ole Miss alumni. And, of course, it's just across the way from Drew.

So we will surely spend more of our weekends there. Every time there are two home games in a row you can bet Olivia will want to stay over. We've become nomads, Olivia and I. Always on the road—driving to Oxford, driving to Philadelphia to see her folks, driving to Auburn or Starkville or wherever for an Ole Miss game, or flying to Indianapolis to see the Colts.

We cope with an empty nest knowing that the independence you wish on your kids—praying they'll be able to handle it, working hard toward the day when they try—is holding up all around. We thank God that it's been a happy transition up to now. As different as they may be, we probably get more joy out of our sons than ever. It makes the separations palatable.

Eli settled easily into college life, just as Cooper predicted. The academic side was a surprise. He made the Chancellor's List the first semester and the Dean's List the second, and actually told us about it. A communications breakthrough. He carried a 3.7 grade point average, and switched from liberal arts to business. He had joined Sigma Nu, and survived with no further missteps the frat party fiasco that had drawn the police. He told one reporter that he felt "honored, not pressured," to be compared with his brothers and his father. (Olivia said, "Don't you just love that?")

We were worried all season long that his coaches wouldn't be able to red-shirt him. He was getting way too much media attention, and at one point, in the last home game, Georgia was beating Ole Miss and Romaro Miller got hurt. In the stands, I thought, "Uh-oh, this is it." But Miller sucked it up and played the game through, and Eli finished the season a year older and smarter—but still a freshman in eligibility. Obviously, I was relieved. He went into his second season right behind Miller, now a senior, on the Ole Miss depth chart.

Cooper, meanwhile, added some new moves to being Cooper. He changed jobs to an institutional investment firm and he and Ellen had bought a home. He converted to Catholicism at Ellen's request to accommodate marital harmony ("the family that prays together . . .). She's a special young lady, Ellen. Beautiful, smart, and doesn't know a stranger. The kind of gal if they go to a party and he says, "I'll be right back," and wanders around like he usually does, she winds up making four or five new friends by the time he returns. Take Ellen along anywhere and people are glad to see her.

Now when Cooper and I get together we are more into real-life issues, but with no discernible reduction in his antic quotient. He's twenty-six, but when he comes into the house and gets the urge, he'll still dance on a chair. That's not "breaking the rules," that's Cooper. Peyton took him to the NFL's big sponsor party before the 1999 Super Bowl and they were sitting with the Gatorade people, surrounded by tables of NFL bigwigs, when Cooper went to use the restroom. He was gone for a while, and somebody asked Peyton where he was. Peyton shook his head—then caught a glimpse of Cooper across the room at the table of some corporate vice president. He was dancing on it. Peyton said, "As Dad would say, 'That's my boy.'" Actually, what Dad would have said was, "At least he has his clothes on."

Cooper and I started *The Archie and Cooper Show,* for call-ins on Thursday-night radio. Cooper runs it and I field most of the questions, but he puts us on the brink every now and again just to stay in shape. He told a guy who called to complain about his son's high school coach that he thought maybe the son "ought to just forget football and play in the band." One woman called to praise Olivia for raising three football players. She said, "I don't know about your mom, but I don't know a tight end from a runningback." And Cooper said, "Well, I guarantee you Miz Olivia has a tight end."

I could have strangled him.

Nowadays I seem to spend a lot of time being humble about Peyton. Trying to be modest. Trying to put it in perspective when people make such a big deal out of him. What I'd really like to say, of course, is, "Boy, ain't it wonderful?" I'd like to stick my head out a window and yell, "Damn, he's good!"

Sorry, it's just not in me to do that as a dad. Strike those remarks from the record. But the quarterback that still lurks beneath this graying head knows when to appreciate success when he sees it. And toughness. And leadership. And talent. And this above all: that it was just like Peyton to be more pleased over being named one of the Ten Most Outstanding Young Americans by the U.S. Junior Chamber of Commerce in Washington in 1999 than he was over any other award he got. He was surprised they recognized a football player for such recognition. I told him he shouldn't be. But I was just as surprised when I received it in 1988.

Peyton and Ashley Thompson plan to marry, and Peyton's building a house now, from a tear-down in an old section of Indianapolis that reminds me of the Garden District. He wants to plant the flag there. But he has a room with us whenever he wants it, and when he comes back, he still picks up around the house and checks all the locks before he goes to bed. We hunt more now and play golf. He likes golf the way I do, for the discipline and all the skills it requires. He had a hole-in-one at the Avalon Course in Knoxville but never saw it. He said it was like launching a touchdown pass the exact moment you get buried by two defensive tackles. The green was elevated, and he couldn't see if the ball stayed on or what. His group couldn't find it anywhere—until somebody looked in the cup.

The hole-in-one was a thrill, he says, but nothing like a touchdown pass in a big game. He says even if he had started young, he never would have preferred golf to football. Like Red Grange said after playing it for several years, there's something missing in golf. Maybe for your opponent to be able to whack you as you're swinging.

Peyton still gets highly animated when we talk football, and I marvel how cerebral he is. And unselfish. How much he understands that statistics don't matter, except as indicators. That only the score matters. The first part of the 1999 season, he had great figures; then the defenses started adjusting. Marvin Harrison didn't see single coverage more than ten times in the last half of the season. In those circumstances, Peyton took what they gave him. He put it on the shelf against the Jets, using a dink-and-dunk game of short passes (for less than 200 yards), and the Colts won anyway.

Against the Browns late in the season, he had his record of consecutive games with a touchdown pass broken at 27 when he checked off on a pass play that had been called right at the Browns' goal line. Instead, he handed off to James for a touchdown. The surer way to go, record be hanged. That's smart. And unselfish. And impressive. By "doing whatever it takes," he led the Colts six times to come-from-behind victories in the fourth quarter in '99. As a result, the coaches said, the Colts no longer "expect" bad things to happen at the end.

But, of course, when they do, Peyton suffers as much as

ever. And for every bit as long as he did after a loss at Newman . . . or Tennessee . . . or that first bittersweet year in Indianapolis.

Right after the loss to the Titans ended the season, we went hunting, and when we stopped for gas on the way home, I saw a Monday edition of *USA Today* on the newsstand. Thinking Peyton might like to see what was being written about the Super Bowl, I said, "Want a copy?" He said, "Unh-unh."

When we driving again, he said, "You know, Dad, you've gotten over this a lot sooner than I have."

And I realized the difference now in our perspectives— and that he was right. I'm beyond living and dying over football games. I hurt when my kids lose, but not for myself, for them. If he hadn't been on that team, in that game, I really wouldn't have cared. A game is a game is a game. I cared about Tennessee because he played there, but my team was Ole Miss. I care now about the Colts because he plays for them, but it'll take a while for me to feel anything close to the allegiance you naturally feel for "your team." That's just the way it is with us fans.

Football or any sport, for the unattached, can be fun to watch, even exciting, but if you have no real rooting interest, the outcome doesn't matter. It's like what Duane Thomas of the Cowboys said all those years ago when somebody asked him if playing in the Super Bowl was "the ultimate." Thomas said, "How can it be the ultimate? They play it every year." There's always another season, just as it was for me, though Lord knows I'm relieved already that Peyton won't have to wait fourteen years for a winning record—and still leave the game unfulfilled.

In the end, Peyton handled that final defeat well. (Or at least better.) He was able to put it in the larger context of knowing everything else happening to the Colts was positive. That they were a team on the move. And that they were doing it with young players—Harrison, James, Dilger, the two tackles, Tarik Glenn and Adam Meadows, who were drafted one and two the year before Peyton, and so forth. Already people were comparing Peyton, Harrison, and James to the great Dallas teams with Troy Aikman, Michael Irving, and Emmitt Smith.

But to win thirteen games again right away wouldn't seem likely. The Colts would no longer be able to sneak up on anybody. They could be as good or better offensively, and better on defense and special teams, too, and still not be the "dynasty in the making" some suggested. That's just not realistic these days. Teams don't hold together like they used to. Too much player movement (going to the bigger bucks), too little team loyalty. Top players get peddled off to adjust to the salary cap and as a result teams don't have the depth in talent the Cowboys had when they won three Super Bowls with virtually the same roster in the mid-90s.

For Peyton's and the Colts' sake, however, and their fans' sake, I hope they find a way to hold it together. Because if they do, you can forget everything I said in that last paragraph.

Me, I'm just proud. Very, very proud of Peyton, as I am of Cooper and Eli. I love it when Mora talks about Peyton being "special," and about the "good feeling" he gets coaching him. Several regulars in the media have called him the best quarterback in the NFL. I don't get into that, but I know for sure he has "arrived" way ahead of schedule. To be in the league just two years and have people talking like that is extraordinary. For sure when they name the best in the game right now he'll be in the same paragraph with Brett Favre, Troy Aikman, Drew Bledsoe, and Mark Brunell.

People ask me if I knew all this would happen. Or any of it would. If in my wildest dreams I thought that Peyton would be so good, and that right on his heels would come his little brother with similarly developing skills and credentials. The short answer would be, Of course not. As proud as I am, I didn't know. And wouldn't have dared to dream it.

But I do know this. It wasn't a fluke.